Depression in Long Term and Residential Care

Robert L. Rubinstein is Senior Research Anthropologist and director of Research at the Polisher Research Institute of the Philadelphia Geriatric Center. He has conducted research in the United States and in Vanuatu (southwest Pacific). His research interests include death and dying, the culture of long-term care, and social relations and home environments of older people.

M. Powell Lawton was Director of Research at the Philadelphia Geriatric Center for 30 years and is now Senior Research Scientist. He is also Adjunct Professor of Human Development at the Pennsylvania State University and Professor of Psychiatry, Temple University School of Medicine. His doctorate was in clinical psychology from Teachers College, Columbia University. He is Editor-in-Chief of the *Annual Review of Gerontology and Geriatrics.*

Depression in Long Term and Residential Care

Advances in Research and Treatment

Robert L. Rubinstein, PhD

M. Powell Lawton, PhD

Editors

Springer Publishing Company

Springer Publishing Company, Inc.
536 Broadway
New York, NY 10012-3955

Cover design by: Margaret Dunin
Acquisitions Editor: Helvi Gold
Production Editor: Susan Gamer

97 98 99 00 01 / 5 4 3 2 1

Library of Congress Cataloging-in Publication Data

Rubinstein, Robert L.
    Depression in long-term and residential care / Robert L. Rubinstein, M. Powell Lawton.
        p.   cm.
    Includes bibliographical references and index.
    ISBN 0-8261-9550-4
    1. Depression in old age—Congresses.   2. Nursing home patients—Mental health—Congresses.   I. Lawton, M. Powell (Mortimer Powell), 1923- .   II. title.
    [DNLM: 1. Depressive Disorder—in old age—congresses.
    2. Aging—psychology—congresses.   3. Long-Term Care—in old age—congresses.   4. Nursing Homes—congresses.
    WM 171 R896d 1997]
    RC537.5.R8   1997
    618.97'68527—dc21
    DNLM/DLC
    for Library of Congress   97-16281
                                                                        CIP

Printed in the United States of America

Contents

Part III: Implications for Policy and Future Research

Contributors

Ivo Abraham, Ph.D., R.N.
Center on Aging and Health
University of Virginia
Charlottesville, Virginia

Gene Cohen, M.D., Ph.D.
Center on Aging, Health, and the
    Humanities
George Washington University
Washington, D.C.

Deborah N. Frazer, Ph.D.
Genesis ElderCare
Kennett Square, Pennsylvania

Dolores Gallagher-Thompson, Ph.D.
Gerontology Research Programs
Veterans Affairs Medical Center
Palo Alto, California

Ira Katz, M.D., Ph.D.
Department of Psychiatry
University of Pennsylvania
Philadelphia, Pennsylvania

M. Powell Lawton
Polisher Research Institute
Philadelphia Geriatric Center
Philadelphia, Pennsylvania

Barry Lebowitz, Ph.D.
Mental Disorders of the Aging
    Research Branch
National Institute of Mental Health
Rockville, Maryland

Mark Luborsky, Ph.D.
Polisher Research Institute
Philadelphia Geriatric Center
Philadelphia, Pennsylvania

Jana Mossey, Ph.D., M.P.H., M.S.N.
MCP Hahnemann School of Medicine
Philadelphia, Pennsylvania

Lisa L. Onega, Ph.D., R.N.
Gerontology Division, School of
    Nursing
Oregon Health Sciences University
Portland, Oregon

Patricia Parmelee, Ph.D.
Center for Clinical Epidemiology and
    Bio-Statistics
University of Pennsylvania
Philadelphia, Pennsylvania

Edward N. Polisher
Cozen & O'Conner
Philadelphia, Pennsylvania

Sally J. Reel, Ph.D., R.N., C.F.N.P.
School of Nursing
University of Virginia
Charlottesville, Virginia

Elizabeth M. Riley, M.A.
Department of Anthropology
University of Pennsylvania
Philadelphia, Pennsylvania

Barry Rovner, M.D.
Department of Psychiatry
Thomas Jefferson Medical University
Philadelphia, Pennsylvania

Robert L. Rubinstein, Ph.D.
Polisher Research Institute
Philadelphia Geriatric Center
Philadelphia, Pennsylvania

Linda Teri, Ph.D.
Psychology and Behavioral Sciences
University of Washington
Seattle, Washington

Larry W. Thompson, Ph.D.
Gerontology Research Programs
Veterans Affairs Medical Center
Palo Alto, California

Amy B. Wofford, M.A.
University of North Carolina
Department of Sociology
Chapel Hill, North Carolina

Foreword

EDWARD N. POLISHER

The chapters of this book point us to fundamental understandings about aging in our society. While there is a popular image or myth about the elderly, that all old people are depressed or unhappy, this is far from the truth. For the most part, elders are not depressed, but in fact lead active and fulfilling lives. This book reports on the experience and treatment of depression among elders in very special circumstances: those who are chronically ill and live in nursing homes. Even among them, although depression occurs more frequently than among elders who do not live in nursing homes, the vast majority of residents are not depressed; also, as the chapters here show, there are many ways of treating depression.

That brings us to a second important point raised by this book: the very important role played by research about the elderly. Research, such as that presented here, is very important in counteracting, step by step, misconceptions and myths about the elderly. People simply do not change and become ineffective at age 65 or 70. Indeed, the elderly have many strengths and make many positive contributions to society at all levels. Unfortunately, we live in a society that does not always value or nurture the aged.

Thus research, such as that conducted at the Philadelphia Geriatric Center and many universities and hospitals, has been crucial in developing our understanding of what old age is really like and what it can be optimally, and in not bowing to negative myths and popular misconceptions about the aged. At the very least, research is critical because it presents us with a map of what is and what can be, across all dimensions of the aging experience.

One characteristic of the research presented in this volume is that it represents work undertaken by many scholarly and professional disciplines and perspectives: medicine, psychiatry, psychology, nursing, sociology, anthropology, and others. Aging is not experienced just biologically or just socially. It is experienced on all levels and requires many specialized skills to be understood fully.

Research also directly confronts the problems and difficulties experienced by elderly people and their families. This brings us to a third point: Research such as that presented here enlightens us about medical, psychological, and social aspects of aging and old age and about how best to deal with the problems that do occur in later life. In this regard, a fourth important point made clear by the chapters to follow is that the treatment of depression, even among people who are sick and in diminished circumstances, can be effective. Committed, caring teams of practitioners, armed with the best knowledge, can and do make a profound difference in the lives of the people for whom they care.

The chapters presented in this book were based on papers delivered at a conference in Philadelphia in April of 1994, sponsored by the Polisher Research Institute of the Philadelphia Geriatric Center. The conference was attended by more than 300 practitioners and researchers. It is my hope that, through this presentation in published form, the knowledge these papers contain will be further used to improve the lives of our elderly.

Introduction

ROBERT L. RUBINSTEIN
M. POWELL LAWTON

Over the last few years, and despite definite progress, a social fog has persisted that has prevented us from acknowledging, understanding, and alleviating the disease of depression. And even the modest improvement in understanding and treating depression has brought with it bad as well as good news.

The bad news about depression takes several forms. It is important to note that, when an effort is made to identify it, depression is, in fact, found to affect many victims and their families. Several chapters in this book report on rates of depression among community samples. More bad news about depression is the reality that depression disproportionately affects certain categories of people. Elderly nursing home residents, for example, experience some form of depression at a rate exceeding that of elderly community residents. Similarly, while there are a number of good interventions that can be used to treat depression, the rate of application of treatment has yet to match the frequency and severity of this disease, especially in senior residential care and in nursing homes. Also, depressive states have not yet been fully accepted as disease states. Culturally, there still remains a widespread sense that depression is largely a function of lack of personal willpower, or that it is mere moodiness. Such false ideas still strongly permeate both popular and clinical cultures.

At the same time, however, there is good news about depression and its treatment, as the chapters that follow will attest. Research over the last decade has brought a vastly improved, age-specific understanding of depression. There has been continuing exploration of the biopsychosocial factors contributing to the etiology of depression in later life. And there has been very great progress toward its control and cure. Several techniques have been shown to be highly effective. As Chapter 11, by Barry Lebowitz, demonstrates, the efficacy of treatment for depression rivals or exceeds that for other diseases.

The book begins with an overview—Chapter 1, by Ira Katz and Patricia Parmelee—which treats the phenomenon of depression in nursing home and residential care. Katz and Parmelee note the widespread prevalence of mental disorders in nursing homes and the elevated frequency of depression in nursing homes. The unfortunate reality is that direct-care staff are often unequipped to handle or treat depression in such settings. The salience of the problem of depression in nursing homes, they note, is clear and compelling. There are significant unmet needs for mental health services; comparatively high frequencies of major depression among nursing home residents; depressive reactions to the experience of chronic illness, disability, and pain accompanying medical illness; and profound consequences for morbidity and mortality from depression. Although the authors' focus is on chronically ill nursing home residents, they also note that findings about the consequences of depression can be sensitive indicators of associations that may also be present, if more subtly, in younger and healthier patients.

Katz and Parmelee report that, depending on the study, the prevalence of mental health disorders in nursing homes ranges from 41% to 87%, and the prevalence of depression itself from 6% to 25%. They note the close and frequent association of depression with chronic illness and pain from illness, and the role of depression in particular in amplifying the experience of pain.

It is important to note, as they do, that people with a psychiatric history of depression are not admitted selectively to nursing homes. Rather, the origin of residents' depression is closely associated with their health conditions as well as their adjustments to nursing home life.

Katz and Parmelee note that depression may also be experienced along with the cognitive decline associated with dementia, a disease often found among nursing home residents. Depression can contribute to the behavioral disturbances and agitation often found among demented nursing home residents. Depression, Katz and Parmelee conclude, can also be persistent and therefore often challenging to the most proactive treatment plans. They end their discussion with a brief, general overview of psychopharmacologic and nonpsychopharmacologic methods of treating depression in the nursing home.

Part I, Research on the Nature of Depression in the Elderly, presents several research studies on depression in nursing homes and residential care. Each chapter in Part I discusses a different facet of the interplay between the personal experience of depression and the medical construction of depression as a diagnostic category. Further, each chapter develops a theoretical position with respect to depression and other affects, and each provides implications for treatment.

Chapter 2, by M. Powell Lawton, continues in part the theme of the overview, but it broadens the overview by discussing a general theory of the emotions in later life and a research program on positive and negative emotions (including depression) as experienced by residents of nursing homes and senior apartments, as well as other elders. Lawton thus expands the discussion of depression in the nursing home per se from the clinical diagnosis of depression to a general examination of negative and positive affect in later life. He notes that *depression* is not only a clinical and medical term—that is, not only a term describing disease—but also a term used to describe an emotion or a personal state of being. The relationship of depression as an emotion to depression as a clinical syndrome is important, he notes. Lawton relates his research project to theories of personality development in adulthood and later life, particularly the long-standing debate about the stability of personality over the life span. While evidence suggests that personality has considerable stability, he notes that emotions and moods are much more transitory components of the personality system. These more changeable features are an extremely salient component of quality of life.

An important but unexpected finding presented in Chapter 2 is the imperfect correlation between positive and negative affects. A two-factor structure to emotion has been found in many studies, although the details of how the emotions are linked to each factor may vary. He notes that positive, diverting, environmentally engaging experiences heighten positive affect but do not lessen negative affect; and that negative internal experiences (such as poor health or poor personal relationships) that reflect upon the self contribute to negative affect but are less likely to impair positive affect. The therapeutic implications of this disjunction between positive and negative affect for the nursing home setting are significant: While programming activities may not diminish depression and other negative emotions, diverting and engaging programming can buffer or augment positive emotions and thereby strengthen the self. This argument also anticipates the discussion by Larry Thompson and Dolores Gallagher-Thompson, in Chapter 8, of work done in the nursing home to stimulate positive moods or develop a sense of pleasant events.

Turning to the question of how depression is experienced by residents of a nursing home and people in congregate residential care, Lawton reports on research designed to illuminate the temporal aspects of the experience of depression and other components of mental health, through a series of 30 consecutive daily ratings of affect states. Of great significance here is his finding that, contrary to expectations, people with major depression do not experience it, or other negative affect, as pervasive and unrelenting. Rather, negative affect is experienced as variable—more so among depressed people than among so-called "normals." Thus, while people with major depressive disorders experience relatively little positive affect, they do have days characterized by an absence of negative affect intermixed with bad days, or despite a dominant sense of emotional negativity or affective anomie. An important conclusion here is that for most people depression is not unrelenting. In addition, an excellent rationale is given for increasing the frequency and intensity of positive experiences within the nursing home. This has clear implications for programming social components and activities.

Jana Mossey, in her chapter on depression among the medically ill—Chapter 3—reports on findings from three research studies. Whereas Lawton's chapter addresses depression in the context of other emotions and reports on variations in the daily experience of depression and other emotions, Mossey focuses on another poorly understood area of depression research: subdysthymia. *Subdysthymia* here refers to elevated symptoms of depression that are self-reported but do not meet clinical criteria for depression or dysthymia. Subdysthymia has also been called (among other terms) "mild depression" or "subthreshold depression." Subdysthymia is, Mossey notes, a serious condition with important ramifications, one that is defined with reference to baseline clinical parameters as a "low-key" type of depressive syndrome. It may be more similar to the nondepressive array of negative emotions outlined by Lawton in Chapter 2. It may also be a kind of depression that is more integrated into the natural experience of everyday life and that may be phenomenologically less separated from "normality" or from the natural experience of daily life.

Mossey notes that among community populations of elderly persons, prevalence rates for depression of this type range from 15 to 30%, depending on the study. Mossey addresses several important questions: Are subdysthymic conditions related to medical illness or predictive of more acute forms of depression? Is depression in the medically ill a new condition, born of adjustment to the illness, or does it occur in more continuous or chronic conditions? What are the consequences of subdysthymic conditions for illnesses? How do people with subdysthymic conditions differ from those who have no depressive symptoms at all? What therapies are available and effective for subdysthymic symptoms?

Mossey treats these topics with reference to three studies. Two of these are studies of hospitalized residents of nursing homes and senior housing; the third is a study of hospitalized community dwelling elderly people. Mossey finds that subdysthymia seems to be definable and clinically significant. Indeed, she finds that health care resources are used disproportionately by subdysthymic persons and that their recovery from medical illness is delayed or of poorer quality.

Chapter 3 has clinical implications and implications for therapy. A key issue in the institutional setting is adequate identification not only of persons with syndromic depression but also of those with subdysthymic depression. Much work remains to be done on ''unpacking'' the nature and experience of subdysthymia in the nursing home. As a whole, Mossey's chapter demonstrates the advantage of moving away from a rigid, binary, ''clinical versus normal'' approach to the identification and treatment of psychological disorders in these environments.

Chapter 4, by Mark Luborsky and Elizabeth Riley, like Mossey's chapter, summarizes research from several studies; and, like Lawton's chapter, it deals with the ''natural'' experience of depression in the nursing homes, although in a different way. Luborsky and Riley are concerned with residents' own experiences and understanding of depression. Thus a key question in Chapter 4, one that is significant in understanding the natural experience of depression in the nursing home, is: How do residents themselves, rather than the clinicians, understand and interpret their own depressive states? The research reported in Chapter 4 uses ethnographic and qualitative research techniques to assess this and other questions.

In one study, respondents in nursing homes, of whom some were not depressed and others exhibited a range of depressive diagnoses, were asked to explain what the word *depression* means. There were significant differences in responses between the depressed and nondepressed nursing home residents. Informants were also asked to compare ''depression'' with other descriptors of kinds of negative emotions such as ''sad'' or ''blue.'' They were asked what they thought causes depression, who gets depressed, what the stages of depression are, and what folk or lay management strategies for handling depression they could describe.

At the very least this reminds clinicians, therapists, and practitioners that in assessing treatment issues in the nursing home and residential care, they will face preexisting worlds and preexisting systems of meaning that are already in operation and that may have an important role in depression.

How people manage their own depression, how a scrutinizing ego assesses or interprets its own depression, and how depression relates to a foreshortened or ''end of life'' worldview appear to be virtually unresearched. These issues are also touched on in Chapters 5, 6, and 9.

A second study described by Luborsky and Riley investigated the perceived lifetime personal identity of informants in relation to depression. The study found a time-based structure in self-reports of depression and other affects. A third study examined personal themes and the structure of life stories in nursing home residents, and their relationship to depression. There are clear differences in how depressed and nondepressed long-term care residents narrate their life stories.

These studies describe how depression and other components of negative affect are interwoven into everyday life and into the experiences of nursing home residents. The research by Luborsky and Riley reveals, in a highly original way, how depression may be an object of thematic organization, temporal orientations, constructed meanings, cognitions, and "folk" management procedures, and how these relate to elements of personal identity, to biography, and to the perception of the life course.

It has long been noted that aging reduces a person socially, making people somehow "less than" or "less whole than" they once were. Barry Rovner's provocative chapter—Chapter 5—refers us to the embodied self, the self of mortal hearts and bones, of things that can and do go wrong and of the world as a changed place. In the nursing home, this problem may be magnified, as residents are seen as patients—frail, sick, demented or depressed—rather than as whole people with dignity and a biography. But clearly adumbrated here are hearts and bones of a more metaphoric or transcendent nature, the realm of human striving, envisioning, imagination, and pleasure.

Rovner returns us to a reality that should be stressed: Why is major depression *not* more common in old age? He reviews some reasons why old age may be incorrectly associated with depression, including the increased possibility of depression in some specific forms of disease that are associated with old age. He concludes that the most telling reason for this association is our tendency to see old age, metaphorically, as something else: not as life, but as loss, pain, disease, death. Thus there is a cultural association of old age with a variety of declines. As part of this complex of declines, depression becomes just another one of several expected negatives. But, Rovner suggests, we must look beyond the pathological processes of old age to processes that lead to growth, enrichment, and wisdom.

The chapters by Rovner (Chapter 5), Cohen (Chapter 10), and Luborsky and Riley (Chapter 4) are related in that they all see a person-centered, biographic, life course, or historical dimension in the experience of depression. This anchors clinical diagnosis in the context of the whole person and a wide array of capacities and possibilities.

Part II, Research on the Treatment of Depression, consists of four chapters that concern the treatment of depression in the nursing home. Chapter 1 (by Katz and Parmelee) and Chapter 3 (by Mossey) in Part I briefly review some treatment methodologies. In Part II, all the chapters describe, in varying detail, the link between treatment and research about treatment.

While this book discusses several therapeutic techniques, the greatest attention is given to psychotherapy and related cognitive and behavioral interventions. The text touches on five techniques that can alleviate depression or buffer the self in dealing with depression.

Predominant among all treatments for depression is pharmacologic intervention. For this book, a decision was made not to review psychopharmacologic interventions, because that has recently been done in a number of excellent articles, cited in Chapter 1. However, Chapter 11, by Barry Lebowitz, does present some of the issues that have governed the use of psychotropic medications in the nursing homes, including the effects of OBRA in 1987.

Particular attention is given to psychotherapy and cognitive and behavioral methodologies. These modalities represent a category of techniques that can be used effectively in the nursing home and in senior residences. The four chapters in Part II directly concern these techniques.

In Chapter 6, Linda Teri examines a research program about a clinical application for alleviating depression. In particular, she is concerned with depression that is experienced with dementia. In this case, depression is an ''excess disability'' that can be treated effectively even if the underlying dementia itself cannot. She notes that the combination of these two disorders is quite common among demented elders, and that such patients have significantly more dysphoric mood, vegetative signs, social withdrawal, loss of interest, feelings of guilt and worthlessness, and suicidal ideation; are more likely to have delusions and hallucinations; experience more behavioral disturbances; and have more problems with restlessness, falling, agitation, suspiciousness, incontinence, and functional disability. Teri notes that depression can affect not only the victim but also the family.

Chapter 6, like the other chapters in this section, as well as Chapters 1 and 11, highlights the significant relationship between depression and dementia. Teri outlines why nonpharmacologic approaches may be especially effective for dealing with depression in dementia patients. Drugs may not always be effective, may engender iatrogenic disorders, or may not be useful in patients with multiple disorders and polypharmacy; and they may further reduce cognitive capacity. Similarly, while traditional therapeutic approaches may not be useful for patients with cognitive impairment, there are a number of behavioral techniques, Teri argues, that are useful. Chapter 6 describes one such intervention, called the Seattle Protocol, which uses behavioral strategies shown initially to be helpful for depressed adults who were not demented. The usefulness of this technique for caregivers and for depressed, demented patients is described. The treatment involves nine weekly 60-minute sessions. An evaluation of this program is also described.

Chapter 7, by Abraham and colleagues, also has a perspective derived from cognitive and behavioral therapy. This approach is tailored to the capacities of frail, depressed, cognitively impaired nursing home residents. These authors note that although their own previous interventions—group therapy involving cognitive-behavioral techniques and focused visual imagery—did not produce significant changes in several criteria of depression and distress, these interventions did produce significant improvements in the overall cognitive status of nursing home residents. The authors also examine further cognitive group intervention for depression among nursing home residents. The chapter offers a brief review of cognitive-behavioral therapy and focused visual-imagery therapy for depressed elders. Research that evaluates these interventions on the affects and cognitions of depressed nursing home residents is summarized, particularly with reference to the factor structure of the Geriatric Depression Scale.

The reanalysis probes possible reasons why cognitive group interventions with depressed nursing home residents failed to reduce symptoms of depression. Several possible reasons are explored, and these are useful in considering therapeutic interventions with cognitively impaired depressed nursing home residents. One possible implication of these findings, Abraham and his colleagues note, is that elevated depression among the aged, as scored by established instruments such as the CES-D, often occurs primarily because of high scores on subscales that represent lack of well-being. Thus this may not be depression per se, but rather some more global situation in which people come to grips with finitude or constrained life space. Relating depression to more generalized concerns of the whole person is a theme taken up in Chapter 5 (by Rovner) and Chapter 10 (by Cohen).

The focus on psychotherapeutic interventions in the nursing home is expanded in Chapter 8, by Thompson and Gallagher-Thompson. This chapter discusses elders in outpatient and extended-care settings and briefly reviews both psychodynamic and cognitive-behavioral approaches to treatment of the aged in general. Specifically, the chapter discusses how cognitive therapy could be useful in treating depression among residents of nursing homes and other long-term care settings. Cognitive techniques that help patients identify dysfunctional thoughts contributing to depression and lowered self-esteem are outlined. Procedures for treating depression by examining and evaluating dysfunctional thoughts and using "pleasant events" inventories are discussed.

Thompson and Gallagher-Thompson's use of the "pleasant events" inventory was derived from the work of the psychologist Peter Lewinsohn.

Lawton's work (Chapter 2) also owes much to Lewinsohn's work. Thompson and Gallagher-Thompson follow Lewinsohn in suggesting that increasing pleasant events acts to diminish depression or negative affect in cognitively impaired residents. These authors provide a list of behavior therapy interventions used in the nursing home that can significantly strengthen the self and increase positive affect.

The last chapter in Part II—Chapter 9, by Deborah Frazer—concerns psychotherapy in residential settings for the elderly. There have been few studies of the processes and outcomes of psychotherapy in the nursing home and in residential care. Frazer notes, nevertheless, that there is clear evidence—from a variety of research projects with several perspectives, including psychodynamic and cognitive-behavioral approaches—that therapy is effective in treating depression in other geriatric settings.

Chapter 9 presents findings from three preliminary studies of processes and outcomes of psychotherapy in the nursing home and in residential care. The first of these is a study of social skills training, a form of focused behavioral training, using techniques developed by Allen Bellack and his associates. Problems that can be addressed by such techniques include a wide variety of everyday difficulties in the nursing home (such as getting along with a roommate, and other issues in interpersonal interactions) that are stressors or are lightning rods for depressive affect. The second study examined psychotherapy for the oldest old: it considered the psychotherapeutic experiences of ten residents of a nursing home and senior apartment complex, whose average age was about 87. The third study assessed the process and course of psychotherapy in residential care settings.

Frazer's research indicates that with elderly people, the dropout rate from psychotherapy is considerably less among nursing home residents than among community residents. The study described here analyzes data on use of psychotherapy by 329 residents of a nursing home and a senior apartment complex, treating diagnostic categories, persistence, patterns of use of therapy, and diagnostic change over time. These are important data.

In Chapter 9 (as in Chapters 6 and 8), the details of therapeutic practice are significant. The account of steps in planning psychotherapy in this environment will be highly useful to professionals responsible for such a study.

Several other techniques for alleviating depression are also described or touched on in this book. For example, Chapter 2 (by Lawton) suggests that an increase in positive experiences can lead to an increase in positive affect, which may serve to buoy up well-being. "Positive events" or "pleasant events" techniques are also described by Thompson and Gallagher-Thompson in Chapter 8; they provide a detailed explanation of the use of "positive events" techniques in the nursing home. Such techniques share some of the characteristics of cognitive-behavioral, intrapsychic, and environmental interventions because they provide for external stimuli of internal states, including fantasy.

A final technique with potential to alleviate depression—environmental modification—is not discussed directly in this book, although the "pleasant events" technique may be seen as a form of environmental modification. Environmental interventions are theoretically linked to Lawton's concept of positive and negative affect and may increase positive affect through less direct pathways. An example might be planning travel or a holiday through the imagination—a process in which the immediate psychic environment is altered. Environmental modifications may also diminish negative affect by promoting competence through adjusting "environmental press" to an individual's level of competence.

Some environmental modifications may be difficult to achieve. In a nursing home, the burden of change and adaptation is on the individual. Social skills training, for example, may improve interpersonal performance, but these skills may be brought to bear on interaction situations that are constrained by the structure and demands of the environment: a nursing home or residential care.

The public image of nursing homes as depressing institutional environments characterized by death, dying, and human misery, could be used to explain some of the negative affect found among residents. In fact, research evidence is not at hand to document depression as an inevitable consequence of life in a nursing home. Neither is such a view consistent with the idea that the majority of people in nursing homes are not depressed or dysphoric.

In Part III, Implications for Policy and Future Research, Gene Cohen's chapter—Chapter 10—directly addresses society's failure to attend to mental health needs adequately or compassionately. Cohen suggests that this is a major public health failure. He highlights the nursing home as the major arena for the treatment of mental health problems of the aged, particularly when physical and mental health problems together produce health conditions that simply cannot be handled by family caregivers, no matter how dedicated and loving. Key policy questions emerge, especially the question of how quality of life can match increasing longevity and issues of cost. Cohen places mental health issues in later life in the larger context of what he calls the "geriatric landscape," a construct for examining the depth and breadth of human experience in later life. This is an attempt to place clinical concerns in a wider context of experience. Cohen turns, finally, to the topic of creativity and aging, and, like Rovner (in Chapter 5), to the possibilities for expression and growth with age, an antithesis to geriatric depression.

The final chapter—Chapter 11, by Barry Lebowitz—addresses developments and prospects for research and treatment of depression in long-term care. Lebowitz reminds us that "alternatives" to nursing home care are not likely to erase the need for nursing homes, and thus that issues concerning physical and mental health in the nursing home, and the relationship between them, are not likely to disappear. Lebowitz identifies a historical barrier to the care of the mentally ill in nursing homes and traces it to policies developed for funding, primarily so that states would not identify state hospitals as "nursing homes" for possible reimbursement. Later, for purposes of Medicaid, Alzheimer's disease was relabeled as a "neurological and behavioral disorder." Thus there is a tacit denial of mental illness as a significant problem in nursing homes—which, despite their high prevalence of mental problems such as depression and physical problems that may induce depression, give an appearance of being concerned primarily with physical disorders.

Lebowitz reminds us that depression is not only a clinical disorder and an experience, but also a historical and cultural construct. That construct has been subjected to powerful forces in conflict over its definition and its treatment. The nursing home is not the only solution to the most profound health problems of later life, but the development of nursing homes is the product of history and of economic, moral, cultural, and political forces. It is useful to remember that there is little set in stone about the nature and conduct of nursing homes and that, although such places are not likely to disappear—since they are germane to the needs of so many people—they can be rethought and reinvented.

In concluding this introduction to an important and neglected topic, it may also be useful to look into the future. One cannot help feeling some pessimism about the ability of the health-care system to change enough to accommodate the needs of elders in these settings who suffer from depressive illness. Managed care for those living in noninstitutional settings (including residential care) has so far been disinclined to include mental health services on an equal basis with other services. State responsibility for institutional services, in the form of locally administered block grants, may also slight mental health services. The editors hope that this book will document the need for treatment and provide evidence for the treatability of depressive states, in both the community and the institution.

Acknowledgments

A work of this sort cannot be undertaken without the help of many people. We wish to acknowledge, with gratitude, the help we have received.

The editors are grateful to Edward N. Polisher for his support of the research conference from which the chapters in this book derive. Mr. Polisher has been, for many years, a key supporter of the Philadelphia Geriatric Center (PGC) and its research program.

We also wish to acknowledge the support of Frank Podietz, President of the Philadelphia Geriatric Center; and Arnold Kramer, Chairman of the board of Directors of the Philadelphia Geriatric Center.

We also gratefully acknowledge the efforts of Kimberly Wagman and Shelly Benedict in organizing the conference on which the chapters are based, and of Bernice Albert, Anita Garber, and Mary McCaffrey, of the PGC staff, for their help.

CHAPTER 1

Overview

IRA R. KATZ
PATRICIA A. PARMELEE

Depression in long-term care was recognized as one of the key problems in the mental health of the elderly by the recent National Institutes of Health (NIH) Consensus Statement on the Diagnosis and Treatment of Depression in Late Life: "Among the 1.5 million older people living in nursing homes, the prevalence of depression is high. Despite the special vulnerability of old persons in nursing homes and despite the federal regulation that a facility must ensure that 'a resident who displays mental or psychosocial adjustment difficulty receives appropriate treatment and services . . . ,' few nursing homes have the staff capability to intervene in an appropriate and timely fashion. In the nursing home, as in the community, depression goes unrecognized, undiagnosed, and untreated" (Friedhoff, 1992).

This topic warrants attention for several reasons. First, it is important because depression among the elderly in residential care represents a practical clinical problem: Patients in long-term care have significant, largely unmet, needs for mental health services. Second, it is an exemplar of more general problems related to geriatric depression. As a result of the increased prevalence of affective symptoms occurring in association with chronic physical illness, disability, and dependence, residential care facilities can serve, in a sense, as laboratories for studies of the psychopathology of late life. Findings about depression as it occurs in long-term

Note: This chapter, a revision and expansion of material presented at the Consensus Development Conference (Katz & Parmelee, 1993), summarizes the research results that led to the National Institutes of Health conclusions and supplements them with more recent findings.

1

care patients are relevant to the far larger group of older patients living in the community with varying degrees of chronic disease and disability. Finally, it is important because the frailty and vulnerability of long-term care patients lead to a compression of the morbidity and mortality associated with depression. Therefore, findings about the consequences of depression here can be sensitive indicators of associations that may be present, but subtler, with younger and healthier patients.

In addition to the approximately 1.5 million older Americans in nursing homes, a comparable number live in other forms of planned housing for the elderly. At any time, approximately 5% of the elderly are living in nursing homes, but the probability that any individual will require nursing home care at some time in his or her life is far higher, approximately 20% to 25%. The residents of nursing homes are drawn largely from the oldest old: Nursing homes house 1% of those aged 65 to 74 years, but 22% of those 85 and older. Accordingly, in parallel with the aging of the population as a whole, it is expected that the number of nursing home residents will double shortly after the year 2020 and triple by 2040. Given that current costs of nursing home care are estimated to be approximately $50 billion per year, nursing home care is obviously a major issue, in both human and economic terms.

The importance of the mental health aspects of nursing home care was stressed in the nursing home reform provisions of the Omnibus Budget Reconciliation Act of 1987 (OBRA, 1987; Public Law 100-203). Components relevant to mental health include the provisions for Preadmission Screening and Annual Resident Review (PASARR), designed to ensure that patients who require inpatient psychiatric care are not inappropriately placed in nursing homes where they cannot receive necessary treatment; that residents will be free from unnecessary drugs and physical or chemical restraints, and from inappropriate use of antipsychotic drugs; and that residents who are in a nursing home and belong there receive the mental health care that they need. In addition to the regulations of the Health Care Financing Administration (HCFA, 1991) about "mental or psychosocial adjustment difficulty," other regulations require that specialized rehabilitative services, including "health rehabilitative services for mental illness," be available to those who need them. The law thus has provisions that are intended to keep "psychiatric" patients out of the nursing home, to keep physicians from using psychotropic drugs inappropriately, and to make mental health services available when needed. Enforcement of these laws requires that relevant regulations and guidelines be adapted and implemented. It is ironic that, at this time, development of regulations that mandate treatment when it is needed are lagging behind the others. This is especially important in light of studies suggesting that as few as

10% of the needs of nursing home residents for mental health services are being met (Burns & Taube, 1990), that nursing home residents with a diagnosis of depression in their medical records are more likely to be treated with neuroleptics or benzodiazepines than with antidepressants, and that only 10% receive appropriate antidepressant medications (Heston, Garrard, Makris, et al., 1992).

EPIDEMIOLOGY OF DEPRESSION IN THE NURSING HOME

Although federal legislation regarding mental health components of nursing home care is a recent development, it has long been recognized that most residents have diagnosable psychiatric disorders. In his classic early studies, Goldfarb (1962) found that the prevalence of psychiatric disorders in metropolitan old age and nursing homes was 87%. Although the populations served by nursing homes and the types of services provided have evolved over time, this estimate remains valid three decades later. Early studies of psychiatric disorders in these facilities were conducted when it was common to admit deinstitutionalized chronic psychiatric patients. Yet the presence of psychiatric disorders among nursing home residents cannot be attributed solely to the admission of patients known to have chronic mental illness. This was demonstrated by Stotsky (1967), who studied "allegedly nonpsychiatric patients in nursing homes" and found a high prevalence of psychiatric disorders including "chronic brain syndrome" with or without behavior disturbances, psychoses, and depressions.

The high prevalence of mental disorders has repeatedly been confirmed, as has the finding that dementia is the most prevalent type of psychiatric disorder and depression the second most common. Using data from medical records and nursing reports, the 1984 National Nursing Home Survey Pretest (Burns, Larson, Goldstrom, et al., 1988) found a 69% prevalence of mental disorders, including a 6.9% prevalence of depression. The 1985 National Nursing Home Survey (Strahan & Burns, 1991) found prevalence rates of 65.3% for any mental disorder and 11% for depression. The National Institute of Mental Health (NIMH) Epidemiological Catchment Area Study of nursing homes in the Baltimore area (German, Shapiro, & Kramer, 1986) used a structured interview, the Diagnostic Interview Schedule (DIS), and found a 41% prevalence for any psychiatric diagnosis, with 6.8% prevalence of affective disorders.

Recent data, however, suggest that both medical records and the DIS grossly underestimate the presence of psychiatric disorders in general, and depression in particular, among long-term care patients. Recent reviews of the epidemiology of depression in residential care facilities (Ames, 1991, 1993; Abrams, Teresi, & Butin, 1992) suggest that significant depressive symptoms are present in 30% to 50% of nursing home residents, with the exact figures dependent on the type of facility surveyed, assessment methods, and subjects selected. Although there is some ambiguity about the true prevalence of depressive symptoms, it is clear that they are substantially more common in the nursing home than among elderly community residents. Moreover, these findings are consistent across na-tions, cultures, and health care delivery systems; thus, the problem cannot be attributed only to deficits in American nursing homes. Nor is the excess in depressive symptoms limited to the nursing home; it is also apparent in other long-term care settings. Gurland, Copeland, Kuriansky, et al. (1983) found increased symptoms of depression in all residential care settings; in New York (but not in London) the level of symptomatology increases with the level of care from limited home care through adult homes to nursing homes.

PREVALENCE AND INCIDENCE IN LONG-TERM CARE

Estimates of the prevalence of major depression in the nursing home range from 6% to 25%. Our own data, drawn from ongoing research of our Clinical Research Center at the nursing home and congregate apartments of the Philadelphia Geriatric Center (PGC), appear as Table 1.1.

Using the Geriatric Depression scale (GDS; Yesavage et al., 1983) in conjunction with a symptom checklist based on Spitzer and Endicott's (1979) Schizophrenia and Affective Disorders Schedule, we found the overall prevalence of a major depression among PGC residents to be 14.1%. "Minor" depression—significant dysphoria that did not meet the criteria of the *Diagnostic and Statistical Manual of Mental Disorders* (*DSM-III-R*; American Psychiatric Association, 1987)—was observed in another 19.3% of residents. Paralleling the findings of Gurland et al. (1983), we observed much higher rates of major depression among nursing home patients (23.3%) than tenants of congregate apartments (8.5%); for minor depression, this difference was much less pronounced (23.3% in the nursing home; 16.7% in the apartments). Depression occurred as frequently in cognitively intact persons as in people with dementia. Note, however, that these percentages apply only to those residents who were sufficiently intact to respond meaningfully to questions; like other investi-gators, we were unable to assess depression among the most severely cognitively impaired (see Parmelee, Katz, & Lawton, 1989, for related data).

TABLE 1.1   Prevalence of Research-Diagnosed Depression as a Function of Location and Cognitive Status

	Nursing home		Apartments		Total	
	n	(%)	n	(%)	n	(%)
Cognitively intact						
Major depression	44	(8.2)	47	(5.9)	91	(6.8)
Minor depression	50	(9.4)	83	(10.4)	133	(10.0)
No depression	100	(18.7)	411	(51.6)	511	(38.4)
Cognitively impaired						
Major depression	84	(15.7)	21	(2.6)	105	(7.9)
Minor depression	74	(13.9)	50	(6.3)	124	(9.3)
No depression	182	(34.1)	184	(23.1)	366	(27.5)
Total	534	(40.2)	796	(59.8)	1,330	

Fewer findings are available on the incidence of depression in the nursing home. Katz, Lesher, Kleban, et al. (1989) observed a 14% incidence of major depression over a 6-month period and found that patients with minor depression were at increased risk. Foster, Cataldo, and Boksay (1991) report a 14% annual incidence for any depression with a 1:3 ratio of major to minor depression. In a residential care facility consisting of both a nursing home and congregate apartments, our own data (see Table 1.2; see also Parmelee, Katz, & Lawton, 1992a) indicated that the 1-year incidence of major depression was 7.8% overall, and that of minor depression 6.7%, among those with no depression at baseline. The inci-

TABLE 1.2   Change in Depression Over a 1-Year Interval

	Time 2 status					
	Possible major depression		Minor depression		No depression	
Time 1 status	n	(%)	n	(%)	n	(%)
Possible major depression	26	(44.8)	16	(27.6)	16	(27.6)
Minor depression	15	(13.6)	33	(30.0)	62	(56.4)
No depression	20	(4.8)	28	(6.7)	373	(88.6)
Total	61	(10.4)	77	(13.1)	451	(76.6)

dence of major depression was 13.6% among those with minor depression at baseline, suggesting that minor depression is a risk factor for major depression.

HEALTH AND FUNCTIONAL CORRELATES

Taken together, these findings demonstrate that depressions are common in nursing homes and other forms of residential care for the elderly. The reason for the excess is not that patients with psychiatric histories are admitted to nursing homes in large numbers, but that depression is frequently associated with the disabling chronic illnesses that make placement necessary. Data from our own research, presented in Table 1.3, make this point clearly. Cognitive status as indexed by the Blessed Test (Blessed, Tomlinson, & Roth, 1968), functional disability in performance of activities of daily living (Lawton & Brody, 1969), physician-rated physical health, and self-reported pain (Parmelee, 1994) are all associated with depression: More impaired persons are more likely to be depressed, with greatest depression (i.e., meeting criteria for major depression) among the least able.

There must be questions about the extent to which the increased rates of depression result from disease and disability, from the nature of the institutional environment, or from interactions between the two. One study (Zemore & Eames, 1979) attempted to look at this problem by comparing depression in nursing home residents and patients with comparable levels of disease and disability on a waiting list for admission, and found compa-

TABLE 1.3   Functional Correlates of Depression

	Possible major depression		Minor depression		No depression	
	Mean	(SD)	Mean	(SD)	Mean	(SD)
Cognitive status[*]	9.05[a, b]	(6.00)	9.51[a]	(6.02)	7.88[b]	(5.42)
Functional status[**]	13.74[a]	(4.18)	11.46[b]	(3.57)	10.25[c]	(2.75)
Health[**]	1.81[a]	(.34)	1.64[b]	(.32)	1.59[b]	(.32)
Pain[**]	2.44[a]	(1.37)	2.11[b]	(1.13)	1.65[c]	(.95)

[*]$p < .02$
[**]$p < .001$
[a-c]Means with differing superscripts differ significantly at the .05 level or better (Tukey B tests).

rable degrees of depression. The comparison, however, may not be valid, because the group seeking nursing home admission must be considered a group under stress, since current care plans have not worked; anticipation of nursing home placement, in fact, may be a risk factor for suicide (Loebel, Loebel, Dager, et al., 1991). Regardless of the basic causes, it is important to emphasize that depression is the most common reversible psychiatric disorder in residential care patients, and that there are frequent opportunities for treatment and even for prevention of psychiatric disorders in the institutionalized aged.

ASSESSMENT OF DEPRESSION

There has been some controversy about the extent to which standard methods for screening and for the assessment of depressive symptoms can be applied to elderly residential care patients. The Geriatric Depression Scale (GDS) was validated for use in the nursing home by Lesher (1986) and has subsequently been used in several illustrative studies. Kafonek, Ettinger, Roca, et al. (1989) used a cutoff of 13 and found that the GDS identified clinician-rated depression with only 47% sensitivity and 75% specificity. In contrast, Snowdon and Donnelly (1986), using a similar cutoff, found a sensitivity of 86% and a specificity of 87% for identification of major depression. Parmelee, Lawton, and Katz (1989) used a cutoff of 10 and found 74% sensitivity and 82% specificity for research diagnoses of any depression, and 93% sensitivity and 73% specificity for major depression. The differences among these studies appear related primarily to the utility of the scale for the detection of depression in patients with cognitive impairment. Kafonek et al. (1989) reported a deterioration in the sensitivity of the scale from 75% in intact residents to 25% in those with cognitive impairment. Yet Parmelee et al. (1989) found that the sensitivity and the reliability of the scale remain acceptable even in patients with mild to moderate degrees of dementia. In a more recent study, McGivney, Mulvihill, and Taylor (1994) examined the validity of the GDS (with a cutoff of 10) versus psychiatrists' diagnoses of depression and found that the scale was valid (84% sensitivity; 91% specificity) for residents with Mini-Mental State Examination scores greater than 14, but that the validity deteriorated for those with greater impairment. Differences between studies may reflect the methods used. Studies that were able to obtain meaningful data for patients with cognitive impairment administered the instrument as a semistructured interview with probes to determine whether subjects understood the questions and with patience about redirecting subjects to ensure responses in the required ''yes-no'' format.

There is clear agreement among investigators about one major problem in case identification: the reliability of staff ratings of depression in the nursing home. Although Parmelee, Lawton, and Katz (1989) reported a statistically significant correlation between staff ratings of depression (using the Raskin scale) and independent ratings of depression obtained using the GDS ($r = .34$; $n = 370$), the magnitude of this correlation is low. In support of this finding, Rovner, German, Brant, et al. (1991) report that nurses' ratings had a sensitivity of only 58% and a specificity of 66% for identification of patients with psychiatric diagnoses of any depression, and a sensitivity of 65% and specificity of 62% for major depression. Thus, available data suggest that nursing home staffs may have difficulty reliably identifying patients with depression and assessing the severity of their symptoms. Cohen-Mansfield and Marx (1988) and Cohen-Mansfield, Werner, and Marx (1990) have demonstrated that depression can contribute to problem behaviors, such as screaming and agitation, that are common in the nursing home; Rovner, Steele, German, et al. (1992) found that depression contributes to staff ratings of patients as "uncooperative." If depression is not recognized as a specific problem, patients presenting with these symptoms may be mistreated. OBRA regulations have established procedures for the identification of patients with depression that utilize staff ratings of behavior using the Minimum Data Set (MDS) followed by evaluations utilizing standardized Resident Assessment Protocols (RAPs). These methods are, however, being implemented before empirical data are available to demonstrate their reliability and sensitivity. The difficulties with staff ratings observed in previous research document the need for staff education to improve the reliability of assessments. Standardized training programs and more structured approaches to assessment may be necessary before staff ratings can be used for case identification.

COURSE OF DEPRESSION IN THE NURSING HOME

Although there is evidence that depression is common among elderly patients requiring institutional care, and that it covers a spectrum of conditions, there are recurrent questions about its clinical significance and course in this setting.

With respect to depressive symptoms, these questions include the concern that, in the nursing home and related settings, depression may be an existential state rather than a disease and that it may be an understandable and even an inevitable reaction to the stress of institutionalization. A second question concerns major depression. It is possible that diagnostic criteria validated in younger and healthier subjects may lose their predictive value in older patients with chronic medical or neurological illnesses in whom it may be difficult to distinguish between symptoms of medical illness and the somatic or neurovegetative components of depression. In the face of these concerns, it is important to determine whether depressions identified among the institutional elderly are clinically significant disorders having a substantial impact on the lives of the patients.

PERSISTENCE OF DEPRESSION

One measure of the clinical significance of depression as it occurs in residential care patients is its persistence. Evidence for the persistence of self-rated symptoms of depression comes from data from Parmelee, Lawton, and Katz (1989), who found that test-retest reliability for the GDS over the course of 1 month was 0.85; and from Katz et al. (1989), who found that it was 0.48 over 6 months. In our research (Table 1.2), we evaluated the relationship between depressive symptoms (major and minor) observed at two assessments separated by 1 year in a sample of patients living in a nursing home and congregate apartment facility and found again that depression was generally persistent. Approximately half of the patients who were identified as having major depression at the initial assessments were improved at 1 year, but fully half of those still had symptoms of minor depression. Although some patients with minor depression had deteriorated over 1 year, most were in remission; nonetheless, 43.6% still had significant levels of depressive symptoms. This rather poor long-range prognosis for depression echoes the report of Ames, Ashby, Mann, et al. (1988), who found that only 17% of (surviving) patients with depression had recovered at follow-up after an average of 3.6 years; and that of Ames (1992), who found that 59% of the depressives identified in a survey of nursing home residents died, 15% became demented, 20% remained depressed, 2% became psychotic, and 47% were left with "subcases" of depression after 4 to 5 years.

There are questions about the extent to which depression observed after admission to an institution can be considered an adjustment disorder, and hence likely to resolve spontaneously over time. Snowdon and Donnelly (1986), in a cross-sectional study, found a decrease in the intensity of self-rated depression as a function of time since admission to the nursing home. However, our own data (Katz et al., 1988; Parmelee et al., 1992a) compared the prognosis of depression over a 1-year period in patients who were newly admitted to the nursing home with that in veteran residents and found no evidence suggesting a better prognosis for depression observed at the time of admission.

As discussed earlier, depression occurs in both cognitively intact and impaired residential care patients. One-year test-retest reliability for the short form of the GDS suggests that symptoms are equally persistent in the two groups (Parmelee, Lawton, & Katz, 1989). In the residential care facility, where cognitively intact patients are likely to have required supportive care as a result of physical illnesses that cause disability, there appears to be little cross-sectional relationship between depression and cognitive impairment. However, findings from one longitudinal study indicated that depression may predict increased rates of cognitive decline over the subsequent year (Parmelee, Kleban, Lawton, & Katz, 1991). Further evidence for the clinical significance of depression comes from studies of its relationship with the need for care; with morbidity (pain, physical health, and functional status); with markers for subnutrition; and with mortality.

NEED FOR CARE

Fries, Mehr, Schneider, et al. (1993) used measures of nursing staff time spent in the care of patients with and without mental dysfunctions in developing case-mix models for reimbursement for nursing home care. They found that the diagnosis of depression was associated with an increase of approximately 6.5% in direct nursing staff time, even after controlling for impairments in activities of daily living (ADLs). The effect of depression was most significant among residents with intermediate self-care deficits; on the basis of these findings, depression is used in the Resource Utilization Groups Version III (RUG-III) as one of the diagnoses differentiating subgroups of residents with major medical conditions, such as hemiplegia, aphasia, or terminal illness, who will require additional care.

MORBIDITY

One way to assess the effects of depression as they occur in patients with physical illness is to probe the association of symptoms of depression with complaints of pain. Parmelee, Katz, and Lawton (1991; see Table 1.3) used a pain questionnaire derived from the McGill Pain Scale (Melzack, 1975) and found that major and minor depression are associated with both the intensity of self-reported pain and the number of complaints of localized pain. More recently, Cohen-Mansfield and Marx (1993) corroborated the association between depression and pain; they found that depressed affect is predicted by greater pain, a greater number of medical diagnoses, and a poorer social network. The investigation by Parmelee et al. (1991) of the association between specific complaints of pain and physician-rated disease on a system-by-system basis showed that depression was associated with increased pain in those patients for whom physicians could identify physical illnesses as possible causes. It therefore appears that depression amplifies complaints of pain referable to diseases recognized by physicians but does not, as a rule, lead to the generation of meaningless symptoms. Although further longitudinal research is needed to evaluate the extent to which pain is a cause as opposed to an effect of depression, the observed associations provide further evidence for the clinical significance of depressive symptoms in elderly people in residential care. The implication of the interactions between physical illness, pain, and depression is that physicians should attend carefully when a patient complains of pain, even if the patient is depressed.

A recurring, and troublesome, question is the causal link between depression and physical health among frail older persons. Certain health problems—including Parkinson's disease (Cummings, 1992; Mayeux et al., 1984); diabetes (Lustman et al., 1992); and, depending on the location of the lesion, stroke (Robinson et al., 1986)—are known to cause depression because of inherent biochemical or neuroanatomical changes. However, broadly based studies of the association between late-life depression and physical health (e.g., Borson et al., 1986; O'Riordan et al., 1989) have generally revealed few specific physical disorders that are consistently linked with depression. We have attempted to address this question among our sample of residents at the Philadelphia Geriatric Center by examining physicians' ratings of the seriousness of their patients' health problems for 13 separate organ systems, using the Cumulative Illness Rating Scale for Geriatrics (CIRS-G; Miller et al., 1991). Results of an initial multivariate analysis of variance (MANOVA), examining average ratings for persons with major, minor, or no depression, appear as Table 1.4. Significant differences appeared for 6 of the 13 systems, although the direction of the effect for hypertension—a "silent" disease in terms of its functional effects—was opposite that expected (i.e., healthier persons were more depressed). However, when we reanalyzed these data controlling for functional disability, the overall effect was eliminated, and only lower gastrointestinal and neurological problems remained significantly associated with depression. The nature of those effects needs further study. But overall, it appears that the high rates of depression observed among elderly long-term care residents are more closely related to their general frailty than to specific diseases.

This point is further reinforced when one examines the course of depression in tandem with the cause of functional decline. Figure 1.1

TABLE 1.4   Specific Health Conditions Associated With Depression[a]

	Major depression	Minor depression	No depression
Cardiac	2.18	2.14	2.14
Hypertension[b]	1.63	1.69	1.81
Vascular	2.02	1.88	1.84
Respiratory	1.60	1.50	1.43
Eyes, ears, nose, and throat	2.14	2.17	1.97
Upper gastrointestinal[c]	1.62	1.61	1.42
Lower gastrointestinal[d]	1.81	1.67	1.57
Hepatic	1.12	1.13	1.08
Renal	1.36	1.28	1.23
Other genitourinary	1.61	1.56	1.51
Musculoskeletal	2.32	2.32	2.17
Neurological[e]	1.87	1.59	1.53
Endocrine/metabolic[b]	1.62	1.40	1.43

[a]Hotellings $F (26,1362) = 2.16$; $p < .001$
[b]$p < .05$
[c]$p < .005$
[d]$p < .01$
[e]$p < .001$

presents 1-year changes in cognition, functional disability, and physical health as a function of change in depression over the same period. For this figure, we combined major and minor depressives and examined change over the 1-year period. Thus, "remitted depression" refers to persons with either major or minor depression at time 1 who were free of depression a year later; "incident" depression includes time 2 major or minor depressives who were not depressed at time 1, and "persistent" depressives had some depression at both points. As Figure 1.2 shows, changes in physical health status were of relatively small magnitude and inconsistently associated with depression. Cognitive and ADL declines, however, were strongly associated with depression. Note first that persons whose depression remitted over the 1-year period displayed no greater decline than the never-depressed group. This suggests that some of the functional deficits observed among frail, depressed older persons may be "excess" disability, linked to the depression itself and equally reversible. In contrast, persons who became depressed over the course of the year showed marked declines in cognitive and functional status, and functional declines were particularly marked among the persistently depressed group.

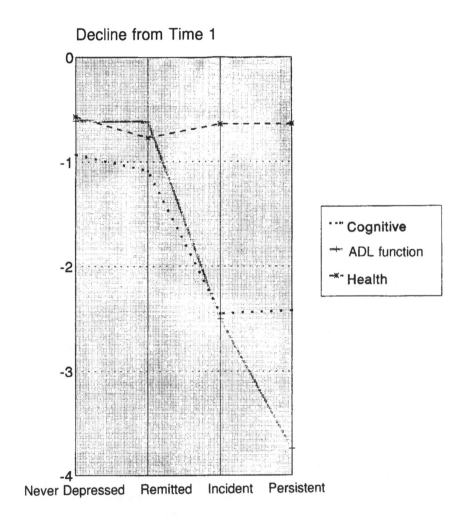

FIGURE 1.1   One-year decline in functional status as a function of change in depression.

NUTRITION

Morley and Kraenzle (1994) recently suggested that depression may be the most common cause of weight loss in community nursing homes. Previous studies have shown that biochemical evidence for subnutrition based on markers such as serum albumin is common among nursing home residents and in patients with disabling chronic illnesses who live in other settings. However, low levels of albumin may reflect either protein calorie undernutrition or the more direct impact of chronic disease and inflammation (through negative acute phase effects). These apparent deficits may be due to the inability of patients with disability to maintain dietary intake, to their inability to catch up after periods of catabolism related to episodes of acute illness, or to the effects of chronic disease on protein synthesis. Albumin levels are related to several clinical markers of frailty in elderly people in residential care, including depression as well as cognitive impairment, measures of physical disability, and summary measures of physical illness (Katz, Beaston-Wimmer, & Parmelee, 1993). Regression models suggest that the association of depression with low albumin is complex, that there is a component in which the effect of depression is mediated through its association with disability, and that there is another component in which depression is more directly associated with evidence for subnutrition. Further research is needed to determine causal directions and to delineate the nature of the biochemical disturbance associated with depression and frailty. From the perspective of this review, it is significant that depression emerges as a state associated with abnormalities in physiological status as well as with psychiatric symptoms.

MORTALITY

The most compelling evidence that symptoms of depression identify a clinically significant state comes from observations that nursing home residents with symptoms of major depression exhibit increased rates of mortality. Katz et al. (1989) found that nursing home residents with major depression exhibit approximately a twofold increase in mortality rate relative to cognitively intact and mildly impaired controls, and Rovner et al. (1991) found a 1.6-fold effect. In these studies, the increase in mortality was specific for those with a categorical diagnosis of major depression. Ashby, Ames, West, et al. (1991) found a threefold increase in mortality related to depressive symptoms as assessed with the Brief Assessment Scale among residents of British nursing homes; this effect remained significant even after controlling for coexisting dementia. The association between depression and increased mortality was confirmed more recently in studies by Shah, Phongsathorn, George, et al. (1993), who measured depression on a scale that incorporated observations from interviews with patients and their caregivers (1993); they suggested that the symptoms most closely associated with increased mortality were reduced appetite, diurnal variation in mood, and loss of interests (1994).

Given the close relationship between depression and physical illness, it is important to consider the question raised by O'Brien and Ames (1994): Why do the depressed elderly die? Put most succinctly, the issue is whether patients are dying because they are depressed or whether they are depressed because they are dying. Rovner et al. (1991) found that the increased mortality associated with depression in nursing home residents persists even after controlling for the level of disability and the number of medical diagnoses. This finding suggests that depression is contributing directly to mortality, possibly through its contribution to indirect life-threatening behaviors, as suggested by Osgood and Brant (1990); through reluctance to seek or accept medical treatment, as suggested by Gerety, Chiodo, Kanten, et al. (1993); or through physiological mechanisms. However, Parmelee et al. (1992) observed a 2.8-fold increase in mortality associated with major depression in a residential care population that included nursing home and congregate apartment residents. They found, however, that the increased mortality could be accounted for by controlling for disability and physicians' ratings of the severity of medical illness. The difference between these two findings may be a reflection of the differences in the populations or in the methods used to control for the effects of physical illness; the methods used by Parmelee et al. (1992b) were likely to account for a greater component of the variance in health status than those of Rovner et al. (1991). The shared variance between depression and health may have thus succeeded in overcorrecting for the zero-order relationship between depression and mortality.

A recent study by Samuels, Katz, Parmelee, et al. (1995) lends support to the conclusion that depression can directly increase mortality. A factor analysis of the Hamilton Rating Scale for Depression among a sample of long-term care subjects screened for inclusion in a study of drug treatment identified four factors accounting for 46% of variance: (1) core depression (work and activities, general somatic, retardation, weight loss, gastrointestinal symptoms, and suicidal ideation); (2) insomnia and hypochondriasis (terminal, initial, middle insomnia, and hypochondriasis); (3) anxiety (somatic anxiety, psychic anxiety, and agitation); and (4) depressive ideation (guilt, obsessive-compulsive behavior, lack of insight, and diurnal variation). Factor scores for core depression (but not the other factors) were associated with increased mortality, even after controlling for ratings of disease and disability.

In summary, both major depression and other depressive states are, as a rule, persistent. Similarly, both are associated with increased medical morbidity. The relationships discussed previously with both pain and biochemical evidence for subnutrition have been demonstrated with symptom ratings rather than diagnoses. The increase in mortality, however, is apparent only in patients with major depression and those with severe depressive symptoms. Taken together, these findings demonstrate that even in the long-term care setting, both major depression and other less severe depressive states are clinically significant disorders. They refute the suggestion that depressive symptoms are natural and transitory reactions to the stresses of institutional life.

TREATMENT OF DEPRESSION IN THE NURSING HOME

PSYCHOPHARMACOLOGY

The research findings outlined thus far document that major depression in residential care patients is a state of clinical significance. Recognition of the potential difficulties in diagnosis in this population, however, leads to the question of whether the symptoms of major depression define the same disorder that is seen in younger and healthier patients.

Significance of Research on Antidepressant Medication

The question has been addressed by Katz et al. (1990), who conducted a double-blind, placebo-controlled therapeutic trial of the standard antidepressant medication, nortriptyline, in a population of residential care patients, average age 84.1, from an institution consisting of a nursing home and a congregate apartment facility. The goals of this study were essentially the mirror image of those of standard drug trials. In most cases, such studies are conducted using well-defined patient populations and are designed to determine whether novel compounds are therapeutically active. In this case, the study was conducted with a standard agent with dose adjustments calculated to achieve plasma levels of the medication that are known to be effective in younger and healthier patients. This study was designed to use response to treatment as a critical test for characterizing the psychopathology observed in residential care patients. If a difference was apparent between the drug and a placebo, that would support the conclusion that the symptoms of major depression have the same significance in these settings as in other patient populations. If, however, no such difference was observed, it would suggest that the symptoms of major depression identified a different disorder in the frail elderly—either a different pathophysiological state or a combination of existential despair and somatic symptoms from physical illness.

The findings, even from a small-scale study, confirmed that elderly residential care patients did, in fact, respond to nortriptyline. In this study, 58% of patients given active medication but only 9% of those given a placebo were "much" or "very much" improved, whereas 83% of those given medication and 22% of those on a placebo exhibited improvement of some degree. The alleviation of depressive symptoms was accompanied by increases in participation in activities within the institution; it had a significant impact on the day-to-day lives of the patients. However, treatment of major depression in this facility was not accompanied by significant reductions in disability or self-care deficits. This implies that screening criteria for admission to the facility were adequate to detect those patients for whom depression was making major contributions to the disability that led to institutionalization; such patients, however, may be found among residents of other facilities. In this study, the patients who responded were not individuals for whom depression led to inappropriate admission to the long-term care setting. This finding is of special importance in light of recent OBRA regulations. It establishes the fact that patients who by all criteria belong in residential care facilities require and can respond to antidepressant medication. This finding provides further support for the suggestion by Murphy (1989) that, regardless of findings suggesting that other psychotropic drugs may be overused in the nursing home, antidepressants are valuable therapeutic agents that may be underused.

Although the difference between drug and placebo validates the diagnosis of major depression in the long-term care setting, analysis of the predictors of response in a group of 21 patients treated with active nortriptyline provided evidence for a treatment-relevant subgroup of patients. In the study sample, there were highly significant correlations between serum albumin and measures of self-care deficits ($r = .638$; $P = .002$); those patients with the greatest self-care deficits and the lowest levels of serum albumin were less likely to respond to nortriptyline. At present, it is reasonable to consider the possibility that significant self-care deficits together with low serum albumin may characterize a subtype of major depression that is less likely to respond to treatment with nortriptyline. Further research—with other pharmacological treatments, with electroconvulsive therapy (ECT), or with combinations of drug treatment and rehabilitation or nutritional interventions—should be performed.

Medical Complications of Pharmacotherapy

Other findings from this study include the high prevalence of medical disorders that complicate the use of antidepressant medications, and the suggestion that there may be significant variability over time in the pharmacokinetics of nortriptyline in the frail elderly (Katz, Simpson, Jethanandani, et al., 1989). The frequency of adverse medical events that required early termination of drug treatment was high, approximately 30% to 33%. Although it may be difficult to distinguish between adverse drug effects and intercurrent medical events, these findings demonstrate that long-term care patients require careful monitoring during drug treatment for depression.

Further insight into the significance of the high rates of adverse events during nortriptyline treatment comes in a report by Katz et al. (1994). They found that depressed patients who were unable to tolerate treatment with the tricyclic antidepressant had significantly higher mortality rates than those (responders or nonresponders) who completed treatment, but that deaths, in general, occurred long after nortriptyline was discontinued, from causes not directly related to treatment for depression. They suggested that treatment with a tricyclic antidepressant represents a type of autonomic challenge, and that patients who do not have the homeostatic reserve to compensate for drug effects are also limited in their ability to tolerate stressors, such as fever, dehydration, or infection. These authors concluded that both adverse drug effects during nortriptyline treatment and subsequent mortality are indicators of "frailty."

Nortriptyline is probably the most studied and best understood of the antidepressant medications for use in the elderly and was, therefore, the appropriate drug for an investigation of the significance of depressive symptoms in residential care patients. Nonetheless, there is a need for further research to optimize the effectiveness and safety of treatment in this setting. Furthermore, the findings on the efficacy of antidepressant medications in a short-term clinical trial must be contrasted with the finding from more naturalistic observations that depression is, in general, persistent. The conclusion must be that recurrence and relapse are common, and that there is a need for research on the safety and efficacy of maintenance treatment for depression in the frail elderly.

NONPHARMACOLOGICAL TREATMENT

There are few empirical data on alternative treatments for depression in residential care settings. The literature suggests the potential value of interventions designed to modify the interpersonal environment within the nursing home, and of interventions that make specific psychotherapies available to residential care patients (Abraham, Niles, Thiel, et al., 1991; Ames, 1990; Santmeyer & Roca, 1991; Spayd & Smyer, 1988). Of the former, the most promising may be those designed to enhance the residents' sense of control (Rodin, 1986). Among the latter, studies of cognitive-behavioral therapy (Abraham, Neundorfer, & Currie, 1992; Zerhusen, Boyle, & Wilson, 1991) have demonstrated that well-defined treatments can, in fact, be delivered within nursing home settings; outcomes, however, have been variable. Details of such treatment approaches are discussed by Thompson and Gallagher-Thompson (Chapter 8), Teri (Chapter 6), and Abraham (Chapter 7) in this volume.

CONCLUSIONS

The studies reviewed in this chapter have demonstrated that depression is common among long-term care patients and that it exists as a spectrum of disorders that are, in general, chronic or recurrent. Major depression is common in cognitively intact patients living in the nursing home and related settings, and in residents with dementia. Other, less severe forms of depression are also common and are, in general, persistent and clinically significant. Furthermore, they appear to represent sources of increased risk for major depression. The increased prevalence of depression in a residential care setting relative to that seen in the community may be due to the increased prevalence of chronic disease and disability in long-term care patients, or to the nature of the interpersonal environment. Although there may have been reasons for questioning the validity of the diagnosis of major depression among long-term care patients in some of the research, the diagnosis was usually validated through demonstration of an association with greater need for care, increased morbidity, and excess mortality—and through pharmacological therapy: a response to nortriptyline.

These findings are summarized in Figure 1.2. The paths leading to depression indicate that there may be possibilities for primary prevention (e.g., by interventions that enhance control). Interrelationships between depressive states indicate that treatment of both major and minor depressions represents opportunities for secondary prevention of relapses or chronicity. Finally, the paths leading from depression demonstrate further opportunities for secondary or tertiary prevention; they indicate the possibilities that treatment for depression could, in principle, reduce the need for care, refusal of treatment, behavioral symptoms, morbidity, and mortality.

These findings emphasize the similarity between depression as seen in long-term care and as seen in other settings. Differences that may be significant in these settings might include the existence of a subtype of major depression characterized by high levels of disability and low albumin that may be less likely to respond to nortriptyline, high vulnerability of patients to adverse drug effects, or intercurrent medical illnesses and

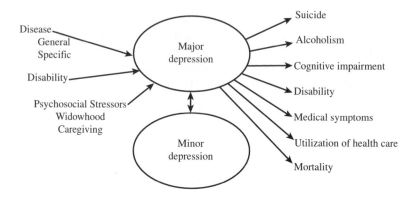

FIGURE 1.2   Depression in late life: causes and consequences.

the discontinuity from earlier lifestyles to the institutional environment. There is a pressing need for further research designed to optimize the effectiveness and safety of drug treatment for depression in long-term care patients. Other special issues that emerge within the long-term care setting include the need to develop and validate psychosocial and behavioral approaches to treatment, and to develop methods for training institution staff to improve case identification and the monitoring of treatment outcome.

The most basic finding from the research reported here is that, relative to community populations, nursing homes and—to a lesser extent—other residential care facilities for the elderly are institutions with an excess of mental illness. Much of this is due to treatable depressive disorders. The federal government has taken important steps in the direction of nursing home reform. It is important that these efforts be extended to ensure that long-term care patients receive the mental health services they need.

REFERENCES

Abraham, I. L., Neunforfer, M. M., & Currie, L. J. (1992). Effects of group interventions on cognition and depression in nursing home residents. *Nursing Research, 41,* 196–202.

Abraham, I. L., Niles, S. A., Thiel, B. P., et al. (1991). Therapeutic group work with depressed elderly. *Nursing Clinics of North America, 26,* 635–650.

Abrams, R. C., Teresi, J. A., & Butin, D. N. (1992). Depression in nursing home residents. *Clinics in Geriatric Medicine, 8,* 309–322.

Ames, D. (1990). Depression among elderly residents of local-authority residential homes: Its nature and the efficacy of intervention. *British Journal of Psychiatry, 156,* 667–675.

Ames, D. (1991). Epidemiological studies of depression among the elderly in residential and nursing homes. *International Journal of Geriatric Psychiatry, 6,* 347–354.

Ames, D. (1992). Psychiatric diagnoses made by the AGECAT system in residents of local authority homes for the elderly: Outcome and diagnostic stability after four years. *International Journal of Geriatric Psychiatry, 7,* 83–87.

Ames, D. (1993). Depressive disorders among elderly people in long-term institutional care. *Australian and New Zealand Journal of Psychiatry, 27,* 379–391.

Ames, D. (1994). Why do the depressed elderly die? [Editorial]. *International Journal of Geriatric Psychiatry, 9,* 689–693.

Ames, D., Ashby, D., Mann, A. H., et al. (1988). Psychiatric illness in elderly residents of Part III Homes in one London borough: Prognosis and review. *Age and Aging, 17,* 249–256.

Ashby, D., Ames, D., West, C. R., et al. (1991). Psychiatric morbidity as prediction of mortality for residents of local authority homes for the elderly. *International Journal of Geriatric Psychiatry, 6,* 567–575.

Baker, F. M., & Miller, C. L. (1991). Screening a skilled nursing home population for depression. *Journal of Geriatric Psychiatry and Neurology, 4,* 218–221.

Beaston-Wimmer, P., Katz, I., Parmelee, P. A., et al. (1988). *Relationship between psychiatric status and clinical laboratory measures in the institutional elderly.* Paper presented at the Annual Meeting of the Gerontological Society of America, San Francisco.

Blessed, G., Tominson, B. E., & Roth, M. (1968). The association between quantitative measures of dementia and of senile change in the cerebral gray matter. *British Journal of Psychiatry, 114,* 797–811.

Borson, S., Barnes, R. A., Kukull, W. A., et al. (1986). Symptomatic depression in elderly medical outpatients: 1. Prevalence, demography, and health service utilization. *Journal of the American Geriatrics Society, 34,* 341–347.

Burns, B. J., Larson, D. B., Goldstrom, I. D., et al. (1988). Mental disorders among nursing home patients: Preliminary findings from the National Nursing Home Survey Pretest. *International Journal of Geriatric Psychiatry, 3,* 27–35.

Burns, B. J., & Taube, C. A. (1990). Mental health services in general medical care and in nursing homes. In B. Fogel, A. Furino, & G. Gottlieb (Eds.), *Mental health policy for older Americans: Protecting minds at risk* (pp. 63–84). Washington, DC: American Psychiatric Press.

Chandler, J. D., & Chandler, J. E. (1988). The prevalence of neuropsychiatric disorders in a nursing home population. *Journal of Geriatric Psychiatry and Neurology, 1,* 71–76.

Clark, S. A. (1992). Mental illness among new residents to residential care. *International Journal of Geriatric Psychiatry, 7,* 59–64.

Cohen-Mansfield, J., & Marx, M. S. (1988). The relationship between depression and agitation in nursing home residents. *Comparative Gerontology (B), 2,* 141–146.

Cohen-Mansfield, J., & Marx, M. S. (1993). Pain and depression in the nursing home: Corroborating results. *Journal of Gerontology: Psychology and Science, 48,* P96–P97.

Cohen-Mansfield, J., Werner, P., & Marx, M. S. (1990). Screaming in nursing home residents. *Journal of American Geriatric Society, 38,* 785–792.

Cummings, J. L. (1992). Depression and Parkinson's disease: A review. *American Journal of Psychiatry, 149,* 443–454.

Diagnosis and treatment of depression in late life. (1991, November 4–6). *NIH consensus development conference consensus statement, 9.*

Foster, J. R., Cataldo, J. K., & Boksay, I. J. E. (1991). Incidence of depression in a medical long-term care facility: Findings from a restricted sample of new admissions. *International Journal of Geriatrics Psychiatry, 6,* 13–20.

Fries, B. E., Mehr, D. R., Schneider, D., et al. (1993). Mental dysfunction and resource use in nursing homes. *Medical Care, 31,* 898–920.

Gerety, M. B., Chiodo, L. K., Kanten, D. N., et al. (1993). Medical treatment preferences of nursing home residents: Relationship to function and concordance with surrogate decision-makers. *Journal of the American Geriatrics Society, 41,* 953–960.

German, P. S., Shapiro, S., & Kramer, M. (1986). Nursing home study of the Eastern Baltimore Epidemiological Catchment Area Study. In M. Harper & B. Lebowitz (Eds.), *Mental illness in nursing homes: Agenda for research* (DHHS Publication No. [ADM] 86-1459). Rockville, MD: DHHS.

Goldfarb, A. I. (1962). Prevalence of psychiatric disorders in metropolitan old age and nursing homes. *Journal of the American Geriatrics Society, 10,* 77–84.

Gurland, B., Copeland, J., Kariansky, J., et al. (1983). *The mind and mood of aging.* New York: Haworth.

Harrison, R., Savla, N., & Kafetz, K. (1990). Dementia, depression, and physical disability in a London borough: A survey of elderly people in and out of residential care and implications for future developments. *Age and Aging, 19,* 97–103.

Health Care Financing Administration. (1991). *Medicine and Medicaid requirements for long term care facilities* (42 CFR 483, Federal Register 56 488 26-48880). Washington, DC: Author.

Heston, L. L., Garrard, G., Makris, L., et al. (1992). Inadequate treatment of depressed nursing home elderly. *Journal of the American Geriatrics Society, 40,* 1117–1122.

Horiguchi, J., & Inami, Y. (1991). A survey of the living conditions and psychological states of elderly people admitted to nursing homes in Japan. *Acta Psychiatrica Scandinavica, 83,* 338–341.

Hyer, L., & Blazer, D. G. (1982a). Depression in long term care facilities. In D. G. Blazer (Ed.), *Depression in late life.* St. Louis: C. V. Mosby.

Hyer, L., & Blazer, D. G. (1982b). Depressive symptoms: Impact and problems in long term care facilities. *International Journal of Behavioral Geriatrics, 1,* 33–34.

Kafonek, S., Ettinger, W. H., Roca, R., et al. (1989). Instruments for screening for depression and dementia in a long-term care facility. *Journal of the American Geriatrics Society, 37,* 29–34.

Katz, I. R., Beaston-Wimmer, P., Parmelee, P. A., Friedman, E., & Lawton, M. P. (1993). Failure to thrive in the elderly: Exploration of the concept and delineation of psychiatric components. *Journal of Geriatric Psychiatry and Neurology, 6,* 161–169.

Katz, I. R., Lawton, M. P., & Parmelee, P. A. (1988, November). *Incidence and stability of depression, and cognitive impairment among institutional aged.* Paper presented at the annual meeting of the Gerontological Society of America, San Francisco.

Katz, I. R., Lesher, E., Kleban, M., et al. (1989). Clinical features of depression in the nursing home. *International Psychogeriatrics, 1,* 5–15.

Katz, I. R., & Parmelee, P. A. (1993). Depression in the residential care elderly. In L. S. Schneider, C. F. Reynolds, B. D. Lebowitz, & A. Friedhoff (Eds.), *Diagnosis and treatment of depression in late life: Results of the NIH Consensus Development Conference* (pp. 437–461). Washington, DC: American Psychiatric Press.

Katz, I. R., Parmelee, P. A., Beaston-Wimmer, P., & Smith, B. D. (1994). Association of antidepressants and other medications with mortality in the residential care elderly. *Journal of Geriatric Psychiatry and Neurology, 7,* 221–226.

Katz, I. R., Simpson, G. M., Curlik, S. M., et al. (1990). Pharmacological treatment of major depression for elderly patients in residential care settings. *Journal of Clinical Psychiatry, 51*(Suppl.), 41–48.

Katz, I. R., Simpson, G. M., Jethanandani, V., et al. (1989). Steady state pharmacokinetics of nortriptyline. *Neuropsychopharmacology, 2,* 229–236.

Lawton, M. P., & Brody, E. M. (1969). Assessment of older people: Self-maintaining and instrumental activities of daily living. *Gerontologist, 9,* 179–188.

Lesher, E. (1986). Validation of the Geriatric Depression Scale among nursing home residents. *Clinical Gerontology, 4,* 21–28.

Loebel, J. P., Loebel, J. S., Dager, S. R., et al. (1991). Anticipation of nursing home placement may be a precipitant of suicide among the elderly. *Journal of the American Geriatrics Society, 39,* 407–408.

Lobo, A., Ventura, T., & Marco, C. (1990). Psychiatric morbidity among residents in a home for the elderly in Spain: Prevalence of disorder and validity of screening. *International Journal of Geriatric Psychiatry, 5,* 83–91.

Lustman, P. J., Griffith, L. S., Gavard, J. A., & Clouse, R. E. (1992). Depression in adults with diabetes. *Diabetes Care, 15,* 1631–1639.

Mann, A. L. T., Graham, M., & Ashby, D. (1984). Psychiatric illness in residential homes for the elderly: A survey in one London borough. *Age and Aging, 13,* 257–265.

Mayeux, R., Stern, Y., Cote, L., & Williams, J. B. (1984). Altered serotonin metabolism in depressed patients with Parkinson's disease. *Neurology, 34,* 642–646.

McGivney, S. A., Mulvihill, M., & Taylor, B. (1994). Validating the GDS depression screen in the nursing home. *Journal of the American Geriatrics Society, 42,* 490–492.

Melzack, R. (1975). The McGill Pain Questionnaire: Major properties and scoring methods. *Pain, 1,* 277–299.

Morley, J. E., & Kraenzle, D. (1994). Causes of weight loss in a community nursing home. *Journal of the American Geriatrics Society, 42,* 583–585.

Murphy, E. (1989). The use of psychotropic drugs in long-term care [Editorial]. *International Journal of Geriatric Psychiatry, 4,* 1–2.

O'Riordan, P., Shelley, R., O'Neill, D., Walsh, J. B., & Coakley, D. (1989). The prevalence of depression in an acute geriatric medical assessment unit. *International Journal of Geriatric Psychiatry, 4,* 17–21.

Osgood, N. J., & Brant, B. A. (1990). Suicidal behavior in long-term care facilities. *Suicide and Life Threatening Behavior, 20,* 113–122.

Parmelee, P. A. (1994). Assessment of pain in the elderly. In M. P. Lawton & J. Teresi (Eds.), *Annual review of gerontology and geriatrics* (pp. 281–301). New York: Springer.

Parmelee, P. A., Katz, I. R., & Lawton, M. P. (1989). Depression among institutionalized aged: Assessment and prevalence estimation. *Journal of Gerontology, 44,* M22–M29.

Parmelee, P. A., Katz, I. R., & Lawton, M. P. (1991). The relation of pain to depression among institutionalized aged. *Journal of Gerontology and Psychological Science, 46,* P15–P21.

Parmelee, P. A., Katz, I. R., & Lawton, M. P. (1992a). Depression and mortality among institutionalized aged. *Journal of Gerontology, 47,* P3–P10.

Parmelee, P. A., Katz, I. R., & Lawton, M. P. (1992b). Incidence of depression in long-term care settings. *Journal of Gerontology: Medical Sciences, 47,* M189–M196.

Parmelee, P. A., Kleban, M., Lawton, M. P., & Katz, I. R. (1991). Depression and cognitive change among institutionalized aged. *Psychology and Aging, 6,* 504–511.

Parmelee, P. A., Lawton, M. P., & Katz, I. R. (1989). Psychometric prospectives of the geriatric depression scale among the institutional aged. *Psychological Assessment: American Journal of Consulting Clinical Psychology, 1,* 331–338.

Phillips, C. J., & Henderson, A. S. (1991). The prevalence of depression among Australian nursing home residents: Results using draft ICD-10 and DSM-III criteria. *Psychological Medicine, 21,* 739–748.

Rodin, J. (1986). Aging and health: Effects of the sense of control. *Science, 233,* 1271–1276.

Rovner, B. W., German, P. S., Brant, L. J., et al. (1991). Depression and mortality in nursing homes. *Journal of the American Medical Association, 265,* 993–996.

Rovner, B. W., German, P. S., Broadhead, J., et al. (1990). The prevalence and management of dementia and other psychiatric disorders in nursing homes. *International Psychogeriatrics, 2,* 13–24.

Rovner, B. W., Kafonek, S., Filipp, L., et al. (1986). Prevalence of mental illness in a community nursing home. *American Journal of Psychiatry, 143,* 1446–1449.

Rovner, B. W., Steele, C. D., German, P., et al. (1992). Psychiatric diagnosis and uncooperative behavior in nursing homes. *Journal of Geriatric and Psychological Neurology, 5,* 102–105.

Samuels, S. C., Katz, I. R., Parmelee, P. A., & Boyce, A. (1995). *Use of the Hamilton and Montgomery Asberg Depressions Scales in the institutional elderly: Relationship to measures of disability and physical illness.* American Association for Geriatric Psychiatry Eighth Annual Meeting and Symposium Paper Session.

Santmyer, K. S., & Roca, R. P. (1991). Geropsychiatry in long-term care: A nurse centered approach. *Journal of the American Geriatrics Society, 39,* 156–159.

Shah, A., Phongsathorn, V., George, C., et al. (1992). Psychiatric morbidity among continuing care geriatric inpatients. *International Journal of Geriatric Psychiatry, 7,* 517–525.

Shah, A., Phongsathorn, V., George, C., et al. (1993). Does psychiatric morbidity predict mortality in continuing care geriatric inpatients? *International Journal of Geriatric Psychiatry, 8,* 255–259.

Shah, A., Phongsathorn, V., George, C., et al. (1994). Psychiatric symptoms as predictors of mortality in continuing care geriatric inpatients. *International Journal of Geriatric Psychiatry, 9,* 695–702.

Snowdon, J. (1986). Dementia, depression and life satisfaction in nursing homes. *International Journal of Geriatric Psychiatry, 1,* 85–91.

Snowdon, J. & Donnelly, N. (1986). A study of depression in nursing homes. *Journal of Psychiatric Research, 20,* 327–333.

Spagnoli, A., Forester, G., MacDonald, A., et al. (1986). Dementia and depression in Italian geriatric institutions. *International Journal of Geriatric Psychiatry, 1,* 15–23.

Spayd, C. S., & Smyer, M. A. (1988). Interventions with agitated, disoriented, or depressed residents. In M. A. Smyer, M. D. Cohn, & D. Grannon (Eds.), *Mental health consultation in nursing homes.* New York: New York University Press.

Spitzer, R. L., & Endicott, J. (1979). *Schedule for affective disorders and schizophrenia.* New York: New York State Psychiatric Institute.

Stotsky, B. A. (1967). Allegedly nonpsychiatric patients in nursing homes. *Journal of the American Geriatrics Society, 15,* 535–544.

Strahan, G., & Burns, B. J. (1991). Mental health in nursing homes: United States, 1985. *National Health Survey: Vital and Health Statistics* (Series 13, No. 105, DHHS Publication No. [PHS] 91-1766). Washington, DC: Department of Health and Human Services.

Trichard, L., Zabow, A., & Gillis, L. S. (1982). Elderly persons in old age homes. A medical, psychiatric and social investigation. *South African Medical Journal, 61,* 624–627.

Weyerer, S. (1992). Prevalence, course and treatment of depression among residents in old age homes. *Clinical Neuropharmacology, 15*(Suppl. 1), 283A–285A.

Yesavage, J. A., Brink, T. L., Rose, T. L., et al. (1983). The geriatric depression rating scale: Comparison with other self report and psychiatric rating scales. In T. Cook, S. Ferris, & R. Bartus (Eds.), *Assessment in geriatric psychopharmacology* (pp. 37–49). New Canaan, CT: Mark Powley.

Zemore, R., & Eames, N. (1979). Psychic and somatic symptoms of depression among young adults, institutionalized aged, and noninstitutionalized aged. *Journal of Gerontology, 34,* 716–720.

Zerhusen, J. D., Boyle, K., & Wilson, W. (1991). Out of the darkness: Group cognitive therapy for depressed elderly. *Journal of Psychosocial Nursing, 29,* 16–21.

Part I

Research on the Nature
of Depression in the Elderly

CHAPTER 2

Positive and Negative Affective States Among Older People in Long-Term Care

M. POWELL LAWTON

Depression is both a set of clinical disorders and a descriptor of an emotion. Despite the central importance of the emotion *depression* to the various clinical syndromes of depression, surprisingly little attention has been given to the details of depressive feelings in the lives of people suffering from depressive illnesses. This chapter attempts to fill some of the resulting gaps by describing research performed on older people in residential care, where the affective lives of depressed and nondepressed older people were mapped as they varied by days, residential location, and changing social and environmental contexts.

Before summarizing this research and its meaning, however, it is desirable to portray the larger context of psychological knowledge regarding human emotion. The affective lives of older people receiving care were studied with the benefit of a much broader base of knowledge regarding emotion and personality.

BACKGROUND

PERSONALITY AND AFFECT

One of the most persistent issues in psychology has been whether personality is relatively stable or whether it evolves with time and experience. In general, hard evidence in favor of discrete stages of adult personality

Note: Research supported by NIMH grant MH22079 and National Institute on Aging grant UAG 10304.

development has been difficult to assemble. A tentative conclusion is possible: that there is no single process of development so universal as to be identifiable in most people or to be composed of stepwise elements that unfold in a predicable order as age increases. It is thus likely that personality development is heterogeneous and therefore needs to be studied in terms of individual differences rather than ''universals.''

From another point of view, however, there has been some compelling evidence for stability in personality over much of the adult life span. Costa and McCrae (1980) demonstrated, first, high stability over 10 years in neuroticism and substantial stability for extraversion. As predicted, although these two personality dimensions were minimally related to one another, each was associated with happiness: neuroticism negatively and extraversion positively. Especially impressive was the finding that low neuroticism and high extraversion measured early in the study were strongly predictive of greater happiness 10 years later. Further evidence of relative (though not total) stability over 6 years was found in another sample (Costa et al., 1987). Another view of a decade of research on this question was provided, however, by Aldwin and Levenson (1994). Their review demonstrates the existence of a variety of types of change within a larger context of relative stability. It also reminds us that knowledge is still scanty on long-term tracking of personality.

Neuroticism (sometimes called *emotionality*) and *introversion-extra-version* (I-E) are classic descriptions of human temperaments dating from William James (1890); Jung (1921); and, more recently, the research of Eysenck (1970). Personality research has generally converged on five major factors (the ''big five,'' Goldberg, 1990), of which these two factors are by far the largest. In fact, neuroticism and introversion-extraversion appear to be different from the other three, in that they are identifiable early in life and may have a strong genetic component. They also describe generalized personality traits. Neuroticism is a tendency to worry, and to be depressed, hostile, impulsive, and vigilant to possible sources of danger and punishment. Introversion-extraversion describes relative sensitivity to internal, compared with external, stimuli. Thus, an extravert is likely to be sociable, active, spontaneous, and dependent on external reward, whereas an introvert is reserved, stable, and relatively autonomous with respect to external reward. It is convenient to think of these two major dimensions as representing limits on or bounds to the amount of variability possible for individuals. That is, neuroticism and I-E may be modifiable to a limited degree by experience but are relatively resistant to major change over many years.

Thus, neuroticism and introversion-extraversion may be called *tempera-ments* that represent the most basic and general response tendencies subsuming several more specific personality traits, termed and measured as "facets" by Costa and McCrae (1989). A *facet*, or *trait*, is a less fixed attribute, a propensity to act, think, or experience emotion in a particular way—a somewhat circular definition, to be sure, but a definition intended to convey the idea of relative, though not absolute, stability. A "trait name" is a probabilistic statement regarding the way a person is likely to respond at some future time.

The "big five" concept of personality includes, in addition to neuroticism and introversion-extraversion, three other factors: *openness to experience, conscientiousness*, and *agreeableness*. (These terms were coined by Costa and McCrae in their NEO Personality Inventory (NEO-PI 2, 1989) and are generally accepted by many personality researchers.) Neuroticism and introversion-extraversion have been shown to have strong genetic components, but heritability has not so far been convincingly demonstrated for the other three traits (Aldwin & Levenson, 1994). A hypothesis worthy of consideration is that responsiveness to individual developmental and contextual change is greater in traits where there is less evidence for genetic influence, especially conscientiousness and agreeableness among the "big five."

If *temperament* is most stable and *trait* slightly less so, then the *state* represented by an emotion represents the most transitory aspect of personality. Among the terms used in association with emotion, the word *emotion* itself refers to muscular, physiological, or subjective activations that are brief; *mood* is a longer-lasting condition whose cognitive and subjective features are more dominant than the physical manifestations. *Affect* is a more general term whose meaning is less time-related, although the term *affective state* can cover both emotion and mood. The distinction between trait and state has been made in psychological tests. For example, anxiety may be measured in terms of "how you usually feel" (trait) or in terms of "how you are feeling right now" (state; Spielberger, 1972).

The relationships among temperament, traits, and states have been difficult to study because the probability that emotional states will recur is a trait, and complexes of traits define temperament. Simply asking a respondent to distinguish between "usually" and "right now" does not necessarily guarantee that the right distinction is being made.

There is also a blurred distinction between personality and mental health outcome, or psychological well-being. A hallmark of neuroticism is anxiety, demoralization, and other negative mental health states. If we think, however, of temperament and traits as predictive statements regarding the frequency with which specified states are likely to recur, then at least a conceptual distinction between the two is easier, although measuring them independently is still problematic. In the usual nomenclature, psychological well-being is sometimes discussed as a stable trait and sometimes discussed as a state. For the present discussion, the term *affective state* will be used to describe the short-term outcome and *psychological well-being* or *mental health* will refer to the more stable characteristic.

To recapitulate, change over time is presumed to occur to a small degree in temperament, to an unknown though plausibly greater degree at the level of the trait, and to the greatest degree in affective state.

Affect is especially relevant to contextual or environmental issues because environment can change or conceivably be manipulated. This principle is the primary argument in favor of including environment in the equation that relates personal characteristics to outcome: If we can find keys to environmental features that can favorably affect well-being, then a redesigned environment can be an element in producing favorable change (Lawton, 1982; Lawton & Nahemow, 1973).

POSITIVE AFFECT AND NEGATIVE AFFECT

Before discussing explicit relationships between affect and environment it is necessary to make a critical distinction between the separate properties of *negative affect* (NA) and *positive affect* (PA). Nearly 30 years ago, Bradburn (1969) found that short separate measures of positive feelings and negative feelings were each related to happiness but not correlated with one another. In other words, in his terms, the sum of positive feelings and the absence of negative feelings contributed to one form of psychological well-being. These results have been replicated many times using Bradburn's Affect Balance Scale (Lawton, 1983; Moriwaki, 1974) but not always when ratings of affect terms were analyzed (Diener & Emmons, 1984; Lawton, Kleban, & Dean, 1993).

More recently, a major stream of research devoted to the structure of subjectively experienced emotion has appeared in the literature. When examined by factor-analytic methods, virtually any representation of emotion, whether in lexical or subjectively experienced form, has been shown to result in two large factors (Russell, 1980; Watson & Tellegen, 1985; Zevon & Tellegen, 1982). Other, smaller, factors also emerge that are reasonably similar across studies as more factors are rotated.

The characteristics of the factors within the two-dimensional structure of affect depend entirely, however, on where one chooses to locate the axes (all rotations will fit the data equally well). Using the loadings on the first two factors to represent each affect on the *x*- and the *y*-axes, a schematic representation of the plot can be made; see the circumplex in Figure 2.1. Adjectives similar to one another occur in closest proximity

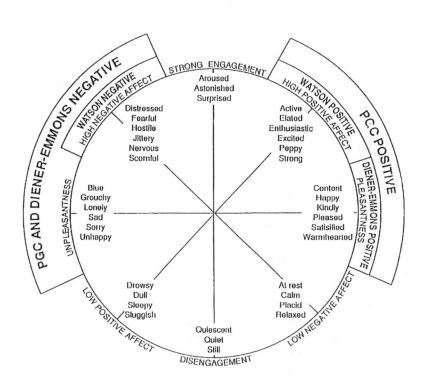

FIGURE 2.1   Circumplex model of emotions, showing affect sectors represented by affect measures of Watson et al. (1988), Diener and Emmons (1984), and Lawton et al. (1992).

Source: Watson, D., & Tellegen, A. (1985). Toward a consensual structure of mood. *Psychological Bulletin, 98,* 221. Copyright © 1985, American Psychological Association. Adapted with permission.

around the periphery; adjectives with opposite affective tone are located at opposite ends of diameters (180°), and adjectives unrelated to one another are at right angles to one another (90°). How to name these first two dimensions is the first task. In their analysis of many investigators' replicated circumplicial arrays of emotion, Watson and Tellegen (1985) showed that two apparently conflicting views of the relationship between positive and negative emotions could be understood by giving more careful attention to the affect terms subsumed under the categories of positive affect and negative affect. When unrotated factor loadings are plotted, the first factor always includes both positive and negative evaluative terms (e.g., *sad* vs. *happy*), whereas the second includes terms denoting activation (*aroused*, *surprised*)—usually a monopolar factor—because deactivation terms are not usually included in affect lists. Because the axes are orthogonal to one another, these two factors are uncorrelated.

If both axes are rotated 90°, one factor (usually the largest) represents agitated negative feelings, whereas the second factor adds a positive affective tone to activation. Watson and Tellegen's terms for factors defined in these two ways are shown at the near periphery of the circle of Figure 2.1. They called the rotated factors *high negative affect* and *high positive affect*. The affect terms falling into each of these factors explain why they are uncorrelated. In much writing on emotion, pleasantness and unpleasantness have often been confused with PA and NA. To the extent that PA and NA are operationalized to include terms in the "pleasantness" and "unpleasantness" sectors of Figure 2.1, respectively, however, they will tend to be negatively correlated. Watson, Clark, and Tellegen (1988), by choosing terms from the appropriate sectors, constructed uncorrelated indices of PA and NA (the Positive and Negative Affect Scales). The indices of PA and NA suggested by Diener and Emmons (1984) and Lawton, Kleban, Rajagopal, Dean, and Parmelee (1992) were deliberately constructed to sample a broader range of both positive and negative affects (shown in the sectors of Figure 2.1), including important states, such as "depressed" and "happy," which are not included in the PA and NA factors of Watson, Clark, and Tellegen. Thereby, negatively correlated indices of PA and NA were ensured, while a partial degree of independence was still maintained between them.

This digression into the structure of affect is relevant for two reasons. First, one cannot help noting the analogies between neuroticism and negative affect and between introversion-extraversion and positive affect. If one carefully analyzes some of the terms used to describe the two temperaments, many exact matches can be found for items on the affect scale. Therefore, it seems less than newsworthy to announce the finding that negative states are more likely among people who score high in neuroticism and positive states more common among extraverts (Costa & McCrae, 1980). What we do learn is that emotion-laden dimensions may be generalized across temporal frames of reference. Temperament, personality, and affective states are different from one another, yet each may be made comprehensible by locating temperaments, traits, or emotions in two-dimensional space. Repeated occurrence of affect states contributes to the definition of a trait, and clusters of traits define temperament. That same ordering typifies increasing stability of personality over time and its decreasing capacity to be influenced by context and changing personal preferences.

Turning specifically to environment, one of the most interesting series of findings has been that the NA and PA have different antecedents. In research performed some years ago, Lawton, Kleban, and diCarlo (1984) found that NA was increased by poor health and poor self-esteem, whereas PA was greater for people who interacted more with friends and participated more in activities; perceived environmental quality was associated with positive affect. In still another context, we examined two subjective dimensions of interpersonal relationships, status, and solidarity (Lawton & Moss, 1987). Relationships characterized as affording status were associated with low NA but were unrelated to PA; those affording solidarity were associated with high PA but not with NA. In another study of caregivers, positive affect was greater for those who reported more satisfactions from this role, whereas those reporting a greater sense of caregiving as a burden were higher in depression (Lawton, Moss, Kleban, Glicksman, & Rovine, 1991). Although there were occasional instances of cross-valence relationships, the general conclusion was clear: Positive, diverting, environmentally engaging experiences heighten PA but do not ameliorate NA; negative, internal experiences, such as poor health and negative personal relationships that reflect on the self, contribute to negative affect but are less likely to impair PA.

BACKGROUND SUMMARY

This review of the psychological concepts of affect and personality thus suggests that affect is an essential aspect of personality, along with other traditional cognitive and behavioral features. The issue of stability versus change is especially relevant in the context of treatment because we need to know what can change and, therefore, where to direct our interventions. It is clear that two of the most general, most basic aspects of personality—neuroticism and introversion-extraversion—are relatively stable. Many of the components of these basic temperaments also show considerable stability. At most, however, the amount of change over adulthood with respect to many of the traits by which we describe personality has not been firmly established. The effect of the length of time over which stability is tested is still unknown. Finally, the conditions under which intervening experiences influence personality, if at all, have not been fully established (Aldwin & Levenson, 1994).

It is also clear that external events, social contexts, and environments influence people's affective states, that is, their short-term subjective states of positive and negative affect. A plausible hypothesis is that although temperament sets bounds on change, everyday experience may still be highly responsive to external influences. The task is to try to understand better how such stability and change play out over spans of time ranging from moments to decades or even to a lifetime.

The distinction between positive affect and negative affect must always be part of a general concept of mental health. Mental health is not simply the absence of negative affect but just as much the presence of positive affect. Adding the temporal dimension enables us to state three assumptions that guided the research to be reported here.

1. Any excess of positive-affect state over negative-affect state constitutes a definition of favorable mental health.
2. Mental health is a concept relevant to any period, from brief to permanent.
3. Any external influence, such as a treatment or a manipulable context that increases positive affect or decreases negative affect, is, therefore, a potential contributor to mental health.

DEPRESSION AND THE RESIDENTIAL ENVIRONMENT

Proceeding from these assumptions, it is clear that we need to know more about how affect states change or remain stable over time and what factors are associated with change when it does occur. Because (as other chapters amply document) depression is a major problem in frail elders and in nursing homes, depression has been a focus of some of the research done at the Philadelphia Geriatric Center. The bulk of this chapter discusses research findings on the temporal aspects of depressive affect and other indicators of mental health, as well as data that help identify some of the influences on affect state. The overall conclusions of several such projects are emphasized because the details of each investigation have been, or will be, published in full elsewhere.

ENVIRONMENTS UNDER STUDY

Because of the importance of both intrapersonal and external factors in the view of mental health espoused here, it is necessary to describe the environments in which the data were gathered: congregate housing, nursing home, and a special care unit for patients with Alzheimer's disease.

The *congregate housing* consists of two high-rise buildings where 500 elders live (York House North and York House South of the Philadelphia Geriatric Center). The housing is traditional—private apartments with full bathrooms and efficiency kitchens. The housing is considered "congregate" because an essential part of the environment is the service package, which includes lunch and dinner served in a common dining room, an on-site medical clinic, weekly major housekeeping services, and a staff for activities and social work staff. The buildings were 25 and 30 years old at the time the research was performed, ample time for aging in place (Lawton, Moss, & Grimes, 1985; Tillson, 1990) to have occurred. In fact, the mean age was 85, and the general impression was the residents had become frail. Although competence in activities of daily living (ADL) was required, many tenants would have been unable to remain in independent housing without the supportive services.

The *nursing home* cares for about 530 residents in 12 care areas and a small acute-care hospital. All residents have major physical or mental disabilities. The mean age is about 86. There are few short-term rehabilitation admissions. Virtually all social, psychological, nursing, and medical services except surgery are performed on the premises.

Two buildings of the nursing home were designed for the special needs of *patients with Alzheimer's disease*; these buildings are designated here as special care units. One—the Weiss Institute—has been widely reported (Cohen & Day, 1993; Lawton, Fulcomer, & Kleban, 1984; Liebowitz, Lawton, & Waldman, 1979), but the present research was done in a more recent building with special features that include a large activity space open to the corridor and the nurses' station; a smaller peripheral activity space; a corridor with telescoping width designed to allow some nontraffic use and to reduce the constriction and disappearing perspective of the long corridor; and a variety of design features to increase color, texture, variety, and personalization.

The differences among these three environments derive from the type of occupant, the physical design, and the services offered, attributes that are clearly related to one another. Despite their increasing frailty, the residents of the congregate housing are in notably better health than the residents of the nursing home. Thus the supportive services are far more intense in the nursing home. The social milieus are less easily quantified. Life is more autonomous in the housing because, for the most part, residents manage their own apartments, come and go as they please, and treat private space and communication in a way that is reasonably similar to life in the community. Many activities in both the housing and the nursing home are performed in congregate style, however, such as meals, some group activities, and informal use of public seating. A greater proportion of both formal scheduled and informal social activity is prescribed in the nursing home. It is difficult to estimate the quantitative difference between the two locations as regards the probability of interacting with another resident, visiting with family members, or participating in an activity. What is certain is that the housing tenants have a greater degree of choice available and a greater range of activities outside the residential environment.

The critical feature of the special care unit is the moderate to moderately severe level of cognitive impairment of residents, not only in the units studied here but also in the earlier Weiss Institute. Coupled with their high level of ADL impairment and the consequent total-institution organization of services, this reduced level of competence effectively removes most daily decision making from the residents. The nursing home as a whole maintains a high level of services by professionals, including therapeutic activities, volunteers, social work, clinical psychology, and all nursing and medical specialties. Thus, the differences in service levels between the special care areas of the nursing home and those housing less impaired residents are somewhat indistinct. In the areas housing relatively intact residents, however, there is considerably more individual decision making and use of a variety of physical spaces and activities in the institution. In the special care unit, by contrast, informal interaction and planned activities have a strong tendency to be concentrated in the single large activity space (including group activities and meals).

These environments and the characteristics of the people who populate them have been described in detail to portray something of what is meant when subjects living in congregate housing are compared with those living in the nursing home in terms of their affect states. In sum, the attributes of the people differ, they live in radically different service contexts, and the stimulus characteristics associated with the social relationships and activities in the several environments differ considerably.

COMPONENTS OF THE RESEARCH

The research to be reviewed here emerged from a study of emotion that had the following six components:

1. Design and testing of brief measures of affect state
2. Study of individual patterns of variability in affect state
3. Determination of how depression relates to affect state and affect variability
4. Residential environment, affect sate, and affect variability

5. Study of the relationship between the context of daily events and affect state
6. Study of the relationship between care context and affect in dementing illness

1. Brief Measures of Affect States

Research on the structure of affect, as reviewed earlier, led to the decision that separate measures of positive and negative affect should constitute the beginning of any research on affect states. The circumplex structure and an analysis of the terms used most frequently by previous investigators to represent positive and negative affect states led to the choice of appropriate emotion terms (see the outermost sector of Figure 2.1). The list also needed to be short, to make the measure useful within a relatively low level of cognitive competence. Pilot work with a longer list of affect terms led to the choice of two five-item indices (Lawton et al., 1992). Positive affect (PA) was represented by *happy, interested, energetic, content*, and *warmhearted*. Negative affect (NA) was represented by *sad, annoyed, worried, irritated*, and *depressed*. Note, in Figure 2.1, that this choice of terms was not designed to produce uncorrelated measures of positive and negative affect, unlike the Affect Balance Scale (Bradburn, 1969) or the Positive and Negative Affect States (PANAS) (Watson et al., 1988). Rather, terms clearly relevant to everyday psychological well-being were seen as necessary. Therefore, terms such as *happy* fell into a boundary area between high PA and low NA. *Sad* fell into the boundary area between high NA and low PA. This decision to represent in our scales desirable and undesirable states over a broad range resulted in a built-in negative correlation between the measures that we called PA and NA. Because it is difficult to feel both PA and NA at the same moment, the negative correlation between PA and NA was greater ($r = -.48$) when we asked people to state how they were feeling at the moment (state affect) than when we asked them how frequently they usually experienced each ($r = -.33$, trait affect).

A series of exploratory and confirmatory factor analyses of ratings of these 10 affects were performed in different age groups, different samples, and different modes of administration. The scales derived to measure PA and NA are shown in Table 2.1. The results confirmed that these affects can represent the two relatively independent types of affect. This research demonstrated further that these affect terms can represent positive and negative affect across three age groups, and (with some minor structural inconsistencies) are generally applicable to both state and trait affect, and to both healthy and frail elders.

TABLE 2.1 Maximum-Likelihood Factor Structure in Four Affect Rating Sets

	Older adults (trait)		Older adults (state)		Older adults (state)		Residential sample (state)		Daily affect (state)	
	PA	NA	PA	NA	PA	NA	PA	NA	PA	NA
Happy	.85	.00	.88	.00	.90	.00	.81	.00	.60	.00
Interested	.82	.00	.61	.00	.58	.00	.51	.00	.46	.00
Energetic	.55	.00	.53	.00	.49	.00	.63	.00	.54	.00
Content	.71	.00	.76	.00	.77	.00	.78	.00	.55	.00
Warmhearted	.74	.00	.50	.00	.46	.00	.48	.00	.35	.00
Sad	.00	.79	.00	.76	.00	.77	.00	.88	.00	.62
Annoyed	.00	.45	.00	.37	.00	.44	.00	.84	.00	.49
Worried	.00	.65	.00	.65	.00	.68	.00	.86	.00	.41
Irritated	.00	.55	.00	.50	.00	.54	.00	.86	.00	.51
Depressed	.00	.93	.00	.89	.00	.89	.00	.89	.00	.73
N	434		434		490		486		945	
r (PA-NA)	−.41		−.50		−.53		−.21		−.67	
X^2 (df = 33)	123.51		157.1		201.2		111.1		56.3	
"Goodness of fit" index	.93		.95		.96		.96		.99	
Bentler-Bonett	.94		.90		.91		.96		.96	
Bollen δ_2	.92		.96		.96		.97		.99	

Note: PA, positive affect; NA, negative affect.
From Lawton, M. P., Kleban, M. H., Rajagopal, D., Dean, J., & Parmelee, P. A. (1992). The factorial generality of brief positive and negative affect measures. *Journal of Gerontology: Psychological Sciences, 47*, P233. Copyright © 1992, Gerontological Society of America. Reprinted with permission.

The 10 affects typically require 3 to 5 minutes for a subject to rate. Their brevity makes them useful measures in a variety of situations.

2. Individual Patterns of Variability

The focal process with which much of this research program was concerned was variability in affect states over time in the same individual. Cattell (1952), who originated the idea of a family of approaches to factor analysis based, alternatively, on replications of subjects, tests, and occasions, suggested that the factors arising from factor analyses of tests replicated over many subjects on one occasion (R analysis) should be the same as those arising from analysis of tests repeated over many occasions with a single subject (P analysis). In other words, the higher-order dimensions that account for individual differences should be the same dimensions on which day-to-day fluctuations of a single person's affect vary.

A test of Cattell's hypothesis was performed by a series of P-factor analyses on 30-day ratings by each of 28 residents, using the 10-item Philadelphia Geriatric Center Positive Affect and Negative Affect rating Scales (Kleban, Lawton, Nesselroade, & Parmelee, 1992). Subjects were "oriented" to the idea that no one feels exactly the same every day, and that there are inevitably times when each of us feels especially good and times when we feel less than perfect. The ratings were made by the subject during a one-to-one interview by a research assistant. Despite these instructions, 45 subjects assigned the same rating every day to one or more of the affect terms and therefore had to be omitted from the statistical analyses involving all 10 items. Forty-five percent of the subjects yielded the expected two-factor solutions, but only 28% of the subjects' individual P factors conformed to the classical PA/NA pattern. Fifty-five percent gave evidence of single-factor solutions; only 22% of the total were single bipolar factors, where the PA items showed positive loadings and the NA items showed negative loadings. Such diversity across individuals (i.e., one vs. two factors and monopolar vs. bipolar) does not confirm the hypothesis that P factors are similar to R factors.

In contrast with the diversity of individual variability patterns, when subjects' ratings were analyzed together (z-scored within subjects), as a group, the two-factor PA/NA emerged strongly (see the "Daily Affect" column in Table 2.1). The conclusion to be drawn from this exploration of patterns of individual variability is that when all subjects' day-to-day ratings are used in the aggregate, the "average" pattern emerged: clear, differentiable, partially independent positive and negative affect factors. Such averaging, however, buried wide individual differences in the way daily fluctuations in emotion occurred in concert or independently of one another. A bare plurality of persons showed the two-factor pattern. For them, on days when they felt sad, they also felt depressed, worried, annoyed, and irritated. If they felt this way, or the opposite (not depressed), they showed only a mild tendency to feel that they were also lacking in the positive feelings. However, on days when they were happy, they also were likely to be interested, energetic, content, and warm. As contrasted with this classic two-factor PA/NA pattern, the second most prevalent pattern was for people to be either up or down: If they were depressed they were not happy, energetic, etc.; if they were happy, they were not depressed, angry, etc. The two-factor and bipolar patterns together accounted for only half of the cases, however. An impressive 50% showed individual patterns that were idiosyncratic; their patterns were neither a mix of relatively independent positive feelings and negative feelings nor unilateral good or bad feelings. For example, for several people only the two hostility items and the positive items clustered as two separate factors; depression and anxiety were not part of any pattern of variability. Another subject, whose rating yielded only a single factor, was happy, content, and not sad or depressed on days when he was annoyed and irritated—he was happy when he could indulge his hostility!

The conclusion is that we learn a lot more when we study people as individuals in addition to studying them as groups. There are many possibilities for studying ongoing processes, such as the course of treatment or rehabilitation, or the unfolding of an illness, by repeated measurement of the same individual over time.

3.   Depression, Affect State, and Affect Variability

The major purpose of the daily affect study was to map the course of day-to-day affect state among depressed elders. Subjective distress is one of the major distinguishing features of clinical depression. Gurland et al. (1983) described the ''pervasive'' quality of the depressed person's mood as a distinguishing feature of major depression—pervasiveness in terms of lasting all day, continuing over days, and being resistant to efforts to change. Actually, little research has been devoted to determining the temporal flow of the feeling of depression or other affects in depressed elders. We know even less about PA—the research on the relative independence of PA and NA would suggest the utility of determining whether there is also such a thing as ''pervasive anhedonia.'' Anhedonia, or the absence of pleasure in things, is another criterion of clinical depression.

The ''daily affect'' subjects were recruited so as to yield groups of nondepressed normals, residents suffering from dysthymia or depressive adjustment reaction (together called *minor depression* here), and residents with a diagnosis of *major depression* according to the *Diagnostic and Statistical Manual of Mental Disorders* (3rd ed. rev., *DSM-III-R*; American Psychiatric Association, 1987). A total of 78 people were recruited for 30-day self-assessments (Lawton, Parmelee, & Katz, 1996).

We hypothesized that the three groups would differ in the expected way—that is, increasing NA and decreasing PA—from normal to minor to major clinical depression. Comparisons of the means of the three groups displayed exactly this regular pattern for both PA and NA as well as for virtually every single affect term.

The question of pervasiveness was addressed by testing differences by diagnosis in each subject's variability over 30 days in the way the affects and affect indexes were rated—the standard deviation was used as an individual index of variability over 30 days for the single affects and the summed PA and NA indices. The results were revealing. Contrary to the investigators' initial hypotheses based on the pervasiveness concept, major depressives did not experience unrelenting depression and other NAs. Although both depressed groups exhibited significantly more NA, depression and other affects were, in fact, variable, more so than for "normals." The normals' NA was low and showed little variability. For PA, conversely, major depressives reported consistently low positive affect, with little variability; minor depressives and normals were not consistently in positive spirits but were more variable in this respect than were major depressives.

Major depression was thus typified by episodic depressive and other negative moods, but, on the whole, relatively good days were mixed in with the bad, despite an average NA that was on the dysphoric side. More characteristic was the relative absence of positive affect; pervasive anhedonia thus was a frequent phenomenon in major depression.

Minor depressives, on the other hand, showed considerable variability in both positive and negative affects. Mood swings of both types were frequent. Although they typically could count on depressive feelings to lift, they could not trust positive feelings to last.

Normals reported few negative feelings. Compatible with the two-factor model of affect, their positive feelings were variable. The unusual days for normals were rarely anxious, depressed, or hostile days; their unusual days were more often marked by high positive affect, as contrasted with usual days where negative affect was absent and positive affect fluctuated around a moderate, rather than high, level.

For illustrative purposes, a single subject's 30-day ratings of *depression* and *happy* were randomly chosen from each of the major depression, minor depression, and nondepressed groups (see Figure 2.2). Note that the "minor depression" subject showed high variability; the "major

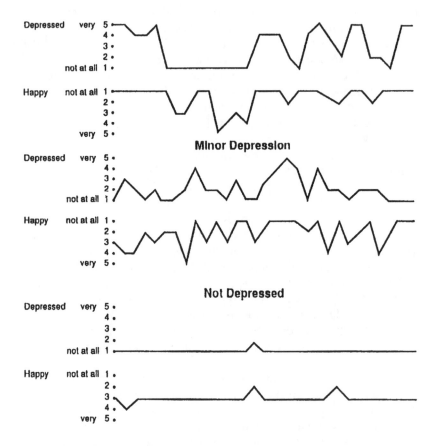

FIGURE 2.2   Thirty-day plots for ratings of "depressed" and "happy" by a randomly selected subject from groups with major depression, minor depression, and no diagnosed depression.

depression'' subject showed moderate variability, with several days of being "not at all depressed" as well as "not at all happy"; and the presumably normal resident showed extreme invariance around "not at all depressed" and "moderately happy."

Knowing that depressed people are not always depressed, caregiving families and staff would do well to sharpen their observational skills to recognize really low days and be cautious about any assumption that a day or so when negative moods are absent necessarily means an upswing in the larger course of the illness. Knowing that not all days are "black" days also provides us with a less bleak view of the life of depressed people. Minor depressives, especially, show even more variability in both positive and negative feelings. Emotional instability is their distinguishing feature. Further, knowing that the pathology is especially evidenced in major depressives' lack of ability to experience pleasure should point professionals toward increased exploration of pleasure-oriented treatment. This theme arises in relation to other research to be discussed later.

4. Residential Environment, Affect State, and Affect Variability

Affect type and variability were explored in the same "daily affect" study as a function of type of living environment. As noted, the subjects were recruited from both the congregate housing and the nursing home. Differences associated with type of living environment were separated from those due to diagnosis. Interestingly, there was no tendency for diagnosable clinical depression to be more prevalent in the nursing home than in the congregate housing. In contrast, location was found to be associated with the prevalence of some of the affects. The total PA index score (but not the score for any separate affect) was higher in congregate housing, whereas the NA index and each of the five individual NAs were more prevalent in the nursing home.

In terms of day-to-day variability, location was not associated with variability of positive affects, but variability was greater for all NAs except depression in the nursing home.

Because the two living environments differ in so many ways, it is difficult to ascribe these findings—better mental health and less variability of negative affect in the congregate housing—to a single cause. There was greater autonomy, choice, and normality in the congregate housing, but these factors are confounded with the better health of the housing residents, compared with those in the nursing home. However, all these factors together provide an adequate explanation for the preponderance of positive over negative affects in the residents of congregate housing, despite the fact that there was no difference in the prevalence of depressive diagnoses between the residents of housing and the nursing home. Why nursing home residents should be more variable in negative affect is less comprehensible. Conceivably, the greater vulnerability associated with their physical frailty may manifest itself in more frequent ebb and flow of anxious and hostile affects.

5. Context of Daily Events and Affect States

Contrasting environments were represented by congregate housing and the nursing home. The contrast between the two is relatively gross, however. A more differentiated facet of the environment is the types and frequency of events that occur in different physical or social settings. An event is less measurable and more complex conceptually than physical, personal, or social aspects of an environment, which may be measured objectively. An event is more subjective: that is, it is personally relevant to the person who experiences it. Events are sometimes things that happen to a person: accidents; behaviors of significant others; or historical episodes, such as a war. Sometimes their origin is within a person, as with a change in health, an idea, or a sudden rush of emotion. Most often, events are transactional, that is, their origin lies in both the external world and the person, and one simply cannot assign the event to either. Attending a party, making a visit, falling in love, and attending a play are all transactional events. Further, what might seem to an outside observer to be an event may not be considered so by the actor; salience is a subjective judgment.

As transactional phenomena, events have varying probabilities of occurrence depending on the person and the environment. In the present research program, different types of elders populated the two environments, and the environments themselves varied greatly in their physical, personal, and social characteristics. Although the residents are active participants in the creation of events, what may be called the "event texture" of the setting constitutes a potential cognitive, affective, or behavior-activating stimulus field for the individual.

Another problem investigated during the "daily affect" study was the relationship of the residential environment and depression to the event context (Lawton, DeVoe, Parmelee, & Katz, 1995). Are some types of events more likely to occur in congregate housing than in the nursing home? Do major depressives, minor depressives, and "normals" report events differently? A second question addressed a more basic issue in the environmental psychology of emotion (Russell & Snodgrass, 1984): To what extent are the affective states that characterize a person's day influenced by the flow of events, including their positive and negative quality? (See Tennen, Suls, & Affleck, 1991, for a state-of-the-art review of the relatively new area of event research; and Zautra, Affleck, & Tennen, 1994, for a general discussion of events and aging.)

At the same time they made their daily affect ratings, residents reported salient events that had occurred within the past 24 hours. Trained coders classified the events into content categories, the most prevalent of which were health-related, self-initiated, family, group activities, personal care, indicators of quality of care, and other social events. Events were also categorized as positive, neutral, and negative.

Comparing the residential environments, congregate housing tenants reported fewer events in general, and fewer negative events. However, few locational differences in frequency of the specific types of events were observed. The diagnostic groups did not differ in the total number of events reported, but residents with major depression reported more negative, fewer positive, and health-related events of all three valences combined than "normals."

The test of event-affect congruence was performed in such a way as to remove the effects of location, diagnosis, and all other individual differences. In other words, the test lay in determining whether each individual's daily affect rating fluctuated up or down from that person's mean in concert with the valence of the event reported that day. For all positive events considered together and for all negative events, congruence occurred to a significant degree, as it also did for two specific event categories: self-initiated positive uses of time and negative health-related events. In other words, a day's positive emotion was greater if a positive event occurred; and the same was true of negative emotions and negative events. Although the frequency of many other events was low, and therefore statistical power was low, congruence measures were, without exception, in the predicted direction even if not statistically significant.

The major finding of this part of the research program was event-affect congruence, which is relevant to the theory of person-environment relations. In addition, the finding that the dominant affect state of any given day has a lot to do with which events occur has many implications for care. The task clearly is to intervene actively, or encourage residents to be proactive, in creating a total array of events in which positive events predominate.

On the whole, however, the effects of two different residential environments and degree of diagnosed depression were associated only moderately with the types and valences of events. It is possible that the highly scheduled activities and the more intense caregiving in the nursing home accounted for the greater frequency of events of all types there. Depression affected the overall distribution of event valence—more negative and fewer positive events. It is also noteworthy that major depressives reported more health-related events of all types (not necessarily negative) than did minor depressives or "normals." This finding is consistent with clinical criteria for depression that emphasize the close relationship between physical illness and depression.

The conclusions to be drawn from the event-affect research are:

• The generic event types used to classify elders' reports differed only slightly between the two environments. Later research should continue to develop taxonomies of events that will better reflect the dynamic salience of events to the particular environments and individuals being studied.

- Event valence was strongly related to clinical depression in the expected manner.
- The clearest relationships between events and affect were displayed in the variability of both events and affects within individuals. That is, the ebb and flow of an individual's affect is related to events of personal salience. Cross-individual analyses—which ask the question, "Does event X have a common affective outcome for everyone?"—were less likely to identify significant event-affect relationships. The treatment task is thus to identify the needs, preferences, and aversions of individuals and to attempt to maximize the occurrence of events that are consonant with such individual characteristics.

6.   Care Context and Affect in Dementing Illness

Depression may often co-occur with Alzheimer's disease and other dementia illness (Alexopoulos, Abrams, Young, & Shamoian, 1988; Gurland, Golden, Teresi, & Challop, 1984; Teri & Wagner, 1982). Prevalence data from the Philadelphia Geriatric Center, for example, estimated rates of about 14% for major depression and 29% for minor depression among nursing home residents with cognitive impairment (Parmelee, Katz, & Lawton, 1989). Despite the repeated demonstration of such dual diagnoses, few clinical studies of dementia have been concerned with the affective states experienced by such patients. Cognitive impairment and pathological behavior have typically constituted the major focus of such research, as if the personalities and inner lives of patients with Alzheimer's disease were irrelevant once dementia began.

The last research to be reviewed here (Lawton, Van Haitsma, & Klapper, 1994) attempted to describe the affective lives of nursing home residents whose impairment was moderate to moderately severe, and to determine the contextual correlates of residents' affect states. Although depression was one of the affects studied, the emphasis in this research was on six states thought to be particularly relevant to treatment—sadness, anxiety, anger, pleasure, interest, and contentment—all chosen from the Philadelphia Geriatric Center PA and NA Rating Scales. A treatment program on the special care unit was evaluated in this research. Many of the cognitively impaired residents could not verbalize their preferences and aversions; therefore, some of the assessment devices that depend on self-response could not be used. Affect states, however, could be evaluated by observers from facial expression, motor behavior, and any relevant verbal cues. The larger research project was one of 10 projects in the National Institute on Aging's Cooperative Study (Ory, 1994) of special care units for Alzheimer's disease patients (Lawton, Van Haitsma, & Klapper, 1994). The general hypothesis was that observed affect could provide clues to the subjective responses of patients with Alzheimer's disease to the treatment and care offered in the unit. Although variation within individuals is being studied here, as in the "daily affect" study, the only results that have been analyzed to date deal with variance between individuals (i.e., relationships between contexts and affect states). These early data will be described in terms of measurement methods, prevalence of affect, and affective correlates of care context.

Measuring Affect   The six states were described in terms of observable indicators. Research assistants' training included an introduction to the Ekman-Friesen (1978) facial affect coding system and many trial observations under supervision. A single subject was observed for 10 minutes, during which time ongoing behavior was coded into a handheld event recorder. At the end of 10 minutes, the observer rated each affect in terms of its estimated duration. The data included in this report were derived from 16 time-sampled 10-minute observations on 158 residents of two identical special care units for people with dementias, studied at baseline.

The reliability of 243 sessions where two raters observed the same 10-minute segment was uniformly high (kappas ranged from .76 to .89). Ratings by family members and staff provided several indicators of the validity of the affect ratings.

Prevalence of Affect States   Affects that can be called "hot"— sadness, anger, anxiety, and pleasure—were relatively infrequent (observed in 5% to 34% of all observation periods). By contrast, contentment was observed in 68% and interest in 87% of all observations. A small group of 43 cognitively intact residents were observed on 143 occasions to provide a rough standard against which the affective lives of patients with dementia might be compared. The unimpaired residents exhibited significantly less anxiety and anger, and more pleasure, contentment, and interest than the demented residents. These differences were rather small, however, and the groups did not differ in depression. Thus, although the evidence for continued affective engagement among patients with Alzheimer's disease was clear, in comparison with some of the nursing home's highest-functioning residents, the impaired residents exhibited more negative and less positive affect.

Context and Affect   Evidence for the association between context and affect was indirect. One such analysis was performed with ratings of

amount of participation in the planned activities and informal social interaction obtained from activity therapists and nursing assistants. Factor
scores from both sources were significantly related to the three positive
affects: Pleasure, contentment, and interest were higher in high
participators.

The second approach used the behaviors coded during the observation
periods, which were accumulated into individual scores and correlated
with summary affect scores. People observed to participate more in various
social behaviors and activities were higher in the positive affects.

Analyses now under way will test the context-affect relationship more
directly by analyzing the relationships between activity and affect as an
individual phenomenon based on an N of 16 occasions, replicated across
all subjects. In this analysis, one would expect that the affect observed
in a single individual would move in a positive or negative direction,
depending on whether the context—stimulating or secure—is congruent
with the person's needs.

The effect of context on affect is influenced by three sources of variation.
First is the long-term, relatively stable personality of the individual, for
example, introversion or extraversion. In our case, we have relatives'
ratings of the personalities of patients with Alzheimer's disease on several
of the "big five" factors. Such highly generalized temperaments, as noted
earlier, determine rough limits over which certain personal characteristics—such as preferences for types of activities, social settings, and motivational processes—vary. The second source is the care setting, or overall
context, which varies widely depending on the time of day, the social
composition of residents and staff, and the specific care activities directed
toward the individual. The third, independent, influence is the congruence
between personal need and environment. The congruence of the environment with individual needs, in turn, leads to different affects observed in
those varying contexts. This three-component model of person-environment congruence has been formulated and tested in other settings by
Kahana and associates (Kahana, 1982; Kahana, Liang, & Felton, 1980).
It remains to be seen whether measurement technology is up to the task
of identifying such relationships among impaired residents. At the very
least, however, the affect measurement of the research on special care
units showed that activities and socialization programs affect the states
of patients with Alzheimer's disease.

CONCLUSIONS AND IMPLICATIONS

This research program has increased our understanding of the daily lives
of older residents suffering from depression as well as those who are

cognitively impaired and not depressed. Perhaps most important was the demonstration that the quality of everyday life needs to be examined in terms of both its positive and negative features. Further, this quality has an inner aspect (PA and NA states) and an outer aspect (positive and negative events), and the two are closely related to one another.

A closely related conclusion concerns the design of programs to improve the level of mental health in nursing homes. Some evidence suggests that enrichment of the stimulating quality of a residential environment may increase PA, even among patients with Alzheimer's disease. It is likely that increased activity programming and attention to the social environment will have a salutary effect on this aspect of mental health. Negative events related to health are associated with more negative affect, underlining the importance of medical, nursing, and psychosocial care for these vulnerable elderly people.

The emotional range of residents' expressiveness was shown to remain broad even in patients with Alzheimer's disease, where the prevalence of depression was equal to that among more intact residents, and differences between "normals" and cognitively impaired people in other affect states was only moderate. The more "micro" look at affect variability in the day-to-day lives of depressed residents was especially revealing, indicating that the negative balance of affective experiences in such people may result especially from the absence of pleasure. Positive-affect scores of many depressed people remained at the same low level day after day, as contrasted with the low but more variable negative-affect scores. If we search for good news in the hypothesis that "positive stimulation equals positive affect," it may be that depressed people will be particularly good targets for such positive activity introduced as part of an intervention.

Depressed mood and anhedonia are only two possible symptoms of clinical depression, however. Equally amenable to study are other symptoms, such as somatic symptoms, fatigue, sleep disturbance, and loss of appetite. The temporal covariation of these symptoms with daily events and other aspects of the care environment deserves study in the same way that events and affects have been examined in the present research.

Finally, looking ahead from questions that were raised but not answered in the present research, the task of matching social context, environment, and care to individual needs requires much more study. The possibilities are evident in the contrast between the apparent universality of the two-factor structure of affect when people are considered in the aggregate and the tremendous diversity when each person is studied more microscopically over time. The diversity of patterns of variability of affect within individuals represents another facet of personality. If such patterns are idiosyncratic, it is likely that interventions designed to optimize quality of life will be similarly diverse. The challenge is to develop clinical and psychometric technology to the point where person-environment congruence and its consequent favorable outcomes are attainable.

REFERENCES

Aldwyn, C. M., & Levenson, M. R. (1994). Aging and personality assessment. In M. P. Lawton & J. A. Teresi (Eds.), *Annual review of gerontology* (Vol. 14, pp. 182–209). New York: Springer.

Alexopoulos, G. S., Abrams, R. C., Young, R. C., & Shamoian, C. A. (1988). Cornell Scale for Depression in Dementia. *Biological Psychiatry, 23,* 271–284.

American Psychiatric Association. (1987). *Diagnostic and statistical manual of mental disorders* (3rd ed., rev.). Washington, DC: Author.

Bradburn, N. M. (1969). *The structure of psychological well-being.* Chicago: Aldine.

Cattell, R. B. (1952). The three basic factor analytic research designs—their interrelationships and derivatives. *Psychological Bulletin, 49,* 499–520.

Cohen, U., & Day, K. (1993). *Contemporary environments for people with dementia.* Baltimore: Johns Hopkins University Press.

Costa, P. T., & McCrae, R. R. (1980). Influence of extraversion and neuroticism on subjective well-being: Happy and unhappy people. *Journal of Personality and Social Psychology, 38,* 668–678.

Costa, P. T., & McCrae, R. R. (1989). *The Neo/FFI manual supplement.* Odessa, FL: Psychological Assessment Resources.

Costa, P. T., Zonderman, A. B., McCrae, R. R., Cornoni-Huntley, J., Locke, B. Z., & Barbano, H. E. (1987). Longitudinal analyses of psychological well-being in a national sample: Stability of mean levels. *Journal of Gerontology, 42,* 50–55.

Diener, E., & Emmons, R. (1984). The independence of positive and negative affect. *Journal of Personality and Social Psychology, 47,* 1105–1117.

Ekman, P., & Friesen, W. V. (1978). *Facial action coding system.* Palo Alto, CA: Consulting Psychologists.

Eysenck, H. J. (1970). *The structure of human personality* (3rd ed.). London: Methuen.

Goldberg, L. R. (1990). An alternative "description of personality": The Big Five factor structure. *Journal of Personality and Social Personality, 59,* 1216–1229.

Gurland, B., Copeland, J., Kuriansky, J., Kelleher, M., Sharpe, L., & Dean, L. L. (1983). *The mind and mood of aging.* New York: Haworth.

Gurland, B., Golden, R. R., Teresi, J. A., & Challop, J. (1984). The SHORT-CARE: An efficient instrument for the assessment of depression, dementia, and disability. *Journal of Gerontology, 39,* 116–169.

James, W. (1890). *The principles of psychology.* New York: Holt.

Jung, C. G. (1921). Psychological types. *Collected works* (Vol. 6). Princeton, NJ: Princeton University Press.

Kahana, E. (1982). A congruence model of person-environment interaction. In M. P. Lawton, P. G. Windley, & T. O. Byerts (Eds.), *Aging and the environment: Theoretical approaches* (pp. 97–121). New York: Springer.

Kahana, E., Liang, J., & Felton, B. J. (1980). Alternative models of person-environment fit: Prediction of morale in three homes for the aged. *Journal of Gerontology, 35,* 584–595.

Kleban, M. H., Lawton, M. P. Nesselroade, J., & Parmelee, P. (1992). The structure of variation in affect among depressed and nondepressed elders. *Journal of Gerontology: Psychological Sciences, 47,* P190–P198.

Lawton, M. P. (1981). Sensory deprivation and the effect of the environment on management of the senile dementia patient. In N. Miller & G. Cohen (Eds.), *Clinical studies of Alzheimer's disease and senile dementia* (pp. 227–249). New York: Raven.

Lawton, M. P. (1983). Environment and other determinants of well-being in older people. *The Gerontologist, 23,* 349–357.

Lawton, M. P., DeVoe, M. R., & Parmelee, P. (1995). The relationship of events and affect in the daily lives of an elderly population. *Psychology and Aging, 10,* 469–477.

Lawton, M. P., Fulcomer, M. C., & Kleban, M. H. (1984). Architecture for the mentally impaired elderly: A postoccupancy evaluation. *Environment and Behavior, 16,* 730–757.

Lawton, M. P., Kleban, M. H., & Dean, J. (1993). Affect and age: Cross-sectional comparisons of structure and prevalence. *Psychology and Aging, 8,* 165–175.

Lawton, M. P., Kleban, M. H., & diCarlo, E. (1984). Psychological well-being in the aged: Factorial and conceptual dimensions. *Research on Aging, 6,* 67–97.

Lawton, M. P., Kleban, M. H., Rajagopal, D., Dean, J., & Parmelee, P. A. (1992). The factorial generality of brief positive and negative affect measures. *Journal of Gerontology: Psychological Sciences, 47,* P228–P237.

Lawton, M. P., & Moss, M. (1987). The social relationships of older people. In E. F. Borgatta & R. V. Montgomery (Eds.), *Critical issues in aging policy.* Beverly Hills, CA: Sage.

Lawton, M. P., Moss, M., & Grimes, M. (1985). The changing service needs of older tenants in planned housing. *The Gerontologist, 25,* 258–264.

Lawton, M. P., Moss, M., Kleban, M. H., Glicksman, A., & Rovine, M. (1991). A two-factor model of caregiving stress and psychological well-being. *Journal of Gerontology: Psychological Sciences, 46,* P181–P189.

Lawton, M. P., & Nahemow, L. (1973). Ecology and the aging process. In C. Eisdorfer & M. P. Lawton (Eds.), *Psychology of adult development and aging* (pp. 619–674). Washington, DC: American Psychological Association.

Lawton, M. P., Parmelee, P. A., & Katz, I. (1996). Affective states in normal and depressed older people. *Journals of Gerontology: Psychological Sciences, 51B.*

Lawton, M. P., Van Haitsma, K., & Klapper, J. (1994). A balanced stimulation and retreat program for a special care dementia unit. *Alzheimer's Disease and Associated Disorders, 8*(Suppl. 1), S133–S138.

Lawton, M. P., Van Haitsma, K., & Klapper, J. (1996). Observed affect in nursing home residents with Alzheimer's disease. *Journals of Gerontology: Psychological Sciences, 51B,* P3–P14.

Liebowitz, B., Lawton, M. P., & Waldman, A. (1979). Designing for confused elderly people: Lessons from the Weiss Institute. *American Institute of Architects Journal, 68,* 59–61.

Moriwaki, S. Y. (1974). The Affect Balance Scale: A validity study with aged samples. *Journal of Gerontology, 29,* 73–78.

Ory, M. G. (1994). Dementia special care: The development of a national research initiative. *Alzheimer's Disease and Associated Disorders, 8*(Supp. 1):S389–S404.

Parmelee, P. A., Katz, I. R., & Lawton, M. P. (1989). Depression among institutionalized aged: Assessment and prevalence estimation. *Journal of Gerontology: Medical Sciences,* M22–M29.

Russell, J. A., & Snodgrass, J. (1987). Emotion and the environment. In D. Stokols & I. Altman (Eds.), *Handbook of environmental psychology* (Vol. 1, pp. 245–280). New York: Wiley.

Spielberger, C. D. (1972). Anxiety as an emotional state. In C. D. Spielberger (Ed.), *Anxiety: Current trends in theory and research* (Vol. 1). New York: Academic.

Tennen, H., Suls, J., & Affleck, G. (Eds.). (1991). Personality and daily experience. *Journal of Personality* (Whole No. 3), *59.*

Teri, L., & Wagner, A. (1992). Alzheimer's disease and depression. *Journal of Consulting and Clinical Psychology, 60,* 379–391.

Tillson, D. (Ed.). (1990). *Aging in place.* Glenview, IL: Scott-Foresman.

Watson, D., Clark, L. A., & Tellegen, A. (1988). Development and validation of brief measures of Positive and Negative Affect: The PANAS scales. *Journal of Personality and Social Psychology, 54,* 1063–1070.

Watson, D., & Tellegen, A. (1985). Toward a consensual structure of mood. *Psychological Bulletin, 98,* 219–235.

Zautra, A. J., Affleck, G., & Tennen, H. (1994). Assessing life events among older adults. In M. P. Lawton & J. A. Teresi (Eds.), *Annual review of gerontology and geriatrics* (Vol. 14, pp. 324–352). New York: Springer.

Zevon, M. A., & Tellegen, A. (1982). The structure of mood change: An idiographic/nomothetic analysis. *Journal of Personality and Social Psychology, 43,* 111–122.

CHAPTER 3

Subdysthymic Depression and the Medically Ill Elderly

JANA M. MOSSEY

Recent studies have shown a 1% to 2% prevalence of major depression and a 2% prevalence of dysthymia in the community-dwelling elderly (Blazer, 1989; Blazer & Williams, 1980). In the institutionalized and medically ill elderly, the prevalence rates of major depression and dysthymia are higher (Koenig, Meador, Cohen, & Blazer, 1988; Parmelee, Katz, & Lawton, 1989). However, although it is recognized that the morbidity associated with major depression and dysthymia is significant, only a relatively small proportion of the population is affected. Elevated levels of depressive symptoms that are detectable by self-report but that do not meet criteria for major depression or dysthymia are much more common. Among community-dwelling elderly people, prevalence rates are reported to range between 15% and 30% (Blazer, Hughes, & George, 1987; Blazer & Williams, 1980; Kennedy et al., 1989). Rates among medically ill hospitalized or institutionalized older individuals typically range from 23% to 40% (Koenig, Meador, Cohen, & Blazer, 1988; Magni, Diego, & Schifano, 1985; Parmelee, Katz, & Lawton, 1989; Saravay, Steinberg, Weinshel, Pollack, & Alovis, 1991). Indeed, in a study conducted by the author (Mossey, Mutran, Knott, & Craik, 1989), 51% of the women who were seen in hospital after hip fractures had elevated levels of depressive symptoms. Until recently, individuals with elevated depressive symptoms in the milder range have been largely overlooked, from the standpoint of both case identification and treatment. There is emerging evidence, however, to indicate that individuals with such symptom levels experience slower and less complete recovery from illness or injury, suffer greater limitations in physical function, and use more health services (Broadhead, Blazer, George, & Tse, 1990; Gurland, Golden, & Lantigua, 1986; Harris, Mion, Patterson, & Frengley, 1988; Johnson, Weissman, & Klerman, 1992; Judd, Rappaport, Paulus, & Brown, 1994; Mossey, Knott, & Craik, 1990; Robinson & Price, 1982; Wells et al., 1989). Moreover, they are reported to be at increased risk of major depression (Howarth, Johnson, Klerman, & Weissman, 1992; Wells et al., 1989) and death (Kaplan & Camacho 1990; Magaziner, Simonsick, Kashner, Hebel, & Kenzora, 1990; Murphy, Monson, Oliver, Soval, & Leighton, 1987). As a consequence of these findings, clinicians and researchers have begun to question whether the milder forms of depressive symptoms, as well as major depression and dysthymia, should be more aggressively identified and treated. Attempts to address this issue have been impeded because of a limited consensus regarding how to define, either conceptually or operationally, the milder depressions and which treatment approaches might be efficacious. Recognizing the dilemmas for the researcher and the clinician that are inherent when there is limited consensus regarding a clinical problem, yet motivated by the data showing the less severe depressions to be associated with morbidity, decreased functioning, and poorer recovery, this chapter focuses on the milder depressions in medically and chronically ill elderly people that do not meet the criteria of the *Diagnostic and Statistical Manual of Mental Disorders* (*DSM*) for either major depression or dysthymia. Several questions are specifically addressed that require clarification before appropriate strategies for case finding and treatment, targeted to medically and chronically ill older individuals with such levels of depressive symptoms, can be developed and implemented. These questions include the following:

1. What constitutes clinically significant elevated depressive symptoms in the medically ill elderly? Particularly, how are the minor depressive symptoms that are clinically significant, but that do not meet standard *DSM* criteria for major depression or dysthymia, defined?
2. Is depression in the medically or chronically ill elderly a new condition in reaction to the illness or hospitalization, or is it a manifestation of a chronic or underlying condition?
3. In what ways do medically ill individuals with milder or subdysthymic depressive symptoms differ from those with few depressive symptoms?
4. What are the consequences of subdysthymic depressive symptoms for the medically ill elderly?
5. What therapies appear effective and efficacious for subdysthymic depression in the medically ill elderly?

The material presented in this chapter is organized around each of the preceding questions. The discussion pertinent to each question draws on published research reports and on the findings from three studies that have been conducted by the author. Methodological information regarding these studies is summarized first. Information specific to each question is presented subsequently. Finally, a summary with conclusions and recommendations suggested by the findings is presented.

STUDY METHODS

Descriptive information pertinent to the three studies—the Philadelphia Geriatric Center–Clinical Research Center (PGC-CRC) Study, the Philadelphia Geriatric Center–Teaching Nursing Home (PGC-TNH) Study, and the Medical College of Pennsylvania–Nurse Intervention Study—is presented in Table 3.1. Each of the studies addressed a slightly different research question; however, they have several characteristics in common. First, they all involved individuals who were hospitalized for a medical or surgical problem. The PGC-CRC Study and the PGC-TNH Study included individuals who were residents at the Philadelphia Geriatric Center; most of these were hospitalized at the PGC Freidman Hospital. The Nurse Intervention Study included individuals who were hospitalized

TABLE 3.1   Description of the Three Studies of Depression in the Hospitalized Elderly

Title	Study location	Sample	Study design
PGC-CRC Study[a]	Philadelphia Geriatric Center	41 Hospitalized elderly PGC residents Age range: 67–102 years	Historical/ prospective
PGC-TNH Study[b]	Philadelphia Geriatric Center	54 Hospitalized elderly PGC residents Age range: 62–100 years	Prospective
Nurse Intervention Study[c]	Three acute care hospitals in Philadelphia, PA	191 Hospitalized elderly Community dwelling Age range: 60–91 years	Retrospective

[a]Funded by a grant from the National Institute of Mental Health (grant no. MHP5040830).
[b]Funded by a grant from the National Institute on Aging (grant no. AG03934).
[c]Funded by a grant from the National Institute of Nursing Research (grant no. NR02642).

at the Medical College of Pennsylvania or the Hospital of the University of Pennsylvania and who resided in the community. Second, information was obtained on history of depressive symptoms as well as on current depressive symptoms. In the PGC-CRC and the PGC-TNH studies, information on depressive symptoms was gathered at a point that preceded the hospital admission. In the Nurse Intervention Study, history of depressive symptoms was obtained retrospectively through a structured clinical interview. Third, the Geriatric Depression Scale (GDS; Yesavage & Brink, 1983) was used as the primary measure of depressive symptomatology. In each study, a cutoff point of 11 identified individuals with elevated scores. Of significance, the three studies did differ in their racial composition. The PGC residents were predominantly Jewish and of Eastern European origin. The Nurse Intervention Study enrolled community-dwelling patients; slightly more than 50% of the subjects were African American.

Details of each of the studies are summarized below. In brief, the PGC-CRC Study was specifically undertaken to answer question 2 above. Two hundred eleven individuals residing in the PGC York Houses, the semi-independent residences of PGC, were screened when they were admitted to the Freidman Hospital. Of these, 41 individuals met the criteria for inclusion in the study and agreed to participate. Ages ranged between 67 and 102 years, with a mean of 87; 44% were male. Data on depressive symptoms (GDS) and other measures were obtained shortly after hospital admission and during the PGC Clinical Research Center screening evaluation done on a yearly basis. The data from the first yearly assessment was used in this study. Typically this initial assessment preceded the individual's hospitalization by 11 months.

The PGC-TNH Study was specifically designed to investigate the relationship of change in cognitive function to change in health state as indicated by hospitalization. One hundred two "medically stable" residents of the PGC York Houses and the PGC nursing care units were enrolled in the study. Assessments of depressive symptoms (GDS) as well as other variables were scheduled at 4-month intervals over a 12-month period. When the individual was admitted to hospital, a specific protocol was initiated that included administration of the GDS. Of the 102 individuals, 54 were hospitalized during the study period; the mean age of this group was 85, and 39% were male. Information on prehospital depressive symptoms was obtained from the 4-month assessment that most closely preceded the individual's hospitalization.

The Nurse Intervention Study was designed to evaluate the efficacy of a nurse-initiated intervention for medically ill individuals with elevated depressive symptoms. Individuals were identified within the first few days following hospital admission. Those who had no mention of cognitive impairment in their hospital admission history, whose GDS was 11 or greater and who did not meet *DSM-III-R* criteria for major depression or dysthymia were invited to participate in the treatment arms of a randomized trial. A similar number of individuals with a GDS of 8 or less were also recruited. One hundred ninety-one individuals were enrolled; the mean age of this group was 72 years, and 31% were male. One hundred three were identified as having a mild form of depression; the remaining 88 were in the nondepressed comparison group. Information on depressive symptoms (GDS) and depressive diagnoses, as indicated by the Structured Clinical Interview for *DSM-III* (SCID; Spitzer, Williams, Gibbon, & First, 1990) was obtained before the intervention was started. Information on history of depressive symptoms was obtained retrospectively during the SCID assessment.

THE FIVE QUESTIONS

1. WHAT CONSTITUTES CLINICALLY SIGNIFICANT ELEVATED DEPRESSIVE SYMPTOMS?

In recent years, there has been increasing consensus regarding the definition of major depression and dysthymia (American Psychiatric Association, 1987, 1994). There has been limited consensus, however, regarding the definition of and the name for elevated depressive symptoms *not* meeting *DSM* criteria for major depression or dysthymia. This has reflected, in part, an assumption by many researchers and clinicians that depressive illnesses represent discrete entities that are qualitatively different from "healthy" states. The notion of depression that warrants treatment as a spectrum of disorders ranging from milder forms to severe major depression is only now becoming more widely accepted as data emerge showing the degree of human suffering and the public health cost associated even with lower levels of symptomatology. The limited consensus reflects as well the fact that distinguishing individuals with significant levels of depressive symptoms from individuals who are experiencing the day-to-day mood fluctuations associated with the human condition involves clinical perceptions that are aesthetic as well as scientific. This difficulty has been heightened in considering the elderly because until recently there has been limited awareness that such states as depressed mood, feelings of helplessness, and loss of interest in life are not inevitable consequences of "normal aging"; the difficulty has also been increased by the overlap between symptoms of illness (e.g., disturbed sleep, diminished appetite, and fatigue) and the psychomotor retardation characteristic of depressive states, and by the frequency with which depressive symptoms present similarly to dementia.

In the absence of a concise definition, the milder levels of depressive symptoms have been referred to by such terms as "depressive symptoms," "subsyndromal symptomatic depression," "subclinical depression," "mild depression," "subthreshold depression," and "minor depression" (Broadhead et al., 1990; Johnson et al., 1992; Mossey et al., 1989; Paykel, Hollyman, Freeling, & Sedwick, 1988; Wells et al., 1989). The term "subdysthymic depression" is used here. The common defining criteria across researchers and terms is the presence of symptoms of major depression or dysthymia, as indicated by *DSM-III-R* or *DSM-IV* (American Psychiatric Association, 1987, 1994), but not in sufficient kind, number, or duration to meet criteria for major depression or dysthymia.

In establishing explicit operational criteria, two different approaches have been taken. In one, subdysthymic depression has been based on a clinical rating; in the other, it has been based on self-reported symptoms. Both approaches are used here. Subdysthymic depression is operationally defined as (a) the presence of elevated depressive symptoms as indicated by two scores of 11 or higher on the GDS, a self-report scale, measured about 1 week apart; (b) the absence of *DSM-III-R* major depression, dysthymia, cyclothymia, or bipolar disorder detected by the SCID (Spitzer et al., 1990), a clinical rating scale; or (c) the presence of an initial elevated GDS and evidence on the SCID of subthreshold dysthymia or subthreshold major depression. The data to characterize individuals according to this definition are available only in the Nurse Intervention Study. In that study, the prevalence of subdysthymic depression in the hospitalized elderly was about 20%. This is similar to that reported by others who have had data on both self-reported depressive symptoms and *DSM* diagnoses (Blazer et al., 1987; Judd et al., 1994; Wells et al., 1989).

2. IS DEPRESSION IN THE MEDICALLY ILL A NEW CONDITION OR A MANIFESTATION OR EXACERBATION OF AN UNDERLYING CONDITION?

Question 2 is considered particularly important because often depression in the hospitalized, medically ill older individual is discounted and attributed to the fact that "Of course older individuals may be depressed. Who wouldn't be if she or he were in the hospital?" The need to clarify this assumption is critical. Specifically, if depressive symptoms in hospital predominantly do represent a reaction to illness or to hospitalization, response of hospital staff and family members might well be to support the individual through the hospitalization knowing that the depressive symptoms are likely to clear up as the illness resolves. If, on the other hand, depressive symptoms identified during hospitalization are a manifestation of a more persistent affective state, a "supportive" or "wait and see" attitude would not be appropriate. Rather, further evaluation would be warranted, and treatment of the underlying depression would be indicated.

In her review article, Kurlowicz (1994) suggests that depression in the hospitalized medically ill elderly may be due to any of several factors: (1) the pharmacological agents used to treat the physical illness; (2) the type and seriousness of the physical illness itself; (3) the emotional response of the individual to the illness and hospitalization; (4) the individual's genetic predisposition. She cites studies that support each factor; these studies were unable, however, to evaluate the contribution of prehospital depressive symptoms. Data from the studies described above permit examination of the association between depressive symptoms in the hospital and the presence of such symptoms before hospitalization. Pertinent data are shown in Table 3.2; as seen here, irrespective of the study, more than 50% of those with depressive symptoms in the hospital had a history of such symptoms before hospitalization.

Indeed, in the Nurse Intervention Study—where the most comprehensive data on past history of depressive symptoms were available—79% of those with depressive symptoms in the hospital reported a past history. These rates would have only limited epidemiological significance if most of the individuals in the acute care hospital reported depressive symptoms before hospitalization. This is not the case. Data from the Nurse Intervention Study are shown in Table 3.3.

Only 13% of individuals with low depressive symptom scores in the hospital reported a prehospital history of depressive symptoms. Table 3.4 shows the odds ratios relating depressive symptoms in the hospital to a history of depressive symptoms before hospitalization. Individuals with depressive symptoms in the hospital were between 14 and 20 times more likely than those without such symptoms to report having depressive symptoms before hospitalization.

TABLE 3.2 Percentage of Individuals with Depressive Symptoms in Hospital Who Had a Prior History of Depressive Symptoms

Study	Percentage with History (%)
PGC-CRC	57
PGC-TNH	74
Nurse Intervention	79

TABLE 3.3   Percentage of Individuals With or Without a History of Depressive Symptoms Before Hospitalization by Level of Depressive Symptoms During Hospitalization[a]

| Prehospital history of depressive symptoms | Level depressive symptoms in hospital | | | |
	Low symptoms	Subdysthymic symptoms	Current major depression	N
Absent	87%	25%	—	88
Present	13%	75%	100%	96
N	75	95	14	184

[a]Data are derived from the Nurse Intervention Study.

These odds ratios are statistically significant and remain so even after controlling for other characteristics of patients that might affect their history of depressive symptoms. These findings are not inconsistent with those supporting the importance of the illness or the treatment for the individual. They indicate that, for most individuals, depressive symptoms observed during the hospital stay predated the hospitalization, either in the immediate preadmission period or at an earlier time point in the individual's life.

To evaluate this further, the seriousness of the reported past depressive symptoms was examined. It was reasoned that the finding noted above would be more compelling if the prehospital symptoms were serious than if they appeared mild or ephemeral. Data from the Nurse Intervention Study were used because the SCID assessment elicits specific information

TABLE 3.4   Odds Ratios for Depressive Symptoms in Hospital Given a History of Depressive Symptoms Before Hospitalization

| Study | Odds ratio | 95% Confidence interval | |
		Lower bound	Upper bound
PGC-CRC	18.2	2.05	157
PGC-TNH	13.6	3.6	49.6
Nurse Intervention	20.3	9.7	40.1

TABLE 3.5   Depressive Symptom History Among Individuals With a Screening GDS > 11 Who Did Not Meet Criteria for Major Depression[a]

No depressive symptoms	25%
Threshold/subthreshold current or past dysthymia	18%
Threshold/subthreshold past major depression	22%
Threshold/subthreshold past major depression and dysthymia	34%

[a]Data are derived from the Nurse Intervention Study.

on past major depression and dysthymia. The distribution of the specific histories for individuals who had a subdysthymic depression during the hospital stay is shown in Table 3.5. Twenty-five percent did not report a history of symptoms; all the remaining reported subthreshold or threshold dysthymia, major depression, or both.

The combined category of dysthymia and major depression constituted the largest percentage. Symptom levels indicated by these histories are not trivial. Even a subthreshold level for major depression or dysthymia is associated with human suffering and diminished functioning. Moreover, in 52% of the individuals, those reporting subthreshold or threshold dysthymia, the symptoms lasted 2 or more years.

Recently, investigators have suggested that subdysthymic depression may represent the waxing and waning of major depression (Sherbourne et al., 1994). Data are not available from the three studies to address this issue directly; however, data from the PGC-TNH study provide important evidence regarding the persistence of depressive symptoms over time. In this study, the number of different GDS administrations an individual had during the 12 study months ranged from two to eight, with most individuals in the never-hospitalized group having four GDS administrations, and those who were hospitalized having eight GDS administrations. GDS scores for 75% of the never-hospitalized sample were unchanged from one administration to another. Most had persistently low GDS scores. Among hospitalized individuals, GDS scores were also persistent. For those whose prehospital and hospital GDS scores were both low, 99% of their other GDS assessments over the 12 study months were also low. Similarly, among those whose prehospital and hospital GDS scores were high, 88% of the remaining GDS assessments were high. Other investigators have observed elevated depressive symptom scores to persist over time as well (Broadhead et al., 1990; Mossey et al., 1989; Thomas, Kelman, Kennedy, Ahn, & Yang, 1992).

To summarize the above: The data suggest that it is the exception rather than the rule for an individual who reports depressive symptoms in the hospital to have developed them for the first time after hospital admission. Depressive symptoms, therefore, do not appear to be a normative response to hospitalization; when observed, rather than being dismissed, they should trigger further evaluation.

3. IN WHAT WAYS DO INDIVIDUALS WITH SUBDYSTHYMIC DEPRESSIONS WHILE IN THE HOSPITAL DIFFER FROM THOSE WITH FEW SYMPTOMS?

An answer to question 3 was considered particularly important because it was a necessary step toward verifying or dispelling the notion that depressive symptoms were a normative reaction by the elderly to hospitalization. Knowledge of the differences, if any, between individuals with and without depressive symptoms may provide insight regarding the etiology and natural history of such symptoms. Cross-sectional comparisons between individuals who had high levels of depression and those with low-level symptoms were conducted. The results from all three studies were almost identical. Because of the ability to distinguish individuals with subdysthymic depression from those with major depression or dysthymia, only findings from the Nurse Intervention Study are presented here. As would be expected, given the study design, the age and sex distribution of individuals with subdysthymia and those with low-level depressive symptoms were similar. Data in Table 3.6 indicate that there were no other differences between groups on the sociodemographic variables, except for education. On average, individuals in the low-symptom group reported 2 more years of completed education.

Data on health and social and physical functioning variables are shown in Table 3.7. In contrast to the sociodemographic variables, individuals with subdysthymic depression differed from those in the low-symptom group on every indicator of physical function and health status measured. For example, self-rated health is measured on a 5-point scale that ranges from 1 ("excellent") to 5 ("bad"). Individuals with subdysthymic depression had, on average, a self-rated health status of "fair," whereas the self-rated health status of those in the low-symptom group was "good." This is not a trivial difference; there is considerable evidence that poorer

TABLE 3.6   Descriptive Statistics for Sociodemographic Variables for Individuals in the Subdysthymic Group and Those in the Nondepressed Comparison Group

	Subdysthymic symptom group ($N = 77$)	Nondepressed group ($N = 77$)
Age (years)		
Mean (SD)	71.0 (7.7)	70.5 (7.5)
Race		
White	44.9	32.5
Black	55.1	67.5
Sex		
Male	21.8	32.5
Female	78.2	67.5
Marital		
Married	40.2	42.4
Widowed	46.3	40.0
Other	13.4	17.6
Years of education		
Mean (SD)	10.4 (3.2)	12.3 (3.3)

self-rated health is associated with increased risk of mortality and less complete recovery (Idler, Kasl, & Lemke, 1990; Kaplan & Camacho, 1990; Mossey & Shapiro, 1982; Schoenfeld, Malmrose, Blazer, Gold, & Seeman, 1994). Differences in self-rated health of the magnitude observed here have prognostic significance. On each of the other measures, individuals with a subdysthymic depression scored much closer to the negative pole than those in the low-symptom group. Members of the depressive symptom group reported more health problems; fewer feelings of vigor; greater fatigue; greater difficulty in performing such activities as stooping, lifting, or carrying; less self-care and fewer instrumental activities of daily living (IADLs) that could be done without assistance; and greater assistance in walking. They also indicated they had poorer interpersonal and social adjustment than the low-symptom group. The consistency of these findings across different dimensions of health and functional status suggests that, even though all study subjects were recruited while in the acute care hospital, the subdysthymic individuals represent a group that is distinct from the low-symptom individuals. The subdysthymic individuals appear in poorer physical and emotional health. Individuals in the subdys-

TABLE 3.7   Means and Standard Deviations for Baseline Psychosocial and Health Variables for Individuals in the Subdysthymic Group and Those in the Nondepressed Comparison Group

	Subdysthymic symptom group ($N = 77$)		Nondepressed comparison group ($N = 77$)	
	Mean	Sd	Mean	Sd
Geriatric Depression Score	15.6	3.7	3.7[*]	2.1
Mini-Mental State	26.7	2.3	27.6[**]	2.1
Self-Rated Health	3.2	.8	2.5[*]	.7
No. of reported conditions	9.7	4.0	6.1[*]	2.7
Days hospital previous 12 months	11.7	20.31	4.4	8.6
ADL, no help (number)	5.3	1.3	5.9[*]	.4
IADL, no help (number)	6.0	2.3	7.4[*]	1.7
Physical activities	9.5	5.8	5.8[*]	5.1
Difficulty walking	5.5	2.5	4.3[*]	2.3
Fatigue	5.7	1.9	2.7[*]	2.2
Vigor	2.4	2.0	5.2[*]	2.5
Social Adjustment				
General	21.7	4.5	16.9[*]	3.8
Extended family	14.4	3.8	11.4[*]	3.4
Close family	6.9	2.6	4.6[*]	2.0
Marital	19.8	5.9	15.6[*]	3.5

Note. High scores on self-rated health, number of reported conditions, days hospital previous 12 months, physical activities, difficulty walking, fatigue, and all measures of social adjustment mean poorer status. ADL, activities of daily living; IADL, instrumental activities of daily living.
[*]$p < .001$
[**]$p < .01$

thymic group were also compared with individuals who met SCID criteria for current major depression or current dysthymia. Consistent with the findings of other investigators (Broadhead et al., 1990; Judd et al., 1994; Wells et al., 1989), the subdysthymic group was more similar to the group with major depression or dysthymia than to the low-symptom group. Additional research is required to clarify the causal relationship between depressed mood and medical illness. In the absence of a clear picture, a past history of depressed mood and a high present level of physical dysfunction represent important predictors of depressed mood in the hospital.

4. WHAT ARE THE CONSEQUENCES OF SUBDYSTHYMIC DEPRESSION FOR OLDER INDIVIDUALS?

The high prevalence of subdysthymic depression makes it especially important to understand the consequences of such symptom levels for the older individual. Specifically, when a condition occurs with relative frequency, it may be associated with a substantial public health burden even if the consequences are modest. This appears to be the case with subdysthymic depressions (Broadhead et al., 1990; Johnson et al., 1992; Judd et al., 1994). The data relevant to this observation have been obtained not from the three studies discussed previously but rather from published research.

The Epidemiological Catchment Area (ECA) Study, a large multisite study of the prevalence of psychiatric morbidity in the community, has permitted cross-sectional and longitudinal evaluation of the relationships between subdysthymic levels of depression and self-reported health conditions, social and physical functioning, incidence of syndromal depression, and use of health services. The findings are consistent across different subgroups of the total ECA sample. Specifically, individuals with subdysthymic depressions reported more health problems, had higher levels of physical and social dysfunction, used more health services, and were at greater risk of major depression than those who did not have such symptoms (Broadhead et al., 1990; Howarth et al., 1992; Johnson et al., 1992; Judd et al., 1994). These findings are consistent with those from several other large epidemiological studies (Sherbourne et al., 1994; Wells et al., 1989; Wells, Burnam, Rogers, Hays, & Camp, 1992).

Studies of the consequences of subdysthymic depressive symptoms for recovery from a medical illness are less extensive. However, when they are considered, a positive association has been observed in which higher levels of depressive symptoms are associated with delayed or less complete recovery. For example, in a study conducted in Philadelphia that involved 196 community-dwelling ambulatory women who were free of cognitive impairment, who were not in the terminal stages of an illness, and who had recently undergone a surgical repair of a recent hip fracture, individuals with persistently high depressive symptoms were 9 times less likely than low-symptom individuals, other things being equal, to return to prefracture levels of physical function (Mossey et al., 1989, 1990). In this study, it was possible to control for the effects of medical status, prefracture physical function, age, and a number of other variables that might affect the recovery process.

As noted earlier, depressive symptoms are reported to have an adverse effect on survival. For example, Magaziner et al. (1990) observed that individuals with high levels of depressive symptoms were more likely than those with low levels to die during the 12 months after surgery for a hip fracture. There are several other studies that demonstrate depressive symptoms to be a risk factor for mortality (Bruce & Leaf, 1988; Kaplan & Camacho, 1990; Murphy et al., 1987; Schekelle et al., 1981). Taken together, these findings suggest that subdysthymic as well as syndromal depressive symptoms have serious negative consequences for the health of older individuals. From this perspective, it is particularly important that they not be dismissed as trivial or normative.

5. WHAT THERAPIES APPEAR EFFECTIVE AND EFFICACIOUS FOR SUBDYSTHYMIC DEPRESSIONS IN THE ELDERLY?

Few studies have been published in which specific treatment programs for subdysthymia have been rigorously evaluated. With the limited consensus regarding the definition and meaning of subdysthymic depressions in older individuals, this is not surprising. Two studies not focused specifically on older individuals, and one in which older medically ill individuals were targeted, have been identified. In one study, Klerman et al. (1987) reported good results with Interpersonal Counseling (IPC), a brief psychosocial intervention (Weissman & Klerman, 1993), with middle-aged adults who were enrolled in a large health maintenance organization in New England. They observed a statistically significant reduction in depressive symptoms, as indicated by scores on the General Health Questionnaire, in those receiving IPC. Paykel et al. (1988) reported findings from another study in which they tested amitriptyline (vs. placebo) with individuals they identified as in the "mild" symptom range. Unlike Klerman et al. (1987), they observed no positive benefit from treatment among the milder depressives. Because of the differences in case definition and the treatments studied, it is difficult to draw comparative conclusions between studies; moreover, the sample sizes and follow-up periods were relatively limited. In the Nurse Intervention Study described above, IPC has been studied as a treatment for subdysthymic depression among older individuals who were recruited during a stay on a general medical or surgical service of the acute care hospital. Results from 77 individuals randomly assigned to IPC or to usual care indicate that by the 6-month follow-up, but not at the 3-month follow-up, individuals in the IPC group demonstrated a statistically significant reduction in their scores on the Geriatric Depression Scale (GDS) and an improvement in their self-rated health (Mossey, Knott, Higgins, & Talerico, 1996). These findings are promising and suggest that intervention is possible with older medically ill individuals who have a subdysthymic depression. More research specific to the treatment of subdysthymic depression, however, is required.

In contrast to the paucity of studies dealing with the milder depressions, there is a growing literature regarding the efficacy of psychotherapy and pharmacotherapy, alone or in combination, with older individuals who are experiencing a major depression, including research performed by authors of other chapters in this book (Gallagher-Thompson et al., 1992; Teri, 1994; Teri & Gallagher-Thompson, 1991). A complete review of that literature is beyond the scope of this chapter; the reader is encouraged to see the review articles on this topic by Reynolds (1993) and Levenson (1992). In brief, several psychotherapies, including cognitive therapy and interpersonal therapy, and several pharmacological agents, including tricyclic antidepressants and selective serotonin reuptake inhibitors (SSRI), have been found effective and efficacious for the treatment of major depression in older individuals. There is no reason to believe that these same therapies would not be effective with older individuals who suffer from a subdysthymic depression.

To summarize the preceding: Although considerably more research is needed, there are substantial data from which to conclude that depression in the elderly, even the milder forms, is treatable. Indeed, the data are so compelling that many individuals view it as unconscionable to permit depression in the elderly to go unrecognized and untreated. Treatment is even more important because many other health problems experienced by older individuals have no effective treatments.

SUMMARY AND RECOMMENDATIONS

Five questions pertinent to subdysthymic depression have been addressed. In reviewing this material, it is evident that considerably more research will be required before the phenomenon is fully understood and appropriate intervention programs can be routinely implemented. Despite the gaps in knowledge and clinical experience, however, several conclusions can be drawn from the results of research completed to date. First, the level of depressive symptoms referred to here as subdysthymia appears definable and clinically significant. Self-report measures, such as the GDS and structured clinical assessments like the SCID, provide a mechanism for case identification and differentiation from syndromal depression. Individuals with a subdysthymic depression score worse than those with low symptom levels on many different dimensions of health status; their prognosis in terms of survival and recovery is compromised. In addition to personal costs, health care resources are disproportionately used by members of the subdysthymic group. Second, although the prevalence rates of subdysthymic depression, and the severer syndromal depressions, occur with greater frequency among institutionalized and medically ill elderly people than elderly people resident in the community, they are not normative for the former group. Most older individuals, even those who are sufficiently sick to be hospitalized, report few depressive symptoms. Among those hospitalized individuals whose depressive symptom level is high, most indicate the presence of such symptoms before hospitalization. Illness and hospitalization, therefore, are not sufficient cause for symptoms of depression. When observed, such symptoms should not be dismissed—rather, they should be investigated further. Third, untreated subdysthymic symptoms appear remarkably persistent over time. Moreover, they are predictive of major depression. Last, as with the more serious depressions, treatment of subdysthymia appears promising.

Several recommendations for clinical practice, education, and development of health services derive from the preceding conclusions.

1.   Within the hospital or institutional setting, evaluation to identify individual patients with subdysthymic and syndromal depressions should be aggressive and comprehensive. A two-stage approach that includes a screening component and a more comprehensive clinical evaluation for individuals who screen positive is feasible and acceptable. Importantly, the program should be structured so that all patients or residents are screened as part of a routine evaluation (e.g., the hospital admission workup). In a long-term residential setting, individuals should be re-screened at regular intervals.

2.   Within a hospital or institutional setting, a treatment capability directed toward individuals with subdysthymic as well as syndromal depression should be developed. In the absence of clinical trial data demonstrating the efficacy of medication for subdysthymic depression, psychosocial interventions should be stressed; this will be useful even if medication proves effective because studies indicate that combined psychotherapy and pharmacotherapy are effective. Expertise of both psychiatrists and other nonphysician mental health practitioners is required. This is especially important in the hospital setting because many older individuals are reluctant to see a psychiatrist. The Nurse Intervention Study used psychiatric clinical nurse specialists who had a master's degree to conduct the clinical evaluation and the treatment. Nurses are usually well received by a medically ill patient, and they are able to address the patient's medical as well as emotional concerns.

3.   Within the hospital setting, an outpatient treatment capability needs to be developed so that the patient may have continuing, coordinated

treatment after hospital discharge. Several programmatic models are possible. For example, the hospital may develop and operate the program as an outpatient service; alternatively, the hospital may develop referral arrangements with a home health care or mental health agency for the delivery of such services. Irrespective of the model selected, it is important to build into the program an outreach component with sufficient staff to initiate the postdischarge visit to the client.

4.   Education programs directed toward health care providers and administrators, family members and caregivers, and older individuals need to be developed and implemented. Much work is being done to educate practitioners and the public regarding the nature and importance of treating major depression. The clinical practice guidelines for depression in primary care developed by the Agency for Health Care Policy and Research (Depression Guideline Panel, 1993) are one example of this effort. Such programs need to be expanded to include subdysthymic depression both in those who are medically ill and in those who are otherwise healthy. Health care providers, especially physicians during their undergraduate medical education, need to be trained to recognize and treat, or refer for treatment, individuals with elevated depressive symptoms. An initial goal of the educational program would be to reduce the tendency of providers, physicians, and nurses to dismiss depressive symptoms reported by their older patients. Older individuals and their family members as well need to be informed that depressive symptoms are not an expected consequence of illness or aging, that they are not a shameful sign of weakness, and that they can be treated.

5.   Research to specifically investigate the epidemiology and clinical course of subdysthymia should be given funding priority. To date, most of the data pertinent to subdysthymia have been derived from studies, such as the Epidemiology Catchment Area (ECA) Study, conducted for other purposes. To develop the knowledge base that will permit effective clinical interventions and eventually preventive programs, this needs to be rectified. The individual and public health costs associated with subdysthymic levels of depression are too great to leave this important research to chance.

REFERENCES

American Psychiatric Association. (1987). *Diagnostic and statistical manual of mental disorders* (3rd ed., rev.). Washington, DC: American Psychiatric Association.
American Psychiatric Association. (1994). *Diagnostic and statistical manual of mental disorders* (4th ed.). Washington, DC: American Psychiatric Association.

72   THE NATURE OF DEPRESSION

Blazer, D., Hughes, D. C., & George, L. K. (1987). The epidemiology of depression in an elderly community population. *The Gerontologist, 27,* 281–287.

Blazer, D., & William, C. D. (1980). Epidemiology of dysphoria and depression in an elderly population. *American Journal of Psychiatry, 137,* 439–444.

Broadhead, W. E., Blazer, D. G., George, L. K., & Tse, C. K. (1990). Depression, disability days, and days lost from work in a prospective epidemiologic survey. *Journal of the American Medical Association, 264,* 2524–2528.

Bruce, M. L., & Leaf, P. J. (1989). Psychiatric disorders and 15-month mortality in a community sample of older adults. *American Journal of Public Health, 79,* 727–730.

Depression Guideline Panel. (1993). *Depression in primary care* (Vol. 1, AHCPR Publication, No. 93-0500). Washington, DC: Agency for Health Care Policy and Research.

Gallagher-Thompson, D., Futterman, A., Hanley-Peterson, P., Zeiss, A., Ivonson, G., & Thompson, L. W. (1992). Endogenous depression in the elderly, prevalence and agreement among measures. *Journal of Consulting and Clinical Psychology, 60,* 300–303.

Harris, R. E., Mion, L. C., Patterson, M. B., & Frengley, J. D. (1988). Severe illness in older patients: The association between depressive disorders and functional dependency during the recovery phase. *Journal of the American Geriatrics Society, 36,* 890–896.

Howarth, E., Johnson, A. J., Klerman, G., & Weissman, M. M. (1992). Depressive symptoms as relative and attributable risk factors for first-onset major depression. *Archives of General Psychiatry, 49,* 817–823.

Idler, E. L., Kasl, S. V., & Lemke, J. H. (1990). Self-evaluated health and mortality among the elderly in New Haven, Connecticut, and Iowa and Washington counties, Iowa, 1982–1986. *American Journal of Epidemiology, 82,* 91–103.

Johnson, J., Weissman, M. M., & Klerman, G. L. (1992). Service utilization and social morbidity associated with depressive symptoms in the community. *Journal of the American Medical Association, 267,* 1478–1483.

Judd, L. L., Rapaport, M. H., Paulus, M. P., & Brown, J. L. (1994). Subsyndromal symptomatic depression: A new mood disorder. *Journal of Clinical Psychiatry, 55,* 4(Suppl.):18–28.

Kaplan, G. A., & Camacho, T. (1983). Perceived health and mortality: A nine year follow-up of the human population laboratory cohort. *American Journal of Epidemiology, 117,* 292–304.

Kennedy, G. J., Kelman, H. R., Thomas, C., Wisniewsky, W., Metz, H., & Bijur, P. (1989). Hierarchy of characteristics associated with depressive symptoms in an urban elderly sample. *American Journal of Psychiatry, 146,* 220–225.

Klerman, G. L., Budman, S., Berwick, D., Weissman, M. M., Damico-White, J., Demby, A., & Feldstein, M. (1987). Efficacy of a brief psychosocial intervention for symptoms of stress and distress among patients in primary care. *Medical Care, 25,* 1078–1088.

Koenig, H. G., Meador, K. G., Cohen, H. J., & Blazer, D. G. (1988). Depression in elderly hospitalized patients with medical illness. *Archives of Internal Medicine, 148,* 1939–1946.

Kurlowicz, L. H. (1994). Depression in hospitalized medically ill elders: Evolution of a concept. *Archives of Psychiatric Nursing, 8,* 124–136.

Levenson, J. L. (1992). Psychosocial interventions in chronic medical illness: An overview of outcome research. *General Hospital Psychiatry, 145*(Suppl.):43S–49S.

Magaziner, J., Simonsick, E. M., Kashner, T. M., Hebel, J. R., & Kenzora, J. E. (1989). Survival experience of aged hip fracture patients. *American Journal of Public Health, 79,* 274–278.

Magni, G., Diego, D. L., & Schifano, F. (1985). Depression in geriatric and adult medical inpatients. *Journal of Clinical Psychology, 4,* 337–344.

Mossey, J. M., Knott, K., & Craik, R. (1990). The effects of persistent depressive symptoms on hip fracture recovery. *Journal of Gerontology: Medical Sciences, 45,* M163–M168.

Mossey, J. M., Knott, K., Higgins, M., & Talerico, K. (1996). Effectiveness of a psychosocial intervention, Interpersonal Counseling, for subdysthymic depression in medically ill elderly. *Journal of Gerontology: Medical Sciences, 51A,* M172–M178.

Mossey, J. M., Mutran, E., Knott, K. A., & Craik, R. (1989). Determinants of recovery 12 months after hip fracture: The importance of psychosocial factors. *American Journal of Public Health, 79,* 279–286.

Mossey, J. M., & Shapiro, E. (1982). Self-rated health: A predictor of mortality among the elderly. *American Journal of Public Health, 72,* 800–808.

Murphy, J. M., Monson, R., Oliver, D. C., Sobal, A. M., & Leighton, A. H. (1987). Affective disorders and mortality. *Archives of General Psychiatry, 44,* 473–480.

Parmelee, P. A., Katz, I. R., & Lawton, M. P. (1989). Depression among the institutionalized aged: Assessment and prevalence estimation. *Journal of Gerontology: Medical Sciences, 44,* M22–M29.

Paykel, E. S., Hollyman, J. A., Freeling, P., & Sedgwick, P. (1989). Predictors of therapeutic benefit from amitriptyline in mild depression: A general practice placebo-controlled trial. *Journal of Affective Disorders, 14,* 83–95.

Reynolds, C. F. (1992, September). Treatment of depression in special populations. *Journal of Clinical Psychiatry, 53*(Suppl.):45–53.

Robinson, R. G., & Price, T. R. (1982). Post-stroke depressive disorders: A follow-up study of 103 patients. *Stroke, 13,* 335–341.

Saravay, S. M., Steinberg, M. D., Weinshel, B., Pollack, S., & Alovis, N. (1991). Psychological comorbidity and length of stay in the general hospital. *American Journal of Psychiatry, 148,* 324–329.

Schoenfeld, D. E., Malmrose, L. C., Blazer, D. G., Gold, D. T., & Seeman, T. E. (1994). Self-rated health and mortality in the high-functioning elderly—a closer look at healthy individuals: MacArthur field study of successful aging. *Journal of Gerontology: Medical Sciences, 49,* M109–M115.

Shekelle, R. B., Raynor, W. J., Ostfeld, A. M., Garron, D. C., Bieliauskas, L. A., Liu, S. C., Maliza, C., & Paul, 0. (1981). Psychological depression and 17-year risk of death from cancer. *Journal of Psychosomatic Medicine, 43,* 117–125.

Sherbourne, C. D., Wells, K. B., Hays, R. D., Rogers, W., Burnam, M. A., & Judd, L. L. (1994). Subthreshold depression and depressive disorder: Clinical characteristics of general medical and mental health specialty outpatients. *American Journal of Psychiatry, 151,* 1777–1784.

Spitzer, R. L., Williams, J. B. W., Gibbon, M., & First, M. D. (1990). *SCID user's guide for the structured clinical interview for DSM-III-R.* Washington, DC: American Psychiatric Press.

Teri, L. (1994). Behavioral treatment of depression in patients with dementia. *Alzheimer Disease and Associated Disorders, 3*(Suppl.):66–74.

Teri, L., & Gallagher-Thompson, D. (1991). Cognitive-behavioral interventions for treatment of depression in Alzheimer's patients. *Gerontologist, 31,* 413–416.

Thomas, C., Kelman, H. R., Kennedy, G. J., Ahn, C., & Yang, C. (1992). Depressive symptoms and mortality in older persons. *Journal of Gerontology: Social Sciences, 47,* S8O–S87.

Weissman, M. M., & Klerman, G. L. (1993). Interpersonal counseling for stress and distress in primary care settings. In G. L. Klerman & M. M. Weissman (Eds.), *New applications of interpersonal psychotherapy* (pp. 265–291). Washington, DC: American Psychiatric Press.

Wells, K. B., Burnam, M. A., Rogers, W., Hays, R. D., & Camp, P. (1992). The course of depression in adult outpatients: Results from the Medical Outcomes Study. *Archives of General Psychiatry, 49,* 788–794.

Wells, K. B., Steward, A., Hays, R. D., Burnam, M. A., Rogers, W., Daniels, M., Berry, S., Greenfield, S., & Ware, J. (1989). The functioning and well-being of depressed patients: Results from the Medical Outcomes Study. *Journal of the American Medical Association, 262,* 914–919.

Yesavage, J. A., & Brink, T. L. (1983). Development and validation of a geriatric depression scale: A preliminary report. *Journal of Psychiatric Research, 17,* 37–49.

CHAPTER 4

Residents' Understanding and Experience of Depression: Anthropological Perspectives

MARK R. LUBORSKY
ELIZABETH M. RILEY

O ur ability to detect and treat depression, and to specify its distribution and causes, is well advanced. We know that the disease is psychologically and physically debilitating, costly, and widespread; we also know that it can be treated successfully at all ages (Scogin & McElreath, 1994; Thompson et al., 1987). However, a better understanding of depression in later life is clearly needed. Depression is more prevalent among elderly people living in long-term care facilities than in the community (Blazer, 1994). Usage rates for psychological services are low among the current cohort of elderly people who prefer to present problems to physicians and to present physical rather than psychological complaints (Bucholz & Robins, 1987; Lasoski & Thelens, 1987). Even after rapid effective treatment for depression, the elderly may still not seek help for new problems (Sadavoy & Reiman-Sheldon, 1983).

Note: Grants to the first author from the National Institutes on Aging (grant no. R0190650), National Institute of Mental Health (grant no. POMH40380-07), and the National Institute of Child Health and Human Development (grant no. R01HD31526) are gratefully acknowledged. Contributions by Dr. Morton Kleban to the design and statistical analyses, and by Rohini Mukand to the interviews and analysis, are gratefully acknowledged. Permission was granted to include excerpts from previous publications by the first author from the Gerontological Society of America for excerpts from *The Gerontologist, 33*, 445–452, and from Elsevier for a passage from *Social Science and Medicine, 40*, 1447–1459.

Today, despite advances in identifying the causes and treating the symptoms of depression, we do not clearly understand the personal meanings, contexts, and natural course of depressive experience (Aneshensel, 1985; Blazer, 1989). The clinical tradition of focusing on pathology tends to obscure the ways people with mental health problems continue to make sense of, manage, and represent their experiences to others in light of past experiences, current situations, and cultural contexts. One marker of the value of a meaning-centered approach is the efficacy of low-cost cognitive and behavioral treatments that operate by ''jump-starting'' the individual's patterns of attributing meaning from depression-prone to non–depression-prone styles. Such interventions are aimed at the level of the whole person, making meaning of his or her experiences, rather than at a biological level.

The goal of this chapter is to describe results of our research on the individual and social understanding and experience of depression among elderly long-term care residents. The studies represent part of a developing paradigm for a culturally and historically contextualized life-history perspective on quality of life (Luborsky, 1993a, 1993b, 1994; Luborsky & Rubinstein, 1987; Scheer & Luborsky, 1991). The aims of this chapter are to describe personal explanations and self-management strategies for depression, the sociocultural ideals and settings that shape the formation and reporting of symptoms, and the personal life themes and identities of depressed and nondepressed residents.

ANTHROPOLOGICAL CONCEPTS AND RESEARCH

GENERAL GOALS AND APPROACHES OF ANTHROPOLOGY

Because this chapter builds on anthropological perspectives, we first provide a brief orientation to ethnographic research. Ethnographic research provides naturalistic data that can represent meanings, concepts, and concerns about depression in the informant's own language. One value of these data is that they provide a comparative perspective that reveals the fit between the concepts of the medical researcher and those of the informants. The ethnographic approach uses idiographic and qualitative methods that assess personal beliefs without forcing responses into nomothetic, standardized formats that require subjects to ''choose the best answer'' from predefined categories of responses. Rather, a major goal is to discover the scope of the universe of phenomena for study and to identify relevant units to use for subsequent sampling and analyses (Luborsky & Rubinstein, 1995).

Anthropological research provides distinctive knowledge. First, it describes the web of cultural values and meanings that are the settings within which individuals interpret and shape experiences, meanings, and daily social life. Second, it describes human experience on the basis of the perspectives, words, and constructs of the population under study. A variety of terms and concepts designate this approach, which is dedicated to exploring the ''insider's view,'' emic perspective, or lived experience, and has also been popularized in terms of ''life worlds'' of patients—in contrast to the ''medical worlds'' of health professionals (Geertz, 1984; Mishler, 1986; Strauss & Corbin, 1990). One basic finding from such studies is that personal meanings and experiences are not predicted by objective factors such as living conditions (e.g., disease, disability level, and income), social norms (e.g., statuses and identities), or ascribed characteristics of the person (e.g., age and ethnicity). The path to such knowledge is via naturalistic, discovery-oriented techniques. A familiar, but false, stereotype should be noted. Although anthropological studies use individual informants, it should not be inferred that they focus solely on subjectivity and psychological issues. Rather, the objective is to learn about the shared cultural values and social practices that shape how individuals interpret their own conditions.

A third contribution of ethnographic research concerns the complexity of cultural meanings and experience. Research has shown that cultural values are not univalent and unproblematic guides to daily life, social relationships, or lifelong biographies. Rather, we find multiple sets of values and ideologies, sometimes conflicting (Clark, 1972). For example, a person needing an adaptive device such as a walker for mobility encounters several dilemmas regarding the value of independence. On the one hand, the device enables the person to move independently (i.e., volitionally). But with gains in independent mobility comes a stigmatized public image due to the inability to walk unaided and to physical dependence on a device. The high rate of abandonment of medically prescribed adaptive equipment testifies to the onerous value conflicts surrounding personal independence (Deppen, Luborsky, & Scheer, 1996; Luborsky, 1993b, 1994a).

The basic building blocks of qualitative research (e.g., meanings, identities, and symbols) are not fixed, constant objects with immutable traits like the variables and factors in standardized research. Rather, meanings and identities are fluid and can change over time, according to the situation and the persons involved. Different methods and concepts are employed to develop knowledge about the realm of human experiences undergone by persons in particular communities or societies. For example, Whitbourne (1984) explores adult identity processes and categories in terms of the constructs held by adults themselves; she thus crosses disciplinary boundaries between developmental psychological and phenomenologically oriented humanistic sciences. Cohler (1991) describes this plasticity as a biographical self or a ''personal life-history self'' that interprets experiences and marshals meanings as a way to manage adversity. Two examples can clarify this point.

A textbook illustration of the fluidity of meanings is presented by Evans-Pritchard (1940). He wrote of his trouble, during his early fieldwork in Africa, in determining the names of villagers. Each person repeatedly gave him totally different names, seemingly at random. In the kinship-based society, the name, or identity, one person provides to another is relative to each person's clan membership, age, and community. The social relativity of identities, now known as the principle of segmentary opposition, was apparent once Evans-Pritchard discovered that the informants indexed their names to provide an identity at an equivalent level of social organization. For example, when traveling abroad, we would identify ourselves by our nationality; however, to greet a new neighbor, we identify ourselves by where we live on the block—not by reference to a level of shared identity as residents of the same state or nation.

Ethnic identity is a familiar example of fluid meanings that vary according to social situation, historical time period, and personal salience over a lifetime (Luborsky & Rubinstein, 1987, 1990). Ethnic identity serves as a source of fixed basic family values during socialization in childhood. It becomes more fluid as an ascribed family identity to redefine or even reject as part of the psychological process of individuation in early adulthood. It continues to be fluid: Sometimes it is a source of social stigma in communities or times of war (e.g., being Japanese American or Italian American during World War II). Finally, it may serve as a valuable source of continuity of meaning and pride in later life that may help individuals adapt to bereavement and losses.

One form of fluid meanings receiving new attention is the personal theme. Research shows that personal themes exist as a discrete level of individual awareness, which people actively monitor and manage (Bruner, 1986, 1990; Luborsky, 1993a, 1994a, 1995). Themes are markers of processes rather than fixed traits or structures. For example, studies of bereavement reveal the central role in survivors' overall life reorganization of the need to form a new sense of meaning and pattern for their life in addition to mourning the loss of a partner or family member (Luborsky & Rubinstein, 1990). Williams (1984) suggests that a person's perception of being ill with a chronic medical disease is triggered only when the disease disrupts the expected roles and trajectory of one's biography and life themes. Some research shows that a break in the sense of continuity in personal meaning (Becker, 1993), rather than the presence of any particular meaning (theme), precedes illness and depression (Atchley, 1988; Antonovsky, 1987). Thematic life stories have been linked with distress and clinical depression (Luborsky, 1993a).

In summary, the ethnographic study of personal and social values and meanings is important to research on depression. Personal and social values and meanings represent domains of great concern to research subjects, who work to reaffirm or to change them over the lifetime. The loss of cherished values or meanings is mourned, just as lost persons and objects are mourned. Themes and meanings are objective and measurable to the extent that they can be identified and described, although specialized methods and concepts are needed to assess and interpret each. Careful attention must be directed toward understanding the personal interpretations of social meanings, the fluidity of meanings and the settings in which they emerge, and also the multiplicity and potential conflicts among values in a given setting.

DEPRESSION IN LONG-TERM CARE
FROM ANTHROPOLOGICAL PERSPECTIVES

To date, despite a large clinical and epidemiological literature, a gap exists in our knowledge of how depression is understood, experienced, and managed by elderly people who are receiving long-term care (LTC). There is anthropological research on depression (Jenkins, Kleinman, & Good, 1991; Kleinman & Good, 1985; Nichter, 1981). Core anthropological questions concern the cross-cultural universality or specificity of idioms of emotional expression (Lutz, 1986; Marsella & White, 1982), and the challenge of comparing standardized clinical categories with concepts used by the subjects. One contribution of research addressed to the historical and community settings of particular symptoms has been to document the social production of diagnostic categories (Locke & Lindenbaum, 1993), as in the case of depression (Gains & Farmer, 1986) and posttraumatic stress syndrome (Young, 1993). These studies added to our understanding of the ways in which the culture and language of a community shape how some forms of distress are expressed as depression. Another contribution has been to identify how the general social positions and esteem provided for people with impairments (physical and mental) in a culture are consistent with the kinds and amounts of medical treatment and resources people with mental illness are deemed to deserve (Estroff, 1981; Langness & LeVine, 1986).

A spate of new ethnographies of LTC facilities provide detailed accounts of the social organization, daily life, institutional and care structures, events, and experiences of LTC (Foner, 1994; Gubrium, 1993; Henderson & Vesperi, 1995; Savishinsky, 1991; Shield, 1988). These ethnographies have incorporated data from the multiple viewpoints of residents, staff, and families (Foner, 1994). Several important findings are clear. First, the studies document the residents' widespread concern with depression and depression-like symptoms (e.g., feelings of loss, sadness, powerlessness, loneliness, helplessness). However, they do not directly examine depression. Second, mental health experiences emerge as the complex outcome of interactions between administrators, institutional life, medical providers, families, and other residents. Prominent in each study are prescriptions by residents for maintaining well-being and avoiding depression by remaining physically, socially, and mentally active. Avoidance of depressed residents by other, nondepressed residents has also been observed (Gubrium, 1993; Keith, 1977; Savishinsky, 1991). In general, the studies show how individual symptoms of distress derive from contextual factors, such as rigid institutional schedules for activities (e.g., eating and bathing); loss of a meaningful home and lifestyle; isolation from people and activities in the wider community; and daily life with other people who are ill and disabled. Third, the studies document the palliative strength of long-held personal life themes and values as resources mitigating the adverse effects of institutional life as well as physical and social losses.

UNDERSTANDING THE CONTENT AND EXPERIENCE OF DEPRESSION IN LONG-TERM CARE SETTINGS: CONTRIBUTIONS FROM THREE STUDIES

The projects described here derive from an extended program of ethnographic research at the Philadelphia Geriatric Center. The program has two broad goals. One goal has been to provide empirical data on the elderly LTC residents' beliefs, experiences, and ways of talking about depression. The other goal has been to develop a conceptual framework for understanding the dynamic interaction between individual and cultural understandings of depression. The conceptual framework can be described as a culturally and historically contextualized life-history perspective on quality of life (Luborsky, 1993a, 1993b, 1994, 1995; Luborsky & Rubinstein, 1987; Scheer & Luborsky, 1991). The three studies described below illustrate aspects and findings of the conceptual framework.

The study site and nature of the mental health data used in these ethnographic analyses are outlined briefly to introduce the studies.

The research site was a large, urban, long-term care (LTC) facility in Philadelphia that housed approximately 1,100 elderly residents. The facility consisted of two high-rise apartment towers for elderly people able to live independently, a nursing home, and specialty units for Alzheimer's disease. The facility provided a full spectrum of medical services and allied health, psychological, and social services. In addition, there were a range of outpatient clinics. Most residents were first- or second-generation immigrants of Western and Central European origin. The average age of the residents was 82 years, and there were approximately 80% women.

Data on clinical diagnoses were drawn from computerized mental health records of annual assessments of each resident. The assessments were conducted using established multidisciplinary clinical procedures performed independently by physicians, psychologists, and psychiatrists. A consensus diagnosis was arrived at by combining these findings during case conferences. Depressive symptoms were assessed using the Geriatric Depression Scale (GDS; Brink et al., 1985) and clinically defined major depression was judged by *DSM-III-R* criteria (APA, 1987). Symptoms of depression (e.g., sadness and loss of appetite) are part of the normal spectrum of affect over the life course. Clinically defined depressive disorders range from 6% to 15% and are less prevalent among the elderly than among people of other ages. Depression is more prevalent in old-age homes. At the study site, 40% of residents exhibited depressive symptoms; 12% met clinical criteria for major depression (Parmelee et al., 1989).

STUDY 1: MEANINGS OF DEPRESSION FOR ELDERLY RESIDENTS

Goal and Design

The first study sought to develop an understanding of the meaning and experiences of depression among LTC residents (Luborsky & Riley, 1994). The goal was to document the content and meaning of what informants perceived as the definitions, features, issues, and processes relevant to understanding depression. The study was designed to compare nondepressed with depressed residents, all without cognitive impairment. Twenty-eight subjects were selected for study: 14 currently nondepressed residents (including 4 with a past history of clinical depression), and 14 representing a range of current depressive symptoms including clinically defined major depression. There were equal numbers of women and men in each group. The mean age was 86; ages ranged from 69 to 101. Subjects were drawn from a computerized database of annual assessments of all residents within the facility, using a randomized procedure based on sex and clinical diagnoses.

Data Collection   Procedures for collecting data consisted of multiple in-depth audiotaped interviews using open-ended discussions, narratives, and structured questions. To administer all the research questions, 75-minute interviews were conducted once per week for 5 weeks for this cross-sectional study. Interview topics included discussion of personal meanings, experiences, and management of depression; collection of a life-history narrative; narratives of daily life from the day before the interview; and current concerns, interests, and social life. The data on depression presented here required approximately 1 hour of interview discussion to elicit. Given the methods, aims, and sample size, we present only ethnographic summaries and descriptive statistics for this first study.

Analytic Techniques   Content-analytic techniques were conducted (Luborsky, 1994b) to examine the full set of verbatim transcripts. The objectives of these analyses were to identify and summarize, first, the main topics expressed within responses to each question, and then the themes and patterns emerging across all the interviews. Extensive use of written summary worksheets and computerized databases aided the analyses. Coders were trained to write summaries of main topics in a way that reported explicitly what the person said rather than inferred the speaker's intent. The main point was stated in a brief phrase or in an apt quotation. Overall, we strove to capture the informant's sense of the topic rather than to reduce it to general categories (i.e., ''work'' or ''family'').

The summary lists of all replies, sometimes referred to as a free-listing, is one of the basic techniques used. It provides the data needed to identify the entire universe of analytic units appropriate to a domain or sample (Luborsky & Rubinstein, 1995). These analytic units then serve to guide the development and evaluation of strategies for sampling and analyses.

A team method was used for the analyses. After familiarizing ourselves with each summary, we conducted an inductive open-coding approach based on pile-sorting techniques to generate categories and topics expressed in the interviews. Results of deductive closed-coding explorations are not reported here. For each question we displayed and worked to locate commonalities across the summaries, and then sorted these summaries into piles—that is, categories. Next, each category (pile) was sorted into subcategories (subpiles) by determining differences within each category. The criteria and rationale guiding the sorting into each pile were recorded. These sortings (piles and subpiles) of responses enabled us to assess which responses were comparable in meaning and which were unique.

This method is valuable because it provides summaries that are close to the expressed ideas and language of the participants. It lends itself to multiple alternative groupings for the data rather than limiting it to a single structure.

Verbatim texts transcribed from audiotapes have clear strengths and limitations. One strength is that they present direct data on beliefs and ideas in people's own words. There is no preset answer to the questions in contrast to surveys. Instead, the person determines both how to interpret the question and the appropriate words to use in response. Texts allow multiple independent reviews by several investigators. One limitation is that information conveyed by body posture and tone of voice is often not encoded in the transcript. The labor and cost required to provide such information militate against it. Also, the process of "making meanings" is not apparent in statements removed from the context of the discourse. In that case, the apparent and intended meaning may not be reflected equally. For example, repetition of a statement may serve to emphasize its importance, or to signal an entirely different meaning or emphasis (Luborsky, 1994b). Careful training of interviewers helps minimize such potential limitations.

Findings

We present the results of questions about personal meanings, signs or symptoms, causes of depression, outcome and recovery, and the evolution of depression. The descriptions of results are organized as follows. For each question, we first summarize the entire range of topics and responses for the whole sample and describe the major groupings or categories of answers. Second, we describe how these vary according to the factors of depression and gender.

Meaning of Depression   "On the basis of your opinion, how would you explain what the word 'depression' means?" The goal of this question was to learn how depression is conceptualized by elderly LTC residents. We describe the results in three sections: the actual meanings of depression, how these meanings may vary by depression or gender, and contrasts in styles of talking about depression.

Forty topics (including one "Don't know") were recorded in the replies of the 28 informants. We identified six *general dimensions* within the responses. These dimensions were (1) mood and feelings; (2) loss, isolation, and separation; (3) analogies to social events outside the LTC setting; (4) personal outlook and philosophy; (5) individual accountability for one's actions; (6) "Don't know." In the case of analogies, the informants drew a connection between the experience of depression and the sense of being part of the larger outside world (e.g., one's religion, family, or the national economy).

Note that these dimensions are not entirely discrete in content. They represent sets of ideas by informants that sometimes overlap or share a fuzzy boundary with other topics. That is, our analytic concern with formally defining factors did not lead us to impose an abstract neatness on these data. For example, one man responded that the depression he felt was related to an arm impairment that kept him from writing greeting cards to stay in touch with people. We interpreted the impairment that made him feel isolated as indicating the dimensions of functional loss (physical impairment) and also social isolation (from lack of contact through letters). The major topics are listed in Table 4.1.

1. *Mood and feelings.* Forty-one percent of all responses indicated the dimension of mood and feelings in identifying the meaning of depression. Among the idioms used to express experiences of depression were "hopelessness," "always feeling sick," and "feeling disgusted with life." Participants also indicated that not caring about anything and feeling down, worried, or sad exemplified depression. Responses that simply provided a label or word indicating mood were assigned to this category. In contrast, responses that referred to some active process by the whole person ("seeing things that way") were assigned to the category of personal outlook and philosophy. Interestingly, as discussed below, these data indicate that nondepressed persons most often defined depression by listing synonyms and images focused on mood and affect, whereas depressed informants tended to use descriptions of feelings of isolation rather than terms describing affect.

2. *Loss, isolation, and separation.* Twenty-one percent of the responses referred to feelings of loss. Informants distinguished three areas of loss: (a) objects and persons, (b) settings, and (c) personal values. In some cases, informants described isolation from their social community and family on the basis of residence in the LTC facility. "It happens when elderly people have a hard time adjusting to rapid change," suggested one 80-year-old woman with severe depression. "I'm depressed now because I'm in a room by myself," related a 79-year-old man with depression. For others, isolation arose from being the last survivor among their peers. Another area was loss of familiar, cherished personal values and lifestyles on entry into the LTC facility. For some, this dimension embodied a loss of personal security in terms of physical safety, personal finances, and the assurance that one's own body would serve for basic activities of daily life. "You aren't capable of doing the things you used to do well,"

TABLE 4.1 Major Topic Dimensions in the Meaning of Depression

Major topic dimension	Percent	Example
1. Mood and feelings	41	"Being very down." "Being disgusted with everything." "Always feeling sick and disgusted." "Not caring about anything."
2. Loss, isolation, separation	21	"Being old and sick, with your friends gone." "The wife of a man with no job." "I'm depressed now because I'm in a room by myself." "You aren't capable of doing the things you used to do well."
3. Analogies	13	"Growing up in Europe during world wars; waiting in bread lines." "Breakup in Depression of [my] business, family, the self-respect, and what you're proud of. It's not like the loss of your TV or radio." "Depression in the 1930s—nothing sadder."
4. Personal outlook and philosophy	12	"Giving up optimistic ways." "Impression left on a person as a result of experiences, causing damage."
5. Individual actions and accountability	10	"It comes from people doing things that aren't right." "They could correct it [being depressed]."
6. Don't know	1	"I don't know."

stated an 80-year-old woman with severe depression. Other informants pointedly noted that ageist stereotypes and residence at the LTC facility exacerbated their feelings of lost identity and lost abilities.

3. *Analogies.* Thirteen percent of the replies involved the construction of an analogy that symbolically linked individual experiences with societal or historical events. In these cases, the analogy established an identification with others in the same age cohort. These analogies represent the kind of contextual information described in the first section of this chapter as a web of cultural meanings and connotations. Several respondents brought

up the Great Depression, and even the bread lines in Europe during World Wars I and II. One woman said, "Depression means a guy without a job. That's the only definition I can give you." Another interpretation provided was as follows: "A depression in a can is an indentation. Depression in a person is something entirely different." This is not entirely unrelated to economic dimensions. Another subject indicated that the hardest part of the Great Depression was the "breakup of family, self-respect, and what you're proud of. It's not like the loss of your TV or radio." This reasserts the cultural perception of depression as a justifiable response to the loss of values and habitual ways of life.

4. *Personal outlook and philosophy*. Twelve percent of the topics stated in informants' responses addressed an individual's outlook. Responses assigned to this domain communicated information on the individual's active interpretation of events or imposition of meanings for events; in contrast, responses that merely stated a mood or feeling were assigned to the "mood and feelings" dimension. The dimension of outlook can be described as the ongoing perception that everything is negative instead of positive. One respondent described depression as "giving up optimistic ways." Another viewed depression as intrinsic to people who are oversensitive, or who are affected more by things than others. "You're feeling somehow dissatisfied or unable to do what you want to" (nondepressed woman, aged 91).

5. *Individual actions and accountability*. Approximately 10% of the responses indicated the dimension of activity or responsibility. The dimension of personal responsibility for one's actions was characterized as guilt, remorse, anxiety, or punishment. One person claimed that depression "comes from people doing things that aren't right," and another spoke of how it was related to bad habits, such as "smoking, drinking, gambling, and chasing women," which all contribute to lost sleep. Activity level was interpreted as a behavioral symptom. Indications of depression were either not sleeping or sleeping too much. Other reported signs were withdrawal and a lack of visiting with others. Others described depression in terms of being inactive, or acting "like a lump."

6. *"Don't know."* This accounted for only 1% of all responses.

To *analyze depression and gender as factors*, we examined the relation between the contents of answers about the meanings of depression and characteristics of the speakers. Results show no difference in content in terms of the number of ideas or topics mentioned by depressed and nondepressed informants. But, perhaps expectably, we observed at least one difference in behavior: Depressed speakers gave shorter, less verbose replies.

Sharp contrasts emerged in the topic focus related to depression status (see Table 4.2). Not one subject in the nondepressed group but every one of the depressed subjects identified topics of loss and isolation, personal outlook, or responsibility for actions in the definition of depression. Overwhelmingly, the nondepressed subjects' focus of attention was on moods and feelings and analogies to the wider world. In contrast, those experiencing depression gave little attention to mood and feelings; instead, they narrated the actual experiences and events to which they attributed their depression. From another perspective, we see that the depressed group represents a more diverse and elaborate set of ideologies (responsibility, personal outlook, social and psychological isolation, and loss) than the nondepressed group. The nondepressed group located depression strictly in intrapsychic space.

Gender differences within each group were clear. Table 4.2 reveals that depressed men emphasized issues of isolation and loss of connections to people, and social or personal values. They did not identify affects. Depressed women, in contrast, conceptualized depression in terms of negative moods and experiences rather than social and psychological loss. These findings are difficult to interpret simply. They may reflect objective facts about the number of social relationships; men may have had fewer ties than women or had a harder time maintaining ties, and the loss of ties may have had a disproportionately larger effect on the men. These results echo Chodorow's (1989) arguments that women have a lifelong orientation of interrelatedness, whereas men tend to orient more toward social indicators of identity and status. One interpretation is that for this cohort, the gender contrasts may reflect a socially conditioned reticence in men—men may be reluctant to voice subjective feelings and therefore prefer to talk about events and conditions. Further data are needed to better explain the observed gender differences.

To understand how depression is communicated, we examined *styles of discourse* about depression. We identified what can be described as concrete as opposed to abstract styles of talking. The abstract style was to provide a terse listing of words and definitions, several of which are outlined above, in the first dimension. Although these terms were provided in reference to lifelong or daily situations, there was no elaborated lengthy conversation. The concrete style of discourse in defining depression involved narrating concrete specific examples and stories taken from episodes in the respondent's life. Such examples centered on a sick friend or family member, or on the informant's place in larger historical events (the Depression) and in family or personal events. In these responses, speakers related to depression in terms not of impersonal distant labels but of immediate experiences in actual settings. One woman offered as

TABLE 4.2 Meanings for Depression

Major topic dimensions	% Total	Depressed	Nondepressed	Total	Depressed			Nondepressed		
					Male	Female	Total	Male	Female	Total
1. Mood and feelings	41	74	26	100	50	50	100	—	100	100
2. Loss, isolation, separation	21	—	100	100	—	—	—	87	12	100
3. Analogies	13	80	20	100	50	50	100	100	—	100
4. Outlook and personal philosophy	10	—	100	100	—	—	—	80	20	100
5. Actions and responsibility	1	—	100	100	—	—	—	—	100	100
6. Don't know		—	100	100	—	—	—	—	100	100

an example occasions when a wife "has to slave" for an unemployed man who cannot support his family. One man described his recent hospitalization, as well as the stomach trouble and other physical ailments that caused him pain, but did not mention his mood. Another mentioned the cost of rent and personal-care attendants.

Analyses were conducted to determine if discourse style—concrete or abstract—was related to other factors, such as the speaker's age, sex, or depression. No differences could be identified in relation to these factors. Thus, there is a heterogeneity regarding beliefs about and experiences of depression that is not reducible to objective factors.

In summary, depression was not viewed by the elderly residents in this sample simply as a decontextualized, free-floating entity or a diagnostic label. Informants talked about it as embodied in specific circumstances and experiences of life. Depression was viewed as a rational, inevitable stance toward one's current fortunes and situation, which included the hardships of later-life infirmities, the social isolation of LTC settings, the loss of lifelong avenues of involvements and stimulation, loss of control associated with institutional routines, and loss of close friends and family. The focus on feelings of loss or separation from social life typified the world of depressed informants, whereas nondepressed individuals do not mention a sense of connection and participation. The latter conceived of depression in terms of internal and affective states. In addition, the analogies to other events used solely by nondepressed people to describe depression may exemplify the more complex thoughts and multiple viewpoints exhibited by nondepressed compared with depressed individuals.

Sadness versus Depression   *"How different is depression from other kinds of unhappiness, such as being 'sad' or 'blue'?"* This question was designed to elicit information about how informants conceptualized depression in the context of other negative moods. Analyses revealed two intriguingly contrary conceptions: one posited a continuum and the other a categorical contrast between the two concepts.

The first concept identified was a continuum between depression and sadness. Reported criteria for differentiating among these states included intensity (e.g., depression is the most extreme kind of sadness) and also duration. Sadness and unhappiness represent brief states, whereas depression represents an enduring condition. A person who is sad or blue temporarily is not depressed, whereas being sad or blue for a lengthy time does warrant the label "depression." One subject described the constancy of depression as "a sort of emotional paralysis." Depression and sadness differ as well in degree of intensity, with depression being perceived as worse or deeper: "A great sadness"; "It's harder." The second concept was a categorical contrast between sadness and depression. In this case, depression was not seen as one end of a continuum from sad to happy. For example, informants noted that bereavement could make a person both sad *and* depressed.

Neither gender nor depression status was found to correlate with these two concepts of depression. However, we did find that within the nondepressed group, all residents with a previous history of depression defined depression as categorically different from being sad or blue.

Origins of Depression   *"What do you think causes depression?"* This question was asked in order to determine beliefs about the causes of depression. Three categories of responses—explanations—were identified. They are described below, ranked in order from most to least frequently stated.

1.   *Forces outside the person* (57% of replies), or social influences, such as living conditions and interpersonal relationships, were the most frequently cited causes for depression. Included here are factors that informants identified as insults and assaults on a person. These influences are complex. For example, informants mentioned as causes for depression both inadequate social contact and isolation, and too much contact with other residents. Also, social contacts were described as evoking painful conflicts with a visiting spouse, child, or other residents (Luborsky, 1995). Other causes cited were a lack of control at the living facility over food choices or housing arrangements, as well as deaths and other losses. Residents voiced strong beliefs about contamination from "living around depressed people." One mildly depressed woman, aged 85, explained the contagion of depression by observing a parallel between the declining health of the residents and the decline of the institution and the surrounding neighborhood. She said, "I was here 22 years. It was much better than it is now. What you see here every day, every day, [is] somebody becoming worse, worse than the others. And you sit and you notice all that. Of course [only], when your mind is still there." In brief, according to these explanations, the burdens imposed by living conditions, experiences of powerlessness, or diminished self-esteem precipitated depressive feelings.

2.   *Somatic processes* (26% of replies), separate from social or psychological factors, were also stated as causes. Informants conceptualized these in terms of "heredity," "bad genes," and "changes in the blood." These factors were described as powerful and overwhelming to the individual. Other somatic causes were bodily discomfort and physical suffering, as well as physical disabilities associated with aging. One man put it this way, "My body bothers me. I'm depressed because I don't see any

improvement." Another man said, "You can't take it as you used to be able to," referring to feelings evoked by even small changes in his body and concerns about weak or brittle bones.

> Well, your body starts to deteriorate. It's your eyes, your hearing, your breathing, your feet, your arm and legs—and your body starts to wear down a lot. You can't take it as you used to be able to. Any little thing out of line, boom! It shows up on you. Before, when you're younger, well, you felt lousy one day; the next day you felt better. But nowadays, it doesn't [happen that way]. (70-year-old man, nondepressed)

3. *Personal features* (17% of replies) was a third explanation given. Among these are bad habits, a bad outlook, and a gloomy disposition. Informants stated that a person's lifelong disposition can foster depression. These explanations link depression to the whole person, not to either a part of the person's physiology or to the living environment. Informants stated, "It affects only sensitive people" and could be inherited; "Depression is degrading"; and "It's such an annoying feeling around your heart." The use of these phrases during the interviews expressed the close connection perceived between depression and the whole person. This perspective highlights personal accountability, both for ways of thinking and for styles of living. For example, one informant attributed depression to bad habits. He explained it to the researcher as follows.

> Well, running around drinking, smoking, women, or uh. . . . Notice that you need a certain time of sleep, a certain many hours. You don't have to run around gambling where you get hyper, you get nervous, and you lose your money. It takes you a long time to earn it and you could lose it in two minutes—most of your money. And your nerves see that excitement, things of that sort. (76-year-old man, nondepressed)

Other person-specific features widely cited were inability to cope or remain upbeat in the face of adversity, and propensity toward worrying. These traits are consistent with the view that some people are inherently susceptible.

Analyses of depression and gender factors were conducted to identify variations in explanations for the causes of depression. The depressed informants as a group conceived of isolation, losses, disability, and the inability to regulate one's behavior or to cope with situations as major causes. In contrast, the nondepressed study group more often cited objective events—world traumas, a poor economy, and disasters—as being causative. That is, the depressed elderly people attributed more to the immediate personal experiences related to health and social life, whereas the nondepressed gave greater weight to adverse, socially shared community conditions.

Susceptibility to Depression   *"Who is prone or susceptible to depression?"* This question was asked to discover if elderly residents perceived everyone as equally at risk for depression or if they thought certain people were more prone to depression. Overwhelmingly, informants told us that depression was most likely to afflict only some kinds of people. One 87-year-old woman with severe depression explained it to us as follows: "grief, sorrow, love, and joy happen to everybody, but some people are more deeply impressed and more deeply depressed than others." Thus, the general belief was that certain people have an underlying predisposition to becoming depressed in the course of typical life events. Variability in susceptibility was attributed to four separate sources: (1) specific individual traits, (2) gender, (3) age, and (4) income. No variation in replies according to depression or gender was found.

1.   *Intrinsic individual traits* (37% of replies) were most often cited as the reason some people are more prone to depression. Personality and psychological traits (e.g., being introspective, easily overwhelmed, and weak) were one such set of factors. Similarly, informants stated that genes account for why some people are likely to experience depression; however, no detailed mechanisms were provided.

2.   *Life stage* (32% of replies). The second most cited depression-prone group were the elderly. Older people were said to feel more physically and psychologically frail than other adults, and more likely to be enduring some physical suffering. For example, one informant contrasted the forces confronting teenagers and the elderly. The teenagers were said to be in danger of becoming depressed because of peer pressure toward conformity or substance abuse, whereas, for the elderly, depression could be triggered by moving to an institution, having to give up one's home, not having sufficient income (see also below), having no friends or having friends die, and not having enough activity or interest in the world around them.

3.   *Gender* (21% of replies) was related to susceptibility. Women were described in 80% of the responses in this category as the most susceptible group. The explanations offered suggested that women were at risk as a consequence of having more involvements in family life than their husbands.

I think women get more depressed. The reason why is because they think more of children, they think more of family, they think more of health.

And they think more about life. A man, he goes out and he is at work, and he gets home—only when he comes back home, then he thinks of it. The woman's always at home; she sees more things than a man. (71-year-old man, nondepressed)

I don't know whether they're weaker or they're more . . . Women pay more attention; their mind pays more attention to—to thing[s] that go wrong than men do. (84-year-old woman, depressed)

4. *Income* (11% of replies) received some mention as a factor that could make people susceptible to depression. However, these elderly informants shared the general opinion that neither low nor high income was a strong factor in fostering depression. Individual character was stated to be the important factor. One subject suggested, "The rich as much as poor and probably more so" were prone to depression because the "more [wealth] you have the more you want."

Management Strategies   "How do you deal with or manage depression?" We designed this question to elicit beliefs about appropriate self-care and management of depression. The question and the ensuing discussion were structured to allow informants to address the entire range of management approaches, both formal medical and informal self-care. Three main types of management, ranked in order of importance, were found: (1) managing personal behavior, (2) regulating social interactions, and (3) seeking professional medical treatment. The first two are self-care strategies (accounting for 90% of all replies), and the third strategy involved seeking professional care (10% of replies).

1. *Self-management of behavior* was mentioned in 64% of the replies. Strategies in this category focused on managing intrapersonal experiences and motivation. Informants described these in terms of recommendations. For example, they cited what they regarded to be shared knowledge of a need to avoid letting depression "settle in," or "settle." Among the prescriptions they offered were doing things to avoid displaying vegetative signs of distress: keeping active, moving around, and going places. An ancillary benefit of this behavior, they argued, was that it effectively preserved or stepped up social contacts. Another strategy in this category focused on behavioral expressions, including presenting a "smooth" face to conceal ones troubles, keeping a "stiff upper lip," and keeping one's mind busy or ignoring trouble. Alternatively, other residents stated that it was important not to "bottle up" depression but rather to "go with it and cry," and to accept that "you have good and you have bad days."

Last, personal prayer and hope were mentioned, though these methods were simply listed and were not discussed at any length or elaborately explained.

2. *Self-management of social interactions* was mentioned in 26% of the replies. In contrast to the preceding strategy, this one focused on regulating contacts with other people. One way to avoid becoming depressed, according to these residents, was to avoid depressed people. Most depressed informants claimed that people avoided them because they did not want to listen to them. This sentiment was endorsed by nondepressed informants: "I don't want to be bothered with people like that"; "It's too depressing to be around an old, sick person"; and "I would avoid them if I had to listen to their same story every day, which is like swallowing a little poison every minute."

Ethnographic studies of nursing homes report similar attitudes by residents (Gubrium, 1993; Savishinsky, 1991). Clearly, such attitudes might increase a depressed individual's sense of isolation and loss. One benefit of ethnographic research is to identify the kinds of cultural-level ideological issues (Clark, 1972) that create value conflicts (such as seclusion or avoidance versus engagement) or impose expectations on individuals. Sensitive appreciation of these social rationales and value issues in experiences of daily life, particularly in congregate long-term care settings, may give clinicians specific avenues for intervention.

3. *Professional medical treatments* (10% of replies) received few mentions. Of these, informants stated that drugs were the preferred medical treatment. Mental health services, such as psychology or psychiatry, were a second choice. Overall, medical treatment was not a prominent topic for informants in any of these discussions. Note that the research site is medically well served; it features an aggressive, multidisciplinary approach to mental health case finding, treatment, and follow-up. Perhaps residents accept a higher level of depressive symptoms as typical and acceptable, not a pathological state requiring professional medical treatment. As we learned from their explanations of the causes and distribution of depression, they assume it is a natural endemic condition, given the health and social experiences of old age and also the experience of living in a long-term care facility. These informants may perceive a high level of mental disability as typical and expectable. Alternatively, because the mental health services are so widely known and active, the informants may have assumed they did not have to state the obvious. Nonetheless, the low priority assigned by residents to formal medical treatment for depression requires further study.

Analyses of depression and gender factors were conducted to identify variations in explanations for how to manage depression.

The nondepressed residents described more types of treatment than the depressed residents. We had expected to find the opposite, given that the residents with personal experiences of depression would have received formal treatment at the LTC setting. These informants might not consider some formal treatments to be therapeutic if the treatments had not been successful for them in the past. Alternatively, the smaller number of treatment options suggested by the depressed informants may reflect symptoms of depression (e.g, low energy and less complex thinking).

Generally, nondepressed respondents cited a need to keep busy and move around. They expected to have a range of feelings each day, expected to have both good days and bad days over time, and saw a need to seek support from other people. But depressed informants spoke of avoiding people in general and indicated that they did not seek support from peers. The reason offered was that they perceived a lack of interest—even an "active" lack of interest—in their problems. They were more likely to seek medical or psychiatric treatments. In a prior study (Luborsky & Rubinstein, 1987), similar beliefs about the value of controlling the outward expression of distress and depression were observed among Irish, Italian, and Jewish widows and widowers; the long-term outcomes of these management strategies included such negative consequences as enduring feelings of disruption and grief. The efforts directed to such expectations for self-control were found to be associated with long-term enduring grief and delayed reorganization of one's life.

Natural Course of Depression *"Were (are) there different chapters or stages in (your) depression?"* Concepts of the natural course of depression were elicited by asking participants to describe its natural evolution in terms of chapters. This method facilitated discussion of experiential stages and transitions and elicited data that provide valuable insights into the longitudinal and variable nature of depression, since the variable experiences of depression were commonly subsumed under the static label "depressive symptoms" or diagnoses of depression.

Analyses revealed a multiplicity of beliefs rather than a single concept of depression. Intervals described between stages ranged from days to weeks and months. Discrete stages were defined by reference to the amount of debility and the intensity of symptoms. For example, one 81-year-old man with a history of depression who was currently nondepressed described his experiences with depression in the past. He stated, "In the first weeks I felt bad, but after that I felt like I was getting back to myself." Several subjects described depression as being undifferentiated or seamless, shifting from one state of mind to another:

It goes off and on. You may . . . you may not hear from it for a while, and then all of a sudden, it'll start popping up for a while, and then go off again. Like an off-and-on thing. (70-year-old man, nondepressed)

Sometimes I would feel, Well, it'll go away; I have to do this. I have to overlook things, or not look into things that I was always looking in. It helps sometimes. I know it—it doesn't change the situation. But, well, these feelings don't take long. They change too fast. I knew it had to change, either for the better or for the worse. (84-year-old woman, depressed)

These descriptions of the course of depression resemble patients' accounts of chronic diseases rather than an acute injury or disease followed by full recovery. Key features of the experience of chronic disease include a sense of continuing vulnerability, variability of symptoms, and uncertainty about future health and functioning—as opposed to the expectation of full recovery after an acute injury (Becker, 1993; Williams, 1984).

Analyses of depression, gender, and discourse style (concrete versus abstract) in relation to beliefs about the course of depression were conducted. Again, depression was an important factor. All the currently nondepressed individuals (including those with a history of major depression) outlined specific and discrete chapters. None described depression as a smooth progression or shift. In contrast, the depressed residents were split equally between describing discrete stages and describing gradual shifts. However, major depression was linked with distinct stages. We surmise that reports of such experiences are relatively state-dependent rather than trait-dependent; that is, the expressed beliefs are strongly influenced by personal history or familiarity with the condition. No gender differences were apparent.

Discourse styles followed the same pattern as we observed in definitions of depression. Changes in depression were stated in abstract terms as having direction, intensity, and duration, or were embedded in concrete details of personal situations in which the subject and the depression were inseparable. These patterns were not related to sex or depression.

Summary: Study 1

Open-ended interviews were conducted to discover and describe beliefs and perceptions held by elderly LTC residents regarding the cause, course, and management of depression. Analyses of interviews from this study revealed content of, beliefs about, and descriptions of depressive experiences by elderly residents in LTC. We identified a diversity in basic concepts of the meaning, cause, treatment, and natural course of depression. Many individual differences in these views were found that cut across the gender of the participants and their depressive symptoms. Gender and depression were related to the topics that informants focused on, experiences of stages in the course of depression, and idioms for expressing depressive feelings. These data add to our understanding by providing data on elderly people's own concepts, idioms, and styles, and their beliefs about depression.

STUDY 2: PERCEIVED LIFETIME PERSONAL IDENTITY

Study 1 provided data specifically on the content of personal beliefs about depression; yet these data represent somewhat abstract knowledge, isolated from the concrete social occasions in which they are put into use. We know that additional factors come into play, derived from the daily-life settings of cultural and personal meanings and values. In this section, we examine constructs at the level of the social processes that shape how people interpret and represent their current conditions for themselves and others, including researchers. That is, we turn from the level of beliefs and values about depression in general, elicited from in-depth interviews, to the level of specific examples where self-reports of well-being and of depression are constructed in clinical research. In this section, we examine linguistic discourse, highlighting processes and contexts. The conjunction of these two levels—knowledge and action—represents the perspective of practice theory (Argrys & Schoen, 1987; Bourdieu, 1977).

The construction of self-reported health and affect among elderly people who have physical impairments and are living in an LTC facility was examined (Luborsky, 1995). The study collected verbatim transcripts of standardized tests administered as part of a separate project to assess daily affect for 90 days among residents (Kleban et al., 1992). The goal of analyzing these transcripts was to identify how subjects chose a standardized clinical label for personal experience. The transcripts of these tests showing the social interaction between the researcher and subject shed light on factors that could not be predicted solely by knowledge of cultural and personal beliefs about depression and health. This ethnographic approach is useful for revealing dimensions, processes, and perceptions that emerge during actual social occasions. The analytic approach followed the paradigm of discourse studies that view conversation as a problematic interaction where participants pursue competing interests and goals, and thus the actual talk is the resulting solution to those problems (Jefferson, 1984; Sacks, Schlegoff, & Jefferson, 1974).

Design, Methods, and Analyses

The data are drawn from a longitudinal study of daily mood among elderly LTC residents that provided an opportunity to observe consecutive clinical diagnostic interviews with elderly subjects. In that project, 12 standardized questions were used to rate pain, health, and moods (e.g., happy, anxious, or sad). Subjects were instructed to answer the question: "How are you feeling today?" by rating each mood on a scale ranging from "not at all" to "extremely." Permission was granted to observe interviews with several subjects and to audiotape five consecutive sessions, starting on the 61st day of research with one subject. The following discussion reports analyses of the five audiotaped assessments. Each interview started with a greeting and small talk—for example, about the weather. Next the researcher began the formal test by inquiring, "Now I want to ask about how you are feeling today." Each occasion lasted about 25 minutes. The researcher ended the interview by thanking the subject and saying, "See you tomorrow."

The discourse observed here was between Mr. K. and a clinical psychologist. Mr. K. was a cognitively intact 78-year-old man. The deaths (from cancer) of his sister, father, and wife remained keenly felt. He described much strife between his daughter, his son, and himself. Two years earlier, a mild stroke had left him with residual weakness in one arm. Continuing symptoms of depression led to a clinical diagnosis of dysphoria. The interviewer was a PhD-level researcher in her mid-30s who had worked for 2 years at the LTC facility. The interviews took place in Mr. K.'s room at the facility.

Analyses consisted of systematic comparisons of transcripts between the five observed occasions with the subject. The transcripts were prepared to specify speech overlap, pauses, and emphases. Texts were reviewed with the interviewer to clarify background information to the interviews. Next, two independent raters identified initiations and closures of topics, discourse cycles, themes, taking turns, and statements of personal identity. Analyses were conducted by comparing the contexts and contents of each topic segment for each test occasion.

Results

The content analyses derived from line-by-line study of the verbatim transcripts were compared with the replies scored on the standardized test form by the clinician. The two kinds of records of the research interview show different pictures of Mr. K. The view obtained from the standardized test form suggests a rapid, nonproblematic test using identical questions each day that captured facts about the subject's state. In contrast, the texts depict lively talk about the questions and answers. An overview of several main findings is presented followed by illustrations of each finding (for a full report, see Luborsky, 1995). The interview dialogue revealed unresolved conflicts and misrepresentation of self-reports related to the subject's perceptions of the relevant time frame, subject matter, issues, and anchor points to use for evaluating current moods.

First, despite repeated instructions to report his "feelings at the moment," Mr. K. often switched the topic to assert a lifelong identity and self-image rooted in his past. He also redefined the meaning of the question or the standardized answers before replying. For example, at one point Mr. K. ignored instruction to state how he felt at the moment and asserted that for his whole life, he "never knew a dull moment" and "always had a lot of energy." Notably, only on these two occasions did he report having "some" energy instead of "no energy at all"—the response he gave on all other occasions. These redefinitions of the question-and-answer categories reveal that personal systems of meanings (Harre, 1984; Muhlhaulser & Harre, 1990) and the cultural network of wider meanings (Good & Good, 1982) guided his self-appraisal. Mr. K. labeled his experience using personalized frames instead of the preset answer categories of the test; however, his intended meanings were not encoded into the permanent research record. Thus, important aspects of the intended self-representation were routinely neglected or "forgotten" in the preparation of scientific models.

A second finding was that subjects' self-reports of internal affect are tied to active monitoring of a variety of features of the interview conversation. We observed that self-reports were influenced by the subject's monitoring of (a) prior (and subsequent) topics; (b) claims to a lifetime identity versus a current identity; (c) management of self-image; and topic switches by the researcher that (d) broke coherence or turn-taking, or (e) juxtaposed topics abrasively (e.g., presenting the test question: "Are you happy?" right after someone reports being in a great deal of pain). These data are consistent with the meanings of depression, described earlier, related to the sense of loss and lifelong personal values.

A third finding was that higher positive health and affect were reported when informants could state a lifelong identity (e.g., "I've always been a pusher" or "I'm the kind of person who . . . "). These findings substantiate the importance of acknowledging that the residents do not perceive affect as decontextualized from settings or from their life experiences. In contrast, negative affect was reported in talk about pain and loss, but never in claims to a past or enduring identity and personal theme. For example, Mr. K. diverted questions about his affect "at the moment" and framed his answer in terms of lifetime images of health and affect. That is, self-reports of positive well-being were situated in contexts framed by claims to personal identity and values, whereas negative reports occurred in talk about physical (bodily) dysfunction and social losses.

A fourth finding was the identification of an "idealized identity" in the discourse, a perception founded on idealized virility, mastery, and productivity. An opposite type, "current identity," was rooted in the subject's current experience of feeling obsolete, incapacitated, unable to master his body (e.g., arms and bowels), his environment (sleep and eating schedules), his social relationships, or his daily activities.

Selected findings are illustrated in the following examples.

Translating Individual Experiences and Beliefs into Research Data
The transcribed dialogues of these research interviews show how individual beliefs are force-fit into standardized categories. The interview settings during which talk about personal experience is transformed into scientific data are problematic, sometimes contentious, interactions even within the constraints imposed by standardized test procedures. Several illustrations are provided below. In these transcripts, italic text indicates louder speech, and the position of the words for each speaker is relative to the sequence of talk; thus, overlapping words indicate that those words were spoken simultaneously by both people.

The excerpt below began just after Mr. K. was asked how much pain he feels and he answered that he was "having excruciating pain." The interviewer posed the next question,

Researcher: Right now, are you feeling sad?
Mr. K: Yes.
Researcher: You answered that you felt sad. Is it extremely sad, or a little bit?
Mr. K: It ain't bad. You know, when you . . . You ask me questions, but—but *when something hurts you, how could you feel happy?*
Researcher: It depends on the person. It is such a personal thing.
Mr. K: *Must be, you are a stupid person to feel good.*
Researcher: Not necessarily. There are many different reasons. Some people have a lot of reasons to feel bad.
Mr K.: *You know I am not stupid!*

The content of this dialogue contradicts a simplistic view of assessment protocols as providing a direct representation. Using parody, Mr. K. challenged the researcher's authority and the basic rationality of the questions, with the comments: "How could you feel happy?" and "Must be, you are a stupid person to feel good." At the same time, he claimed that his reply was intelligent and sensible in the context of his whole life by saying, "You know *I* am not stupid." He decried the fragmentation of his experience and self-representations into the disconnected abstract labels needed for quantitative measurements, such as degrees of pain or sadness (e.g., some or a little). The transcript showed the researcher exercising authority, in order to obtain usable data, to direct a process of selective forgetting of experiences and a dismembering of experiences from the physical body of personal and social contexts.

The subject did not quietly agree to forget, however, as the transcript shows. In the clinical assessment, subjects often debated and reframed the task, the questions, and even the meaning or kinds of set answers provided. The subject did not just focus on the explicit test questions but also monitored cultural expectations for conversation and social interactions. Mr. K. looked to implied composite self-images that built up from the flow of separate questions and answers across the whole interview. Yet respondents' ongoing reinterpretations of the questions and answers were not recorded as data, even though they were prominent in the active give-and-take process of translating individual experiences into standardized reply categories.

Perceived Continuity and Lifetime Identity   This construct was revealed in statements such as, "I've always been on the go," and "I am the kind who could always do anything." In this way, informants asserted a notion of a "true" self that the present-day self only dimly reflects. For example, Mr. K. consistently reported feeling irritated; the one time he reported "no irritation" occurred within a segment of talk about personal identity. "I was always on the go"; "I would've known to do everything a man . . . can do." He asserts a continuity of personal biography with past periods in life that, for him, cannot be disconnected. On all the other test occasions, he did not introduce that element but focused on mundane events or physical pain. The continuity of lifetime identity was very salient to his self-reports of moods at the moment.

Researcher:	Now, the energy that we discussed you having—would you say that you are extremely energetic, moderately energetic, or would you say that you have a little bit of energy? You feel like doing things—remember, you told me you were feeling a little bit better?
Mr. K:	Did you know a dull moment? I never had a dull moment. I was always on the go.
Researcher:	But right now do you feel energetic, extremely energetic, a lot, somewhat?
Mr. K:	A little.

Researcher:	A little bit.
Mr. K:	I have always had.
Researcher:	A lot of energy?
Mr. K:	Lot of energy. I could have done anything in the world. I would've known to do everything a man, a mechanic can do and that a man can do.
Researcher:	You could do it.
Mr. K:	Yeah.
Researcher:	OK. . . . Right now, are you feeling annoyed by anything?
Mr. K:	Nooo.

Mr. K. diverted requests about his feelings "at the moment" by reframing the discourse to encompass a lifelong idealized image of health and affect. In this segment, he communicated a sense of the "true" self that is hidden and limited by his decrepit body, his age, and his living conditions as well as by the discourse. The disjunction is exacerbated by the limits on self-expression imposed by the format of standardized tests (Abu-Lughod, 1985; Mishler, 1991; Tedlock, 1983) compared with, for example, narrative. Again , these confrontations and adjustments to meanings were erased in the clinical research record. Notably, the four occasions when Mr. K. stated that he was more irritated occurred in the absence of talk about his personal identity. They focused exclusively on mundane, present-day events and bodily physical pain.

Multiplicity of Personal, Social Situational, and Cultural Factors This case illuminates the broad scope of contexts and time frames entering into the experiences and labeling of disability. It shows specific aspects of the social situations and cultural contexts that add to variations in self-reports (i.e., external influences on the labeling of inner states), and documents their role in actual question-and-answer sequences. These aspects need to be more adequately incorporated into the research data used to construct scientific models of particular populations. In brief, the standardized questions and the abstract answer categories (e.g., "none," "some," or "a lot") embody multiple meanings rather than the single one intended by the researchers.

Time Frames A multiplicity of temporal dimensions pervaded Mr. K.'s reports. Depression and disability were viewed as if seamlessly connected to experiences and identities from the past, present, and future, whether actual, idealized, or expected. Mr. K. attended to the potential future loss of cherished identities and habits of daily life on the basis of a fit body and a desired personal future. Analogously, research on life stories documents how concerns in the present shape the contents of a life history (Crapanzano, 1980, 1982; Csikszentmihalyi & Beattie, 1979; Luborsky, 1989, 1993a; Luborsky & Rubinstein, 1990). Here we see the past and the future figuring prominently in labeling present conditions. For Mr. K., negative and supportive feedback from others influenced how he labeled his mood and health. More important, the ability to transcend the frame of meaning supplied by the researcher (tied to the immediate moment) and to infuse the interpretation of present conditions into the wide horizon of idealized past self-images and future potential created an important tension between the researcher and subject.

Virulent debates focused on the interviewer's direction to *"forget"* prior answers and earlier life events. For example, the researcher urged Mr. K. to answer each question without relating it to earlier answers. Further, the researcher strove to decontextualize self-appraisals from life-long personal meanings and the immediate conversational context of the questions. Yet Mr. K. spoke of that as contrary to his being a sensible, intelligent, mature man. Two different influences on the data were produced by these specific standardized methods. On several occasions the face-to-face interaction elevated self-ratings of more positive moods and diminished reported depression. For example, some of these increased self-ratings were observed when the conversation enabled Mr. K. to construct a continuity of personal meanings connected to idealized lifelong self-images. In the dialogue, talking about self-identity was linked with better health. Notably, survey questionnaires seldom include items to assess a person's sense of continuity and future prospects. Perhaps they could profit from including such topics.

Alternative explanations for the discourse pattern may be entertained. Perhaps Mr. K. just felt differently when he said he did. However, the succession of transcripts, covering 5 days, provide compelling detailed cultural and sociolinguistic evidence that his talk was the result of a thoughtful response to the messages he perceived in the interview questions. Perhaps on other days, when he was not being interviewed by the clinician, Mr. K. may have created similar patterns of interactions with other people that led to similar supportive and nonsupportive responses, thus fostering the same mood. Such possibilities cannot be ruled out.

In summary, detailed study of the actual dialogues of data collection identified multiple influences on the constructions of self-report or labeling of moods and physical impairment. These data reveal the need to extend our knowledge of how personal values and beliefs emerge in the settings where data are collected rather than limiting our understanding to abstract labels and contents of personal experience. A practical message for ''survey-style'' researchers is to ensure that interviewers adhere to the questions and limit informal talk as a means of minimizing the intrusion of such natural influences. Interactions within the discourse of researchers' data collection reveal important dimensions that individuals use to interpret and evaluate their own feelings; these include both individual and social factors. Some of these factors enhance well-being and others diminish well-being. Perhaps most notable is the construct of idealized or enduring self-images that enter into the interpretation of individual's present-day conditions.

Study 3: Personal Themes in Life Stories

Although study 2 identified the construct of enduring identities and personal themes as components of the personal experience of depression, questions remain about their nature, emergence, and consequences. That is, what kinds of themes are there, and do all kinds lead to the same outcomes? It is important to avoid overgeneralizing or idealizing enduring themes—a trend that is observable in the anthropological, social science, clinical, and popular literature that has idealized the positive value of coherent, fixed, enduring themes and identities (Luborsky, 1993a, 1994b). Many critical questions remain little examined.

A third study examined the construct of personal meanings, operationalized as themes in life stories. Random selection provided 16 informants from a computerized database of the entire population of more than 1,100 residents at the LTC facility. These 16 were selected to provide 8 with a range of depressive symptoms, including major depression, and 8 nondepressed. Included among the 8 nondepressed were 3 with a prior history of depression. Residents with cognitive impairments were excluded from this study. The 16 informants averaged 85 years of age (range, 71 to 99) and 10 years of residence.

Methods

Life stories were elicited during the first of three interviews as part of a larger study. Using a standardized method (the Sequence and Templates in Narratives, STN; Luborsky, 1990), two sets of questions were asked. The goal was to gather brief stories for systematic comparison rather than an exhaustive biography. Four to 20 minutes were typical for the initial story and 14 to 35 minutes for the whole procedure. One standard query was used to elicit the life story: "I'd like to know more about you and your life. Would you describe your life for me—whatever comes to mind about it? Start where you like; take as much time as you need." By design, the prompt has few cultural propositions (D'Andrade, 1985; Metzger, 1974) or cues about scripts to use for the reply (Agar, 1980; Mandler, 1983; Mishler, 1986). Phrases such as "important events" are carefully avoided because, rather than eliciting a rich personal story, they evoke bare outlines of socially normative markers (e.g., school, marriage, and work) and seem to irk people. (Earlier studies using the same prompt but including the word "important" evoked replies such as "Nothing special about me" and "I wasn't president or anything.") Informants spoke uninterrupted until they stopped. Next, informants were asked to depict their whole life using two contrasting images for structure: a sequence of book chapters, and a mural depicting many scenes and themes. This task reveals a person's affinity for a style of representing experience that is intrinsic to the structure of the "chapter" or the "mural" task. The chapter generally dictates a story structure—that is, a linear chronology of socially normative and bounded categories. The mural, in contrast, creates a story structure based on the simultaneous presentation of diverse experiences and events without attention to sequence, boundaries, and coherence. Chapters and murals reveal the personally salient chunks and boundaries of life experience and meanings.

The rationale for these methods derives from the need to be alert to cultural and linguistic conventions shaping self-expression. Some realms of experience are easily described in one medium (e.g., poetry or narrative) but not in others. For example, Vera Brittain's biographers were faced with her pattern of devoting herself entirely to different mediums (novels, letters, and a diary) at different times (Stewart et al., 1988). Thus, we need methods sensitive to how a type of prompt may limit the expression of some types of experience. A review of the prompts used to collect life stories shows that researchers use a host of images: "slices of a pie" (Whitbourne, 1986); "important turning points" (Lowenthal, 1975); "chapters in a book" (Kaufman, 1987; McAdams, 1988); "tell me your story" (Myerhoff, 1978). Each image used for the question may elicit only particular kinds of information and narrative styles. That is, the orienting images given by the researcher in the question (D'Andrade, 1985) aid expression of some identities and experience while hindering others. This implicit prefiguring of frames and genres for telling about a lifetime are of direct concern to the study of personal meanings. As discussed above, the STN method is designed to systematically exploit and control for such variation in the data rooted in the question frames.

Measures

A life theme, similar to a metaphor, provides an overall image or orienting construct (Moore & Myerhoff, 1972) that creates a sense of wholeness and identity. Arguably, it is the wish for feelings of wholeness that explains the power of an image to transform perceptions, rather than any particular trait intrinsic to the image itself (Fernandez, 1986). Ewing (1990) documents the contingent and situated, not continuous, nature of coherence in personal identity. Metaphors sustain the image of wholeness by downplaying disparate elements and dissolving prior images (Wagner, 1986) to give a fresh unity to the many events and periods of a lifetime. Guiding metaphors (Moore, 1972) cross-reference separate domains of meaning to supply information from a familiar to a less-known domain, thus merging them to form a new one. Reference to a central guiding metaphor serves to clarify who and where individuals are and what they are doing.

Metaphors instill the most coherence or wholeness when the images are farthest away from concrete events and experiences (Nisbet, 1969). Familiar metaphors include societal or individual "progress," "growth," and "development." These are cultural concepts that do not exist at any point in a day or year. The images provide a powerful orienting image and set of compelling motivations that serve to guide social and individual life. One such powerful shared orienting image is the cultural life course (Fry, 1990). In our work, we find that the life course is but one socially normative shared image for constructing a lifetime, and that it is unpalatable to some informants.

The transcripts were analyzed to identify two aspects: the orienting image or conceptual template, and the temporal sequence of topics using the standardized STN coding procedure (Agar & Hobbes, 1982; Luborsky, 1987, 1990). Interrater reliability was 82%. Orienting images for the life story were coded as either a *cultural life course pattern* of successive life stages and identities or a central *personal theme*. The sequence of story topics was coded as either *linear*, defined as a single temporal sequence from birth to present; or *recursive*, defined as a nonchronological concatenated series of episodes of life in different eras or settings. Recursive stories, for example, proceed from telling of school, work, and retirement, then circle back to cover dating and marriage, and then cover family life. Such stories tend to marshal a variety of episodes and beliefs to assert a key point, but they lack a linear chronology.

Findings

Structure and Content of Life Stories   Variations in text structures and thematic "templates" were found to relate to current experiences of distress. Among the normal and the depressed informants, the current mood state consistently differentiated the text structures. The eight "normals" presented linear stories using life-course templates. Seven of the eight depressed informants gave recursive texts organized by theme templates. The difference was statistically significant, $p < .001$, using the Fisher exact probability test.

Four examples illustrate differences in themes. The life-story texts are presented in their entirety. Each line represents a "chunk" or unit of meaning as indicated by intonation and by pauses in the speech (Chafe, 1980; Mishler, 1991). The first two stories were told by Marge and Rita; both women were diagnosed as depressed. Their stories were organized around a key personal theme, not a strong chronologically linear structure.

Marge
I'll tell you something.
I have nothing to tell you.
I told you that before.
I, I was a housewife.
I had eight children.
I kept the house clean.
I washed laundry. I ironed. I, I fed my children.
I sent them to school.
What else can I tell you?
I don't have nothing to tell you.

Rita
I was. When I came here I was 14 years old.
I had a sister here to whom I came.
I went to work at 14.
Took some schooling on my own.
This is how I went on and worked.
I paid for my rent, I paid for my food,
I was independent, and I was 14 years old.
I had nobody to depend upon.
My sister that I came to, she didn't know me, I didn't know her.
We were from one father, not from one mother.
And when she went to the U.S. I was an infant.
But she knew just by corresponding there was a little sister here.
So the little sister was 14 years old when she came here.
And that, that's the whole story in a nutshell!

The next two life stories were told by Celia and Steve. These two narrators were nondepressed. Their stories were organized by the culturally defined normative life-course pattern of stages and transitions and were presented in chronologically linear sequence.

Celia
There was nothing unusual about my life.
I grew up here,
met my husband at a very very young age,
   but we didn't know that we were going to marry someday.
His sister, the one that sent me that note, was my Sunday school teacher.
And he was also in my class. I knew his brother very well.
His brother was dating my girlfriend.
And, through him, I started going out with my future husband.
And we married at a very young age.
And we had a wonderful, wonderful life together.
We had two sons.
We, they married at young age too,
   and I would say that they are now undergoing the same type of life
   that my husband and I had.
I have five grandchildren,
I have eight great grandchildren.

Steve
I was born and raised in Philadelphia.
And I went to high school and college.
And, er, some years back then I was in my 20s,
I moved to Florida.
I lived in Florida 4 1/2 years.
And I came back here. And I was interested in art
   and had a gallery where I sold pictures, paintings, framing.
Framing was a profession, was the biggest item that I had.
And I was on Chestnut Street,
   you know where that is?
17th and Chestnut, which was the center of town.
And I used to come to work by,
I had my automobile, but I used to have a bus which brought me
   center of town.
And I met scores of people, I have friends that I've known for years.
In the business that I was in I met judges, congressmen, priests,
   lawyers, doctors.
And then, anyway, I became familiar with a lot of people.
Now sportswise, I was sports-minded.
Played soccer as a, baseball as a boy.
What else could I tell you?

Variations in the narrative structure and content of these stories express the informants' diverse perceptions of their personal biographies. The depressed narrators constructed their story around a personally salient core theme. The theme in Rita's story was the struggle to meet the cultural ideal of independence. Marge's theme was the exploited and now unneeded caretaker; she organized her life story around the pervasive image of a negative lot in life. In contrast, the nondepressed speakers, Celia and Steve, told the tale of their life using several narrative voices that inform us about the interests and concerns they had at different stages. While the second two stories depict a chronologically ordered string of life stages, events, and activities, the first two stories do not present an inventory of the stages of life. Instead, Rita and Marge structured their stories by marshaling several sets of facts and events that substantiated their assertion about a focal concern or central conflict.

The speakers' general stance toward life was reinforced by the topics presented in addition to the structure of the story. Steve and Celia conveyed the stance that their life was normal (e.g., "typical" life or "not unusual"), matching the image of the culturally shared life-course. Steve's account covered the main socially normative points: birthplace, schooling, travel, and career. His closing section depicted the ideal of a well-rounded, whole person: sports-minded, socially well connected ("scores of people"), and successful (cars and job). In contrast, Rita and Marge recounted selected parts of their lifetime story that exemplified their struggles and hardships as a way to reinforce the stance that their lives were difficult.

Briefly, the themes nondepressed speakers preferred were linear accounts based on an image of a collective life cycle. They seemed adaptable to alternative formats for self-representation. The dysphorics, in contrast, preferred styles involving recursive personal themes and exhibited less willingness to adapt to different formats.

Subjective Salience of Story Structure: Chapters and Murals Task   The preceding interpretations about narrative features are inferences made without feedback from the narrators. One important feature of ethnography is that the researchers discuss their interpretations with informants to gain further insight or to corroborate initial findings. Thus, the validity of our inferences about the subjective meaningfulness of narrative structures and content was directly tested in two ways. We examined answers to the task involving structured alternative story frames in order to gauge preferences for a "book chapters" structure (emphasizing a collective, normatively segmented linear script) or personalized thematic scenes in a mural (emphasizing an individualistic topic and a nonlinear script). We also examined the spontaneous comments made by informants while completing the tasks.

There was a sharp difference between the number of chapters and the number of murals provided by depressed and nondepressed informants. A comparison of performances reveals that nondepressed speakers gave far more chapters than murals (mean, 5 to 1.4, respectively). Depressed speakers gave fewer chapters but more murals (mean, 1 and 2.5, respectively). However, the depressed informants' replies were sparser and contained fewer mural scenes or chapters; this may be a function of their generally low effort and apathy. For example, the nondepressed informants required an average of one reading of the interview prompt before they provided an answer; the depressed informants required two or more prompts.

Qualitatively, the commentary or asides made by informants about interview tasks confirms the impression received from the counts of chapters and murals. Among the depressed informants, six of the eight complained that the chapters were not an appropriate format, for example: "I just don't see my life broken up that way; it's all mixed together." "No title for the whole thing; it's more like an empty book with a blank cover." "They are just one on top of another." Depressed informants refused to give a chapter account, claiming, "It doesn't fit into neat categories like that"; and "It's not been a smooth progression for me." Thus, these speakers found the chapter image ill suited to the task. The nondepressed informants performed well on both tasks, but they insisted that the chapters made more sense.

These spontaneous statements of dislike for one image easily meet significance ($p < .01$) for a single Fisher exact probability test. They do not meet the conservative statistical requirement at the .05 level for the Bonferroni adjustment. The findings are presented here to encourage further study of the personal meaning of particular orienting images and structures.

An association between mortality and styles of describing experience was found, based on a 2-year follow-up. Among the speakers using the personal theme, all eight of the subjects had died; among the speakers using the normative shared life-course theme, only one subject had died. These longer-term outcomes, although consistent with the general association between depression and mortality, add credence to the definition of the narrative style structured by expressions of personal themes as a marker of distress. Overall, these findings support the need to develop a more critical understanding of the concept of making meanings, and of its benefits. Certain styles of making meanings clearly are not related to positive well-being and survival.

These findings are similar to those reported from earlier studies of retirement and bereavement and ethnicity that identified these dimensions and their correlates and refined the methods (Luborsky, 1987, 1990; Luborsky & Rubinstein, 1990). Major contrasts in retirement behavior, mourning, and self-concepts are linked with these dimensions. These studies showed that the life narratives are a valid brief index of the personal meanings and thematic structures that emerge in multiple in-depth interviews. Thus, the STN method, which combines codings of the questions involving life narratives, structured chapters, and murals, offers sufficient materials for comparative analyses of personal themes and meanings. The distribution of narrative templates among the bereaved, retirees, and PGC residents is similar, despite major differences in the samples. The widowers' median age was 74; they were first- or second-generation immigrants to Philadelphia. The retirees' median age was 60; they were middle-class, Protestant, longtime residents from the San Francisco region. The median age of the PGC residents was 85+; they were first-generation Jewish European immigrants. Psychological distress was signaled by personal themes and recursively structured stories with few chapters, whereas positive well-being was marked by linear accounts using culturally shared themes.

SUMMARY

This chapter has described results from three studies designed to explore the cultural and personal dimensions of depression. Several of the dimensions described here contribute to the experience, self-treatment, and course of the disease but remain underrepresented in the literature on depression. Ethnographically based findings on the categories of thought and feelings held by the elderly provide data that complement clinical and epidemiological studies that use standardized analytic categories and methods.

The first study described the scope of the universe of shared meanings, belief, and concerns regarding depression. It also documented heterogeneity in beliefs about and meanings for the cause, nature, and course of depression. Differences were found related to traditional normative medical and social categories (e.g., depressive symptoms and gender), and also related to unexpected categories (e.g., life themes and styles for talking about the self and depressive symptoms). The second study identified how these dimensions are put into action during clinical assessments of affect symptoms. It further described how factors from daily social life enter into the reporting of subjective well-being. A key discovery was that the perception by elderly people of an enduring personal identity or life theme alters their evaluation of their current mood. The third study focused on life themes to describe the structure and content and idioms for expressing life themes and distress in brief life narratives. The results revealed homogeneity and diversity in the form and content of such stories, but also an unexpected link between highly thematic accounts and experiences of depression or distress.

Some implications are clear for research and clinical practice in LTC. At a basic level, these findings expand our understanding of the scope of the universe of salient factors and domains that must be assessed to provide a valid representation of depression among the elderly. Some of these beliefs are not isomorphic with those held by medical and research professionals. These data suggest substantial interindividual, and intraindividual and group heterogeneity in the experience of depression, in beliefs about the management of depression, and in social forces that shape how symptoms of depression are labeled by those with the disease.

These studies document that the elderly residents did not view mental health symptoms as the abstract or decontextualized analytic entities of medical classification systems. Rather, these elderly people viewed depression as inseparable from the values and experiences of a whole person's life span and the occasions and conditions of current life. The studies showed that these elderly people evaluated depression (and reported its symptoms) using multiple reference fields or anchor points beyond those specified in standardized assessments. For example, informants perceived categorical contrasts rather than a continuum of severity in reporting certain symptoms. That finding is clinically and methodologically important and needs to be better understood if we are to improve the accuracy and sensitivity of our instruments and the effectiveness of our treatments for depression.

Unexpected findings about the autobiographical constructs (e.g., perception of an enduring life theme) suggest the need for further study to clarify the exact nature, variation, and effects of these factors. The studies described here suggest the pervasive role of personally salient life themes and their contribution to reports of depressive symptoms.

With these studies in hand, the ability of clinicians and researchers to design protocols to detect depression and to develop interventions may be strengthened. Insights into content, idioms for expression, and diversity of views of depression can serve as guideposts that sensitize practitioners to the concerns and expectations of the elderly. However, we need further work to refine and evaluate these factors for measurement and clinical applications. The heterogeneity among beliefs within this population and the dissonance between practitioners' and patients' perspectives suggest the need for further research.

Such caution may not be warranted in other areas. The study documented a continuing overacceptance of high levels of depressive symptoms as either normal or expectable. The fact that untreated depression leads to excess disability, distress, and mortality is well documented. Thus, interventions aimed at the elderly, their families, and their primary physicians must remain a high public health priority.

At the most basic level, we hope to have contributed insights into the cultural and personal foundations of depressive experiences in later life to advance our understanding of depression and to suggest new questions to ask. Today a host of basic research, clinical, and institutional issues remain to be answered. The need is clear to invest our resources to address each of these to benefit current and future generations experiencing depression in later life.

REFERENCES

Abu-Lughod, L. (1985). Honor and the sentiments of loss in a Bedouin society. *American Ethnologist, 12,* 245–261.

Agar, M. (1980). Stories, background, knowledge and themes: Problems in the analysis of life history narratives. *American Ethnologist, 7,* 223–235.

American Psychiatric Association. (1987). *Diagnostic and statistical manual of mental disorders* (rev.). Washington, DC: Author.

Aneshensel, C. (1985). The natural history of depressive symptoms. *Research in Community and Mental Health, 5,* 45–75.

Antonovsky, A. (1987). *Unraveling the mystery of health.* San Francisco: Jossey-Bass.

Argyris, C., & Schon, D. (1974). *Theory in practice.* San Francisco: Jossey-Bass.

Atchley, R. (1988). A continuity theory of aging. *The Gerontologist, 29,* 183–190.

Becker, G. (1993). Continuity after a stroke: Implications of life-course disruption in old age. *The Gerontologist, 33,* 148–158.

Blazer, D. (1989). Depression in later life: An update. In M. P. Lawton (Ed.), *Annual review of gerontology and geriatrics* (pp. 197–214). New York: Springer.

Blazer, D. G. (1994). Epidemiology of depression: Prevalence and incidence. In J. R. M. Copeland, M. T. Abou-Saleh, & D. G. Blazer (Eds.), *Principles and practice of geriatric psychiatry* (pp. 519–522). New York: Wiley.

Blessed, G., Tomlinson, I., & Roth, M. (1968). The association between quantitative measures of dementia and of senile change in cerebral gray matter of elderly subjects. *British Journal of Psychiatry, 114,* 797–811.

Bourdieu, P. (1977). *Outline of a theory of practice,* Richard Nice (trans.). New York: Cambridge University Press.

Brink, T., Curran, P., Dorr, M., Janson, E., McNulty, U., & Messina, M. (1985). Geriatric depression scale reliability. *Clinical Gerontologist, 3,* 57–60.

Bruner, J. (1990). *Acts of meaning.* Cambridge: Harvard University Press.

Bruner, J. (1986). *Actual minds, possible worlds.* Cambridge, MA: Harvard University Press.

Bucholz, K., & Robins, L. (1987). Who talks to doctors about existing depressive illness? *Journal of Affective Disorders, 12,* 241–250.

Chafe, W. (1980). The deployment of consciousness in the production of a narrative. In W. Chafe (Ed.), *The pear stories: Cognitive, cultural, and linguistic aspects of story production.* Norwood, NJ: Ablex.

Chodorow, N. (1989). *Feminism and psychoanalytic theory.* New Haven: Yale University Press.

Clark, M. (1972). Cultural values and dependency in later life. In D. Cowgill & L. Holmes (Eds.), *Aging and modernization.* New York: Appleton-Century-Crofts.

Cohler, B. (1991). The life story and the study of resilience and response to adversity. *Journal of Narrative and Life History, 1,* 169–200.

Crapanzano, V. (1980). *Tuhami: Portrait of a Moroccan.* Chicago: University of Chicago Press.

Crapanzano, V. (1982). The self, the third, and desire. In B. Lee (Ed.), *Psychosocial theories of the self.* New York: Plenum.

Csikszentmihalyi, M., & Beattie, O. (1979). Life themes: A theoretical and empirical exploration of their origins and effects. *Journal of Humanistic Psychology, 19,* 46–63.

D'Andrade, R. (1976). Propositional analysis of Americans' beliefs about illness. In K. Basso & J. Selby (Eds.), *Meaning in anthropology.* Albuquerque: University of New Mexico Press.

Deppen, M., Luborsky, M., & Scheer, J. (1996). Aging, disability, and ethnicity. In J. Sokolovsky (Ed.), *The cultural context of aging: Worldwide perspectives.* New York: Bergin and Garvey.

Esteroff, S. (1981). *Making it crazy: An ethnography of psychiatric patients in a North American community.* Berkeley: University of California Press.

Evans-Pritchard, E. (1940). *The Nuer.* Cambridge: Cambridge University Press.

Ewing, K. (1990). The illusion of wholeness: Culture, self, and the experience of inconsistency. *Ethos, 18,* 251–278.

Fernandez, J. (1986). The argument of images and the experience of returning to the whole. In V. Turner & E. Bruner (Eds.), *The anthropology of experience.* Chicago: University of Chicago Press.

Foner, A. (1994). *The caregiving dilemma: Work in an American nursing home.* Berkeley: University of California Press.

Fry, C. L. (1990). The life course in context: Implications of comparative research. In R. Rubinstein (Ed.), *Anthropology and aging: Comprehensive reviews* (pp. 129–145). Boston: Kluwer Academic.

Geertz, C. (1984). From the natives' point of view: On the nature of anthropological understanding. In R. Shweder & R. LeVine (Eds.), *Culture theory: Essays on mind, self, and nature* (pp. 123–136). New York: Cambridge University Press.

Good, B., & Good, M. J. (1982). Toward a meaning-centered analysis of popular illness categories. In A. Marsella & G. White (Eds.), *Cultural conceptions of mental health and therapy* (pp. 141–166). Dordrecht, Holland: Reidel.

Gubrium, J. (1994). *Speaking of life: Horizons of meaning for nursing home residents.* New York: Aldine de Gruyter.

Harre, R. (1984). *Personal being.* Cambridge, MA: Harvard University.

Henderson, J. N., & Vesperi, M. (1995). *The culture of long term care: Nursing home ethnography.* Westport, CT: Greenwood.

Jefferson, G. (1984). On step-wise transitions from talk about a trouble to inappropriately next-positioned matters. In J. Atkinson & J. Heritage (Eds.), *Structures of social action: Studies in conversational analysis* (pp. 191–222). New York: Cambridge University Press.

Jenkins, J., Kleinman, A., & Good, B. (1991). Cross-cultural aspects of depression. In J. Becker & A. Kleinman (Eds.), *Advances in affective disorders: Theory and research: Vol. 1. Psychosocial aspects* (pp. 67–99). New York: Erlbaum.

Kaufman, S. (1987). *The ageless self: Sources of meaning in late life.* Madison: University of Wisconsin Press.

Keith, J. (1977). *Old people, new lives: Community creation in a retirement residence.* Chicago: University of Chicago Press.

Kleban, M., Lawton, M. P., Nesselroade, J., & Parmelee, P. (1992). The structure of variation in affect among depressed and non-depressed elderly. *Journal of Gerontology: Psychological Sciences, 47,* 190–198.

Kleinman, A., & Good, B. (1985). *Culture and depression: Studies in the anthropology and cross-cultural psychiatry of affect and disorder.* Berkeley: University of California.

Langness, L., & LeVine, H. (1986). *Culture and retardation: Life stories of mildly mentally retarded persons.* Dordrecht, Netherlands: Reidel.

Lasoski, M., & Thelen, M. (1987). Attitudes of older and middle aged person towards mental health interventions. *Gerontologist, 27,* 288–292.

Lindenbaum, S., & Lock, M. (1993). *Knowledge, power, and practice: The anthropology of medicine and everyday life.* Berkeley: University of California Press.

Lowenthal, M., Thurnher, M., & Chiriboga, D. (1975). *The four stages of life: A comparative study of men and women facing transitions.* San Francisco: Jossey-Bass.

Luborsky, M. (1990). Alchemists' visions: Cultural norms in eliciting and analyzing life history narratives. *Journal of Aging Studies, 4,* 17–29.

Luborsky, M. (1993a). The romance with personal meaning in gerontology: Cultural aspects of life themes. *The Gerontologist, 33,* 350–354.

Luborsky, M. (1993b). Sociocultural factors shaping adaptive technology usage: Fulfilling the promise. *Technology and Disability, 2,* 71–78.

Luborsky, M. (1994a). The cultural adversity of physical disability: Erosion of full adult personhood. *Journal of Aging Studies, 8,* 239–253.

Luborsky, M. (1994b). Identifying themes and patterns. In J. Gubrium & A. Sankar (Eds.), *Qualitative methods in aging research* (pp. 189–210). New York: Sage.

Luborsky, M. (1995). The process of self-report of impairment in clinical research. *Social Science and Medicine, 40,* 1447–1459.

Luborsky, M. (1995). The retirement process: Making the person and culture malleable. *Medical Anthropology Quarterly, 8,* 411–429.

Luborsky, M., & Riley, E. (1994). *Categories and experiences of depression in later life.* Philadelphia: Philadelphia Geriatric Center.

Luborsky, M., & Rubinstein, R. (1987). Ethnicity and lifetimes: Self-concepts and situational contexts of ethnic identity in late life. In D. Gelfand & D. Barresi (Eds.), *Ethnicity and aging: New perspectives* (pp. 35–50). New York: Springer.

Luborsky, M., & Rubinstein, R. (1990). Ethnic identity and bereavement in later life: The case of older widowers. In J. Sokolovsky (Ed.), *The cultural context of aging: Worldwide perspectives.* New York: Bergin & Garvey.

Luborsky, M., & Rubinstein, R. (1995). Sampling in qualitative research: Rationale, issues, methods. *Research on Aging, 17,* 89–113.

Luborsky, M., & Sankar, A. (1993). Extending the critical gerontology perspective: Cultural dimensions. *The Gerontologist, 33,* 440–444.

Lutz, C. (1986). Emotion, thought, and estrangement: Emotion as a cultural category. *Cultural Anthropology, 1,* 287–309.

Mandler, J. (1983). *Stories, scripts, and scenes.* Hillsdale, NJ: Lawrence Erlbaum.

Marsella, A., & White, G. (1982). *Cultural conceptions of mental health and therapy.* Dordrecht, Netherlands: Reidel.

McAdams, D. (1988). *Power, intimacy, and the life story: Personological inquiries into identity.* New York: Guilford.

Metzger, D. (1974). Semantic procedures for the study of belief systems. In H. Siverts (Ed.), *Drinking patterns in highland chiapas* (pp. 37–47). Oslo, Norway: Universitetforlaget.

Mishler, E. (1986). *Research interviewing.* Cambridge, MA: Harvard University Press.

Mishler, E. (1991). Representing discourse: The rhetoric of transcription. *Journal of Narrative and Life History, 1,* 255–280.

Moore, S., & Myerhoff, B. (1972). *Secular ritual.* Amsterdam, Netherlands: Van Gorcum.

Muhlhaulser, P., & Harre, R. (1990). *Pronouns and people.* Oxford: Basil Blackwell.

Murphy, R. (1987). *The body silent.* New York: Columbia University Press.

Myerhoff, B. (1978). *Number our days.* New York: Simon & Schuster.

Nichter, M. (1981). Idioms of distress. *Culture, Medicine, and Psychiatry, 5,* 379–408.

Nisbet, R. (1969). *Social change and history: Aspects of the western theory of development.* New York: Oxford University Press.

Parmelee, P., Katz, I., & Lawton, M. P. (1989). Depression among institutionalized aged: Assessment and prevalence estimation. *Journal of Gerontology: Medical Sciences, 44,* 190–196.

Sacks, H., Schlegoff, E., & Jefferson, G. (1974). A simplest systematics for the organization of turn-taking for conversation. *Language, 50,* 696–735.

Sadavoy, J., & Reiman-Sheldon, E. (1983). General hospital geriatrics psychiatric treatment. *Journal of the American Geriatrics Society, 31,* 200–205.

Savishinsky, J. (1991). *The ends of time: Life and work in a nursing home.* New York: Bergin & Garvey.

Scheer, J., & Luborsky, M. (1991). The cultural context of polio biographies. *Orthopedics, 14,* 1173–1181.

Scogin, F., & McElreath, L. (1994). Efficacy of psychosocial treatment for geriatric depression: A quantitative review. *Journal of Consultative Clinical Psychology, 62,* 69–74.

Shield, R. (1988). *Uneasy endings: Daily life in an American nursing home.* Ithaca, NY: Cornell University Press.

Strauss, A., & Corbin, J. (1990). *Basics of qualitative research: Grounded theory procedures and techniques.* Newbury Park, CA: Sage.

Tedlock, D. (1983). *The spoken word and the work of interpretation.* Philadelphia: University of Pennsylvania Press.

Thompson, L. W., Gallagher, D., & Breckenridge, J. S. (1987). Comparative effectiveness of psychotherapies for depressed elders. *Journal of Consulting and Clinical Psychology, 55,* 385–390.

Wagner, R. (1986). *Symbols that stand for themselves.* Chicago: University of Chicago.

Whitbourne, S. (1986). *The me I know: A study of adult identity.* New York: Springer-Verlag.

Williams, G. (1984). The genesis of chronic illness: Narrative reconstruction. *Sociology of Health and Illness, 6,* 175–200.

Young, A. (1993). A description of how ideology shapes knowledge of a mental disorder (posttraumatic stress disorder). In S. Lindenbaum & M. Lock (Eds.), *Knowledge, power, and practice: The anthropology of medicine and everyday life* (pp. 108–128). Berkeley: University of California Press.

Chapter 5

Depression and Growing Old

Barry W. Rovner

New challenges arise as we age, but that's as true for a toddler as a dowager. From the outside, we face changing circumstances that may threaten our stability. On the inside, we experience changes in our physiology and structure that require us to recalibrate ourselves. There are times, though, that involve more extraordinary change than others. Going off to school, adjusting to the growth spurt of adolescence, finding a job in young adulthood, suffering a heart attack in middle age, or losing a spouse in old age are examples. All may feel wrong to the organism when they occur. In old age, in particular, tiring more easily, seeing and hearing less well, and feeling aches and pains that do not abate convey to some people, to varying extents, a sense of loss. Not all older persons respond to these changes in the same way, however. Just as most adolescents do not become angry, resentful, nor rebellious, neither do most older people become depressed, resigned, or discontented. Just as some younger persons fail at love and work and become depressed, some older persons fail to accept life for what it is and become depressed. For them, old age is a time when everything goes wrong.

When things go wrong, some people seek the help of physicians. When a problem involves mood or memory, they may seek geriatric psychiatrists. This means that geriatric psychiatrists often see patients with depression, dementia, and delirium. When we write of our experiences with these patients, we may convey an impression that old age is disastrous. Although we may at times stress the liveliness of the aging mind, more often we focus our research and practice on its deterioration (Nemiah, 1992). Despite this, we know that deterioration is not the rule. To make that point, this chapter modestly reminds us that many persons do well growing old, but that preconceptions about aging, limitations in our research, and statements from our patients may suggest otherwise.

MAJOR DEPRESSION IS NOT MORE PREVALENT IN OLD AGE

Research in geriatric psychiatry has revealed a high prevalence of unrecognized and untreated mental disorders in the elderly. We vigorously exhort policy makers, physicians, nurses, and administrators to listen to what our patients say, and to see the difficult circumstances in which these patients find themselves. Our research shows, moreover, that our treatments work and that patients' distressing conditions can improve. But we may risk characterizing old age itself as pathological, on the basis of the clinical populations we see and the disorders we study.

Are the old more likely to become depressed than the young? When depression is considered as a clinical category, the answer is no (Regier et al., 1988). When depressive symptoms are counted, the answer is less clear (Kessler et al., 1992). This uncertainty arises from biases in case identification, cohort effects, diagnostic uncertainty, and medical comorbidity (Blazer, 1994). Also, we know that suicide rates are higher among the old than among the young, even though young people are more likely to *attempt* suicide. Who, then, is more depressed?

Although there is no easy answer to this question, useful insights can be gained from the words of some older people themselves. These voices show that older people are often less troubled than our stereotypes or even our studies might suggest. They tell of their pleasure in a world perceived through clouded eyes and ossified ears, on bones that creak but with hearts that leap when they are moved. As ever, they forge lives for themselves.

> I have entered a new country—the country of the old. The unknown appears at every juncture. I used to live in a comfortable, civilized land. Now I am living on a frontier. *Survival* becomes a day-to-day, moment-to-moment focus of interest and satisfaction. Though I suffer great physical difficulty, often painful, though I am unable to do most of the things I spent a lifetime doing, I am pleasantly surprised by my changed world. Paradoxically, ordinary moments of life, the prosaic flow of experiences, have become newly interesting. I see things in a fresh way—the picture on the wall, the pillows on the sofa, the tree outside my window. Existence has become adventurous. (Atkin, 1992, p. 3)

Who possesses the flexibility and energy to make old age an adventure? Rather than offer an answer to this question, epidemiological studies more often count the number of ailing hearts and creaking bones. Such studies have, however, helped to identify risk factors for depression, such as race, ethnicity, gender (female), socioeconomic status (low), life events (negative), physical health (poor), and quality of social supports (poor; Wykle & Musil, 1993).

REASONS WHY DEPRESSION MAY BE (WRONGLY) ASSOCIATED WITH OLD AGE

We recognize, of course, that not everyone who grows old becomes depressed, but we also need to recognize why we might associate age with depression. The first reason was noted earlier: decremental change feels wrong to the organism (Clower, 1992). A second reason is that living longer means witnessing more disability and death. A third reason is that symptoms of medical illness often share features with depression, although this overlap may be less of a problem than we think. Multiple somatic symptoms in the medically ill, such as anergia, anorexia, and insomnia, rarely occur without hopelessness, pessimism, and negative attitudes toward the self (Robinson & Rabins, 1989). Patients afflicted in these ways are not just medically ill; they are also depressed. Also, depression may be more common in certain diagnostic groups of patients because it is a symptom of an underlying disorder. Examples include the increased risk of depression in patients with left frontal strokes and in patients with Alzheimer's disease with severe locus ceruleus degeneration.

A fourth reason why old age is seen as specifically associated with depression may have to do with the form depression takes in old age. Older depressed patients often say, "What do I have to live for? I've lived my life?" "I have no energy, I can't think, I can't remember. What can I do now?" "I've made so many mistakes in my life; if only I had. . . . " Such comments may be taken, erroneously, as a consequence of living too long rather than as symptoms of depression. Moreover, just as the prevailing ideas of a culture may influence the content of psychiatric symptoms (e.g., delusions about magnetism in the 19th century and about X-rays in the early 20th century), so might current cultural stereotypes of old age shape the statements of older depressed patients.

A fifth reason why depression is linked to old age is perhaps the most persuasive, and the most misleading. This is the tendency to view old age as a metaphor for something else. For many people, old age symbolizes and intensifies some of our most severe culturally determined fears—

dependency, loss, pain, and death. We may tend to fear these things at all stages of life, but when we are young we can at least push them away to some time in the distant future, or project them onto people who are older than we are. The metaphor of old age as dependency, loss, pain, or death resembles mistaken concepts associated with a number of disorders, such as tuberculosis, cancer, and AIDS—conditions that consume body and mind. Tuberculosis has been imagined as a disease of poverty, deprivation, and romance; cancer as a disease of personal failure or moral decay; and AIDS as punishment for gratification of unacceptable drives. But these are all simply diseases of the body. Far from revealing anything spiritual, they reveal that the body is just a body. Thus, just as physical disease is not a metaphor for anything, neither is old age. Perhaps the most truthful way of regarding old age, and perhaps the healthiest way of growing old, is the way that is most resistant to metaphoric thinking (Sontag, 1979).

In this regard, Blazer (1994) suggests that the source of depression in some patients is inherent not so much in aging itself as in environmental circumstances. Similarly, Lasch wrote that we cannot ''convince people that old age is not necessarily a disaster without challenging the social conditions that cause so many people to experience it as such'' (1978, p. 220). Given the fact that many older persons face social isolation, lower incomes, difficulties with transportation, and inadequate housing, a sociological explanation may be far more relevant than a psychiatric explanation.

THE TROUBLES OF YOUTH MAY PERSIST INTO OLD AGE

Clearly, there are conflicting views about what it means to grow old. One person says:

> Here I am, an old man approaching ninety. The faculties I exercised, the physical powers I depended on don't obey my will anymore. I am very weak. I must navigate with a walker. My equilibrium is uncertain. My control over my movements unreliable. Whatever I do, I do slowly . . . my stool is impacted; my bowel is paralyzed. I have no blood. I can't walk. I can't eat. I am half-blind. But look! I hear, I see, I think, I remember. (Atkin, 1992, p. 10)

Another says:

> If you look closely, you will discover that in the depth of our hearts, even those of us who call themselves happy feel the same gnawing sadness, the

same worm of despair. For how well we know that happiness, transparent as a soap bubble and just as elusive, will be taken away and lost to us forever. (Grossman, 1989, p. 384)

Is the first writer deluded? Is the second depressed?

Most older persons do not ponder these thoughts for long. More likely, they carry on day to day, pausing to mourn misfortune or loss, but they are not cast into the depths unless something else is operative. In the case of prolonged grief, for example, Freud (1957) suggested that individuals so afflicted have incorporated an ambivalently perceived lost person within themselves, and have then inflicted on themselves the vengeful, aggressive feelings they once held toward the other. More generally, Goldfarb (1959, p. 384) suggested that

> the disturbed behavioral functioning of an aged person has at its core the early patterns of that person's behavior. The utilization of illness and inefficiency to punish oneself and others, to justify failure, to symbolize one's wishes, and to substitute for their fulfillment can be developed early and does not disappear with the accumulation of years.

The extent to which such dynamics account for other kinds of depression in old age is unknown, but for most older persons, personal and physical losses do not inevitably lead to depression:

> Usually the individual with normal regard, if unfettered by other predisposing factors, struggles against these feelings, finds other adaptive modes, does not give up, despite the urge to conserve and withdraw. . . . Our ability to cope successfully in relation to the demands of the environment is profoundly influenced by the adaptive styles we embrace. (Whybrow, 1990, p. 185)

Empirical research seems to support this observation. Individuals vary in their tendency to experience dysphoric affect, and this tendency is relatively stable over many years (Costa & McCrae, 1994). Data from the Baltimore Longitudinal Study of Aging suggest that people with high levels of trait depression, who might be considered temperamentally dysthymic or who despair easily, are predisposed to experience depressive episodes (Costa & McCrae, 1994). Cross-sectional evaluations of such older depressed persons may fail to elicit information about their earlier functioning or their predisposition to mild disruptions of mood. If such milder emotional states tend to persist throughout a lifetime, then times of personal stress (such as physical illness), environmental stress (such as placement in a nursing home), or interpersonal stress (such as grief), may lead to more severe emotional states:

> In many older persons, self-reliant, goal-oriented, problem-solving activity may have been at a low level to begin with; when it is further decreased by new functional losses, then previously precariously balanced or already low self-esteem suffers and falls progressively, as failure follows failure. (Goldfarb, 1959, p. 384)

If such persons are identified in an epidemiological study of older populations, they may contribute to the idea of old age as linked with depression. It then becomes difficult to discern whether a current episode is an aspect of an individual's enduring personal characteristics or something specific to old age.

The concept of the "neurotic paradigm" is helpful here. According to this concept, although certain situations can provoke the emotional response of sadness in almost anyone, less extreme circumstances elicit the same response, or even a more intense response, in vulnerable people. Responses elicited by less severe circumstances might, then, be called "neurotic" because they are evoked so much more readily and because their degree and duration seem disproportionate to the situation (McHugh & Slavney, 1983). In this instance, we recognize not disease entities, but rather moods or emotional expressions that can be interpreted and explained in terms of potential, provocation, and response. Personalities are the potential, life circumstances are the provocation, and depression may be the response (McHugh & Slavney, 1983).

More research is necessary to determine the extent to which this paradigm explains depression in old age. We can imagine cases, however, for which it might be explanatory. For some older persons, for instance, the difficulty may be related to their belief that perfect health will persist throughout life and that there is something unnatural about the natural changes of aging. Perhaps those who are overinvested in their appearance or performance, or who have been dependent on others to maintain their self-esteem and functioning, have the greatest difficulty in facing the prospect of a finite existence.

Perhaps, also, aging is less traumatic for those who can redefine themselves and establish new ways of life. Discussing the changes of aging, Clower (1992, p. 75) writes:

> The axiom that one must learn to change what can be changed, to live with what cannot be changed, and to discern the difference, is not just a truism, but a mandate for the elderly.

Nemiah (1992, p. 175) writes:

> Biological aging . . . need not dim the keenness and freshness of inner awareness and experience nor . . . does the passage of time necessarily diminish the flexibility of mind or its capacity for change and growth.

Reynolds Price (1994), when facing his own physical decline and imminent death, wrote:

> [One] finally learns to stand off from all that he has been and done. You are no longer who you were. You will never be that person again. Have one good cry if the tears will come. Then stanch the grief . . . find your way to somebody else, the next viable you.

Adler (1993, p. 25) writes:

> Am I aging? The mirror says so. The calendar confirms it. I must say I realize it is so, but who has time to think about it?

McDonald (1993, p. 178) writes:

> Already some of my coronary arteries have been replaced by veins from my legs, my vision races with my hearing in a downward spiral of self-destruction, and I no longer attempt to entrust to my memory matters that I previously had not hesitated to do. In short, I am very much aware that my past vastly exceeds the thrust of my future. My awareness of reaching the End Zone of my life, however, does not deaden the joys and excitements of my contemporary living.

Nothing in this chapter is meant to diminish the seriousness, suffering, and impact of depression in old age. But we need to look beyond the range of diseases, drugs, and disabilities that research in geriatrics has so ably demonstrated to be associated with depression. It is useful to focus not only on the pathological processes of old age but also on those processes that lead to growth, enrichment, and wisdom. They reflect what it means for most of us to grow old. Even though our bones may creak, our hearts may still sing.

REFERENCES

Adler, S. (1993). [Letter to the editor]. *Johns Hopkins Magazine, 45,* 25.
Atkin, A. (1992). On being old (A psychoanalyst's new world). In G. H. Pollock (Ed.), *How psychiatrists look at aging* (pp. 3–10). Madison: International Universities Press.

Blazer, D. (1994). Is depression more frequent in late life?: An honest look at the evidence. *American Journal of Geriatric Psychiatry, 2,* 193–199.

Clower, V. (1992). Aging in a mirror. In G. H. Pollock (Ed.), *How psychiatrists look at aging* (pp. 73, 75). Madison: International Universities Press.

Costa, P. R., & McCrae, R. R. (1994). Depression as an enduring disposition. In L. Schneider, C. R. Reynolds, B. D. Lebowitz, & A. J. Friedhoff (Eds.), *Diagnosis and treatment of depression in late life: Results of the NIH Consensus Development Conference* (pp. 155–167). Washington, DC: American Psychiatric Association.

Freud, S. (1957). Mourning and melancholia. In *Complete psychological works of Sigmund Freud* (standard ed., Vol. 14, pp. 237–260). New York: Norton.

Goldfarb, A. I. (1959). Minor maladjustments in the aged. In S. Arieti (Ed.), *American handbook of psychiatry* (p. 384). New York: Basic.

Grossman, D. (1989). *See under love.* New York: Farrar, Straus, Giroux.

Kessler, R. C., Foster, C., Webster, P. S., & House, J. S. (1992). The relationship between age and depressive symptoms in two national surveys. *Psychology and Aging, 7,* 119–126.

Lasch, C. (1978). *The culture of narcissism.* New York: Norton.

McDonald, W. (1993). [Letter to the editor]. *Johns Hopkins Magazine, 45,* 25.

McHugh, P. R., & Slavney, P. R. (1983). *The perspectives of psychiatry.* Baltimore: Johns Hopkins University Press.

Nemiah, J. (1992). *De senectute:* Retrospect and prospect. In G. H. Pollock (Ed.), *How psychiatrists look at aging.* Madison: International Universities Press.

Price, R. (1994). *A whole new life.* New York: Maxwell MacMillan International.

Regier, D., Boyd, J. H., Burke, J. D., Rae, D. S., Myers, J. K., Kramer, M., Robins, L. N., George, L. K., Darno, M., & Locke, B. Z. (1988). One-month prevalence of mental disorders in the United States. *Archives of General Psychology, 45,* 977–986.

Robinson, R. G., & Rabins, P. V. (1989). *Depression and coexisting disease.* New York: Igaku-Shoin.

Sontag, S. (1979). *Illness as metaphor.* New York: Vintage.

Whybrow, P. C., Akiskal, H. S., & McKinney, W. T. (1984). *Mood disorders: Toward a new psychobiology.* New York: Plenum.

Part II

Research on the
Treatment of Depression

CHAPTER 6

The Relation Between Research on Depression and a Treatment Program: One Model

LINDA TERI

The clinical application and empirical investigation of treatments to alleviate emotional distress have a long history. The purpose of this chapter is to provide one model to illustrate the type of interplay between research and clinical applications that is, and can be, evident in a diversity of areas. Such interplay can be beneficial to clinicians, researchers, patients, and their families. It can help establish the effectiveness and efficacy of some approaches while identifying ineffective ones, and it can thereby lead to new, creative ideas about as yet unresolved problems. The chapter first provides an overview of clinical and empirical knowledge of depression in older adults with cognitive impairment. It then presents details of one clinical program influenced by that research: the Seattle protocol, an intervention designed to alleviate depression in dementia patients by teaching their caregivers behavioral techniques. The chapter concludes with questions for further research and clinical activity.

Note: Parts of this chapter were presented at the conference of "Shades of Gray: Depression Among the Old and Frail—A Multidisciplinary Symposium," April 11 to 12, 1994, Philadelphia, PA, and have been published elsewhere. Supported in part by grant nos. NIMH-43266 and AG10845 from the National Institute of Mental Health and National Institute of Aging.

OVERVIEW

DEPRESSION IN DEMENTIA

Over the past decade, it has become well accepted that symptoms of depression exist in patients with cognitive impairment, such as Alzheimer's disease (AD), the most prevalent dementing disorder among older adults. Initially, however, clinical writings and research centered on issues of differential diagnosis. The questions were: How can depression be distinguished from dementia? What differences could be identified in etiology, evaluation, or treatment? Over time, clinical opinion and empirical evidence accumulated that depression and dementia were not mutually exclusive. Although a patient could be *either* demented *or* depressed (and although it was important to differentiate these two conditions), a patient could also be *both* demented *and* depressed. Figure 6.1 illustrates the

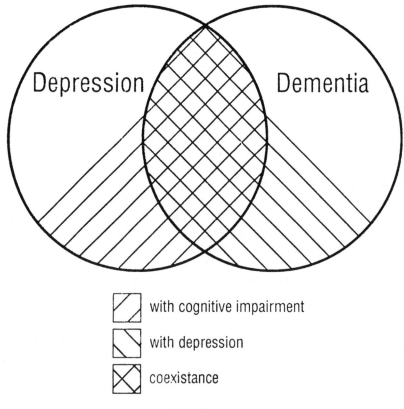

FIGURE 6.1

symptom configurations now known to be possible. Although estimates vary, depending on the sampling strategies and assessment methodologies employed, it is thought that approximately 30% of patients with Alzheimer's disease also meet criteria for the clinical syndrome of depression (Teri & Wagner, 1992; Wragg & Jeste, 1989). This syndrome is characterized by severe affective distress; loss of interest or pleasure in previously enjoyable activities; and associated symptoms, such as disturbances of sleep, appetite, and fatigue. Table 6.1 lists the symptoms characteristic of depression (American Psychiatric Association, 1994). In addition, an even higher percentage of patients exhibit individual depressive symptoms, although not of sufficient severity or duration to merit the diagnosis of depression.

Depression may add "excess disability" to the clinical picture of dementia patients. Kahn (1975) defined excess disability as disability that exists above and beyond the disability that can be explained by the primary disease process. Because depression is not necessarily characteristic of dementia, the depression symptoms themselves may be an area of excess disability. For example, patients with coexistent depression and dementia have significantly more dysphoric mood, vegetative signs, social with-

TABLE 6.1   Criteria for Major Depressive Episode

Five (or more) of the following symptoms have been present during the same 2-week period and represent a change from previous functioning; at least one of the symptoms is either (1) depressed mood, or (2) loss of interest or pleasure. Symptoms 1 to 8 must occur nearly every day.

1. Depressed mood most of the day.
2. Markedly diminished interest or pleasure in all, or almost all, activities most of the day.
3. Significant weight loss or appetite change.
4. Insomnia or hypersomnia.
5. Psychomotor agitation or retardation.
6. Fatigue or loss of energy.
7. Feelings of worthlessness, or excessive or inappropriate guilt.
8. Diminished ability to think or concentrate, or indecisiveness.
9. Recurrent thoughts of death, or recurrent suicidal ideation or a suicide attempt.
10. Symptoms cause clinically significant distress or impairment in social, occupational, or other important areas of functioning.
11. Symptoms are not due to the direct physiological effects of a substance (e.g., drug abuse or medication) or a general medical condition (e.g., hypothyroidism).
12. Symptoms are not better accounted for by bereavement.

Adapted from DSM-IV, American Psychiatric Association, 1994.

drawal, loss of interest, feelings of guilt and worthlessness, and suicidal ideation (Teri, Baer, & Reifler, 1991). They are more likely to have delusions and hallucinations; to experience higher levels of general behavior disturbance; to have more problems with restlessness, falling, agitation, suspiciousness, and incontinence; and to have increased functional disability (Logsdon & Teri, 1988; Pearson, Teri, Reifler, & Raskind, 1989; Raskin & Rae, 1980; Reifler, Larson, & Teri, 1987; Rovner, Broadhead, Spencer, Carson, & Folstein, 1989). Thus, depression is associated with additional problems in patients with coexistent depression and dementia. These associated problems are particularly striking when one considers that depression symptoms appear most prevalent in patients with milder levels of cognitive impairment (Burns, Jacoby, & Levy, 1990; Pearson et al., 1989).

Depression also affects these patients' caregivers. Several studies have found positive associations between patients' depression and caregivers' stress, burden, and depression. For example, Niederehe et al. (1983) reported that caregivers' "subjective strain" was strongly associated with patients' emotional symptoms, such as crying and depression. Drinka, Smith, and Drinka (1987) found the overall level of patients' depression significantly associated with the severity of caregivers' depression and burden. Greene, Smith, Gardiner, and Timbury (1982) found caregivers' burden and distress to be more affected by patients' "passive withdrawn" behavior. Patients' "lack of affect" has also been linked to high levels of stress in caregivers (Barnes, Raskind, Scott, & Murphy, 1981; Haley, Brown, & Levine, 1987). These difficulties experienced by caregivers are not trivial. It is increasingly acknowledged that the rate of depression in caregivers of demented patients is high; estimates are that up to 55% of caregivers experience significant depression symptoms themselves (Drinka et al., 1987; Haley et al., 1987; Pagel, Becker, & Coppel, 1985). Caregivers have also been found to have higher levels of clinically significant anger, anxiety, and guilt than age-matched noncaregivers. In an outpatient geriatric clinic at a university medical center, caregivers of depressed patients reported significantly higher levels of depression and burden than caregivers of patients without depression (Teri, Larson, & Reifler, 1988). Caregivers also reported higher levels of negative reaction in response to depressive behaviors (such as tearfulness and comments about sadness) than they did to memory-related or disruptive behaviors (e.g., asking repetitive questions and feeling agitated, respectively).

In summary, depression is a prevalent characteristic for many patients with dementia and is highly associated with other aspects of patients' disturbance and caregivers' distress. Effective treatment for depression, therefore, may not only improve the patient's depression but also lead to a decrease in depression-associated problems for patients and caregivers.

TREATMENT OF DEPRESSION IN DEMENTIA

Both pharmacological and nonpharmacological approaches to the treatment of depression in patients with dementia have been discussed in the literature. Much of this literature concerns pharmacological treatment, and readers interested in these approaches are referred to excellent reviews by Raskind (1989) and Small (1988). This chapter addresses the nonpharmacological treatment of depression in dementia.

There are several reasons for hypothesizing why nonpharmacological intervention may be effective in reducing depression in patients with Alzheimer's disease. First, in the one controlled clinical trial published, a placebo was found as effective as a commonly prescribed tricyclic antidepressant, imipramine, in reducing depression in this population (Reifler et al., 1989). Second, the often complicated medical conditions and medications used with these patients can sometimes make traditional pharmacotherapy for depression undesirable (Raskind, 1989). Third, the nature of the cognitive deficits experienced by patients with dementia makes traditional psychotherapeutic approaches inappropriate. Such approaches often rely on patients' memory, judgment, problem-solving skills, awareness, and psychological sophistication, each of which can be significantly reduced by the cognitive impairment characteristic of dementia. Therefore, behavioral therapies may be the method of choice.

Behavioral techniques may be particularly useful for depressed demented patients. Such strategies are often included in psychoeducational programs in which caregivers are provided with a variety of ideas to assist them with diverse issues of patient management (Gallagher, Rose, Lovett, & Silven, 1986; Haley et al., 1987; Zarit, Orr, & Zarit, 1985). For example, recommendations often include suggestions that caregivers change various behaviors of patients by modifying the environment or by changing their own response to such behaviors. The focus of such interventions is, however, often on the caregivers, and their effect on patients' depression is largely unknown.

Token economies and more individualized strategies, such as shaping, stimulus control, and social reinforcement, have also been investigated with dementia patients. Behaviors identified for change or reinforcement have included depression, independent eating, social interactions, social conversation, wandering, and seeking exits (Baltes & Zerbe, 1976; Blackman, Howe, & Pinkston, 1976; Hussian, 1983; Hussian & Brown, 1987; Hussian & Lawrence, 1981; Konarski, Johnson, & Whitman, 1980;

Linsk & Pinkston, 1984; McDonald, 1978; Panella, 1986; Pinkston & Linsk, 1984; Pinkston, Linsk, & Whitman, 1988; Rosberger & McLean, 1983; Schnelle et al., 1983). For example, Hussian and Brown (1987) described the successful use of behavioral techniques of stimulus enhancement and control in reducing undesirable wandering behavior. Baltes has shown that dependent behavior in institutionalized elderly people can be significantly reduced through environmental modifications and reinforcement of independent behavior (Baltes & Werner-Wahl, 1987). Pinkston et al. (1988) trained home caregivers to use operant behavioral strategies effectively to manage severe behavior problems in dementia patients.

In summary, clinical wisdom, broad-based studies focused on caregivers' behavior, and behavioral intervention strategies suggest that behavior management techniques can be effective in decreasing problems in dementia patients. Further, in nondemented older patients, behavioral strategies have been shown effective in reducing depression. Consequently, a behavioral intervention for depression in patients with dementia was developed to capitalize on behavioral strategies found effective in nondemented depressed adults, on the clinical wisdom of nonpharmacological management of patients with dementia, and on conceptual and empirical findings regarding depressed demented patients. The resulting intervention, called the Seattle Protocol, is discussed below. (For further information about this protocol, see Teri et al., 1992; and Teri, Logsdon, & Uomoto, 1994.) Before the development of this protocol, no published reports of behavioral interventions for depression or controlled outcome studies had addressed the potential of this type of treatment for patients' depression, or for associated problems of patients or caregivers.

THE SEATTLE PROTOCOL

CLINICAL PROGRAM

The specific goal of treatment is to reduce the patient's depression. In individual meetings between therapist and caregiver, caregivers are taught behavioral strategies to (1) increase pleasant events and decrease unpleasant events, and (2) effectively solve problems involving the day-to-day difficulties of caring for a patient with depression and dementia. Treatment consists of nine 60-minute sessions, once per week. Caregivers rate the patient's mood and monitor the frequency and duration of pleasant events each day throughout treatment. They also monitor changes in the patient's depression as they implement the goals established in the sessions. Caregivers are in a unique position to help the patient. Because of their dementia, patients are limited in their ability to learn new skills, remember the content of treatment, and understand explanations and techniques. Caregivers are able to accomplish each of these goals and, because of their involvement in the patient's care, are often in the best position to institute change. (For more information about the caregiver's role in treatment, the reader is referred to Teri et al., 1994.)

Patients, however, do participate in treatment as much as their level of cognitive impairment allows. Minimal involvement of the caregiver and more reliance on the patient may be appropriate and feasible in the early stages of the disease, when the patient can still function relatively independently and understand and follow through on treatment goals. More severely demented patients will require more involvement by the caregiver as their deficits in communication and memory become more problematic.

Session 1: Education and Rationale

In the first session, the therapist introduces the caregiver and patient to the scientific and clinical logic behind intervention. The behaviors that constitute depression, their impact on and association with other problems, and the potential for treatment are discussed in easily understood terms. Educational information is provided regarding the progressive course of Alzheimer's disease, the importance of long-term planning, and other topics of interest to individual caregivers and patients. Through discussion with the caregiver and patient, examples from their own experiences are used to educate them about the disease process and establish realistic expectations for change.

Session 2: Fundamentals of Behavior Change

In session 2 and throughout the remainder of treatment, caregivers and patients are provided with the fundamentals of behavior change. With examples from their own experience, as well as the therapist's experience with other caregiver-patient dyads, the caregiver is introduced to the importance of behavioral observation and analysis. The caregiver is taught to identify individual behavior problems, observe antecedents and consequences, and consider how altering one or the other can change behavior. This process is called the *ABC*s of behavior change: *A* is the antecedent or triggering event that precedes the problem behavior; *B* is the behavior; and *C* is the consequences of the behavior. Once the ABCs of the problem behavior have been outlined, an intervention strategy targeting either the antecedents or the consequences of the problem behavior can be developed.

(This strategy for identifying and treating problems is detailed in a video training program by the author entitled, "Managing and Understanding Behavior Problems in Alzheimer's Disease and Related Disorders" [Teri, 1990]. It may be obtained by writing to the Northwest Geriatric Education Center, University of Washington, HL-23, Seattle, WA 98195.)

Sessions 3 and 4: Increasing Pleasant Events

Depressed, demented patients are often in a cycle of inactivity and depressed mood. Because of their cognitive impairment, they eventually lose the ability to do many of the activities they once enjoyed. They no longer function as independently as they once could, and often they must rely on others to initiate and maintain activities. The less they do that they enjoy, the more depressed they feel. The more depressed they feel, the less they do. This cycle of depressed mood and inactivity becomes increasingly problematic over time. Involving patients in activities that they still may enjoy can break the cycle and improve their mood.

Starting with session 3, and continuing throughout treatment, this depressive cycle and the importance of identifying, planning, and increasing pleasant events are discussed with patient and caregiver. They then complete the Pleasant Events Schedule—Alzheimer's Disease (PES-AD; Teri & Logsdon, 1991) that is used throughout therapy to generate ideas and to help plan pleasant activities. The PES-AD is a 53-item list of potentially pleasant activities that demented patients may enjoy. It was developed to help caregivers and therapists identify activities that the patient currently enjoys or has enjoyed in the past, determine how frequently the patient engages in these activities, and devise ways of increasing the frequency of selected activities. The therapist works with the caregiver and patient to determine what pleasant activities are still realistic for the patient and helps the caregiver plan and carry out these activities throughout treatment. Table 6.2 shows the PES-AD. As can be seen, the items represent easily accessible and inexpensive tasks. Most involve social interactions but not necessarily so. These activities are intended to be added to the patient's daily repertoire.

Session 5: Maximizing Cognitive Function

Dementia reduces day-to-day abilities. These reductions have far-reaching effects and are directly associated with depression in two basic ways. First, cognitive impairments reduce the enjoyable activities available to the patient. Because so much of our enjoyment is related to what we can

TABLE 6.2   Pleasant Events Schedule—Alzheimer's Disease (PES-AD)

General directions: This schedule contains a list of events or activities that people sometimes enjoy. It is designed to find out about things the patient has enjoyed during the past month. Please rate each item three times. The first time, rate each item on how many times it happened in the past month (frequency); the second time, rate how available it has been (availability); the third time, rate it on how pleasant it has been (enjoyability), either now or in the past. Because this list contains events or activities that might happen to a wide variety of people, you may find that many of the items have not happened to the patient in the past month. It is not expected that anyone will have done all of these things in 1 month. There are no right or wrong answers.

Directions for frequency: How often have these events happened in the patient's life in the past month? Please answer each item by putting an X in the appropriate column according to how often the item has occurred.

   Not at all—This has *not happened* for the patient in the past month.
   A few times—This has *happened a few times* (1 to 6 times) in the past month.
   Often—This has *happened often* (7 or more times) in the past month.

Directions for availability: How available are these events to the patient? Please answer each item by putting an X in the appropriate column according to how available the item is.

   Not at all—This item has *not been available* during the past month.
   A few times—This item has been *available a few times* (1 to 6 times) during the past month.
   Often—This item has been *available often* (7 or more times) during the past month.

Directions for enjoyability: How enjoyable are these events for the patient? Please rate each item by putting an X in the appropriate column/s (one or both if they both apply) according to how enjoyable the item is.

   Now enjoys—The patient has enjoyed doing this item *in the last month.*
   Enjoyed in the past—The patient has enjoyed doing this item in the *past* (in the last 5 years).

Example: Item 1 is "Being outside." If the patient has been outside three times during the last month, place an X in the box marked "a few times," under *frequency*. If the patient has had an opportunity to be outside seven or more times during the past month, place an X in the box marked "often" in the *availability* column. Finally, if the patient has enjoyed being outside in the past, but did not enjoy it during the last month, place an X in the "Enjoyed in the past" column. Even if the patient has not experienced something on the list in the past month, it is still necessary to rate its enjoyability.

Important: Some items will list more than one event; for these items, check how often the patient has done any of the listed events. For example, item 3 is "Planning trips or vacations, looking at travel brochures, traveling." You should rate item 3 on how often the patient has done *any* of these activities in the past month.

(Continued)

137

TABLE 6.2   Pleasant Events Schedule—Alzheimer's Disease (PES-AD)

General directions: This schedule contains a list of events or activities that people sometimes enjoy. It is designed to find out about things the patient has enjoyed during the past month. Please rate each item three times. The first time, rate each item on how many times it happened in the past month (frequency); the second time, rate how available it has been (availability); the third time, rate it on how pleasant it has been (enjoyability), either now or in the past. Because this list contains events or activities that might happen to a wide variety of people, you may find that many of the items have not happened to the patient in the past month. It is not expected that anyone will have done all of these things in 1 month. There are no right or wrong answers.

Directions for frequency: How often have these events happened in the patient's life in the past month? Please answer each item by putting an X in the appropriate column according to how often the item has occurred.

  Not at all—This has *not happened* for the patient in the past month.
  A few times—This has *happened a few times* (1 to 6 times) in the past month.
  Often—This has *happened often* (7 or more times) in the past month.

Directions for availability: How available are these events to the patient? Please answer each item by putting an X in the appropriate column according to how available the item is.

  Not at all—This item has *not been available* during the past month.
  A few times—This item has been *available a few times* (1 to 6 times) during the past month.
  Often—This item has been *available often* (7 or more times) during the past month.

Directions for enjoyability: How enjoyable are these events for the patient? Please rate each item by putting an X in the appropriate column/s (one or both if they both apply) according to how enjoyable the item is *in the last month*.

  Now enjoys—The patient has enjoyed doing this item *in the last month*.
  Enjoyed in the past—The patient has enjoyed doing this item in the *past* (in the last 5 years).

Example: Item 1 is "Being outside." If the patient has been outside three times during the last month, place an X in the box marked "a few times," under *frequency*. If the patient has had an opportunity to be outside seven or more times during the past month, place an X in the box marked "often" in the *availability* column. Finally, if the patient has enjoyed being outside in the past, but did not enjoy it during the last month, place an X in the "Enjoyed in the past" column. Even if the patient has not experienced something on the list in the past month, it is still necessary to rate its enjoyability.

Important: Some items will list more than one event; for these items, check how often the patient has done any of the listed events. For example, item 3 is "Planning trips or vacations, looking at travel brochures, traveling." You should rate item 3 on how often the patient has done *any* of these activities in the past month.

(Continued)

138

TABLE 6.2 (*Continued*)

Event	Frequency			Availability			Enjoyability	
	Not at all	A few times	Often	Not at all	A few times	Often	Now enjoys	Enjoyed in the past
19. Helping others, helping around the house, dusting, cleaning, setting the table, cooking								
20. Combing or brushing hair								
21. Taking a nap								
22. Being with family (children, grandchildren, siblings, others)								
23. Watching animals or birds (in a zoo or in the yard)								
24. Wearing certain clothes (such as new, informal, formal, or favorite clothes)								
25. Listening to the sounds of nature (birdsong, wind, surf)								
26. Having friends come to visit								
27. Getting and sending letters, cards, notes								
28. Watching the clouds, sky, or a storm								
29. Going on outings (to the park, a picnic, a barbecue, etc.)								
30. Reading, watching, or listening to the news								
31. Watching people								
32. Having coffee, tea, a soda, etc., with friends								
33. Being complimented or told he or she has done something well								
34. Being told he or she is loved								
35. Having family members or friends say something that makes him or her proud of them								

(*Continued*)

TABLE 6.2 (*Continued*)

Event	Frequency			Availability			Enjoyability	
	Not at all	A few times	Often	Not at all	A few times	Often	Now enjoys	Enjoyed in the past
36. Seeing or speaking with old friends (in person or on the telephone								
37. Looking at the stars or moon								
38. Playing cards or games								
39. Doing handwork (crocheting, woodworking, crafts, knitting, painting, drawing, ceramics, clay work, other)								
40. Exercising (walking, aerobics, swimming, dancing, other)								
41. Indoor gardening or related activities (tending plants)								
42. Outdoor gardening or related activities (mowing lawn, raking leaves, watering plants, doing yard work)								
43. Going to museums, art exhibits, or related cultural activities								
44. Looking at photo albums and photos								
45. Stamp collecting, or other collections								
46. Sorting out drawers or closets								
47. Going for a ride in the car								

(*Continued*)

TABLE 6.2 *(Continued)*

Event	Frequency			Availability			Enjoyability	
	Not at all	A few times	Often	Not at all	A few times	Often	Now enjoys	Enjoyed in the past
48. Going to a house of worship or attending religious ceremonies								
49. Singing								
50. Grooming self (wearing makeup, having hair done)								
51. Going to the movies								
52. Recalling and discussing past events								
53. Participating in or watching sports (golf, baseball, football, etc.)								

141

and cannot do, maximizing the patient's cognitive function is essential and integral to behavioral treatment of depression. Second, cognitive impairments and their functional correlates increase the potential for conflict between the caregiver and patient. Disagreements about how and when to do certain activities, additional chores for the caregiver, and the patient's decreased functional independence may all contribute to increased aversive interactions. Consequently, treatment seeks to identify individual patients' relative strengths and weaknesses, abilities and disabilities; and to teach caregivers and patients how to maximize strengths and abilities while minimizing weaknesses and disabilities. Common clinical strategies—such as putting labels on cabinets and providing one-step commands—are discussed and tailored to the needs of the particular patient. These strategies are typically introduced during the fifth session and addressed as the need arises in subsequent sessions.

Sessions 6 and 7: Problem-Solving Techniques

As treatment progresses, strategies are developed for identifying and confronting behavioral disturbances that either interfere with planned pleasant activities or cause conflict between the patient, caregiver, and others. Using the skills of behavior observation and analysis taught and reinforced throughout each session, caregivers use the ABCs to devise strategies for modifying problems. The problem behaviors that are addressed include both depressive behaviors (such as crying and self-disparaging statements) and other behaviors (such as wandering and agitation). The therapist introduces behavioral strategies for decreasing problem behaviors and increasing incompatible behaviors, as appropriate.

To aid caregivers and therapists in identifying observable and potentially modifiable behaviors, the Revised Memory and Behavior Problems Checklist (RMBPC) is used (Teri et al., 1992). This inventory of 24 items evaluates the frequency of three domains of problems relevant to dementia: memory-related problems, such as repeated questioning; depression problems, such as crying; and disruption problems, such as verbal aggression. The RMBPC also evaluates the caregiver's reaction to each behavior, providing a measure of the impact of different behaviors on the individual caregiver. Table 6.3 shows the RMBPC. Clinically, administration of the RMBPC is useful for identifying the constellation of problem behaviors of a specific AD patient and the behaviors most distressing to the caregiver. Psychometric data have been published, indicating that the RMBPC is a reliable and valid assessment tool (Teri et al., 1992).

Session 8: Aid with Caregiving Responsibilities

Caregivers' problems, such as depression, stress, anger, and being burdened, are addressed as they relate to treatment plans and the patient's

TABLE 6.3   Revised Memory and Behavior Problems Checklist (RMBPC)

Subject ID # _____ Date: ____/____/____ Patient's name: _____

Name of person filling out form: _____

....

Instructions: The following is a list of problems patients sometimes have. Please indicate if any of these problems have occurred *during the past week*. If so, how much has this bothered or upset you when it happened? Use the following scales for the frequency of the problem and your reaction to it. Please read the description of the ratings carefully. Then answer all the questions below. Please circle a number from 0 to 9 for *both frequency and reaction.*

Frequency ratings:	*Reaction ratings*:
0 = never occurred	0 = not at all
1 = not in the past week	1 = a little
2 = 1 to 2 times in the past week	2 = moderately
3 = 3 to 6 times in the past week	3 = very much
4 = daily or more often	4 = extremely
9 = don't know or not applicable	9 = don't know or not applicable

		Frequency	Reaction
1.	Asking the same question over and over.	0 1 2 3 4 9	0 1 2 3 4 9
2.	Trouble remembering recent events (e.g., items in the newspaper or on TV).	0 1 2 3 4 9	0 1 2 3 4 9
3.	Trouble remembering significant past events.	0 1 2 3 4 9	0 1 2 3 4 9
4.	Losing or misplacing things.	0 1 2 3 4 9	0 1 2 3 4 9
5.	Forgetting what day it is.	0 1 2 3 4 9	0 1 2 3 4 9
6.	Starting but not finishing things.	0 1 2 3 4 9	0 1 2 3 4 9
7.	Difficulty concentrating on a task.	0 1 2 3 4 9	0 1 2 3 4 9
8.	Destroying property.	0 1 2 3 4 9	0 1 2 3 4 9
9.	Doing things that embarrass you.	0 1 2 3 4 9	0 1 2 3 4 9
10.	Waking you or other family members up at night.	0 1 2 3 4 9	0 1 2 3 4 9
11.	Talking loudly and rapidly.	0 1 2 3 4 9	0 1 2 3 4 9
12.	Appearing anxious or worried.	0 1 2 3 4 9	0 1 2 3 4 9
13.	Engaging in behavior that is potentially dangerous to self or others.	0 1 2 3 4 9	0 1 2 3 4 9

(Continued)

TABLE 6.3 *(Continued)*

		Frequency	Reaction
14.	Threatening to hurt oneself.	0 1 2 3 4 9	0 1 2 3 4 9
15.	Threatening to hurt others.	0 1 2 3 4 9	0 1 2 3 4 9
16.	Being verbally aggressive to others.	0 1 2 3 4 9	0 1 2 3 4 9
17.	Appearing sad or depressed.	0 1 2 3 4 9	0 1 2 3 4 9
18.	Expressing feelings of hopelessness or sadness about the future (e.g., "Nothing worthwhile ever happens"; "I never do anything right").	0 1 2 3 4 9	0 1 2 3 4 9
19.	Crying and tearfulness.	0 1 2 3 4 9	0 1 2 3 4 9
20.	Commenting about death of self or others (e.g., "Life isn't worth living"; "I'd be better off dead").	0 1 2 3 4 9	0 1 2 3 4 9
21.	Talking about feeling lonely.	0 1 2 3 4 9	0 1 2 3 4 9
22.	Commenting about feeling worthless or being a burden to others.	0 1 2 3 4 9	0 1 2 3 4 9
23.	Commenting about feeling like a failure, or about not having accomplished anything worthwhile in life.	0 1 2 3 4 9	0 1 2 3 4 9
24.	Arguing, irritability, complaining.	0 1 2 3 4 9	0 1 2 3 4 9

care. Caregivers are encouraged to plan pleasant events for themselves as well as for the patient. They are guided in developing and using a support system to help them care for the patient and to help them maintain their own sense of well-being and their physical health. The availability of respite services and other community assistance is discussed, as needed. Often, caregivers need to be encouraged to care for themselves. They are so concentrated on the patient that their own needs remain unmet, and they often place undue demands on their own time. When the therapist helps to identify others in the caregivers' natural or professional network who can share the demands of caregiving, caregivers can often gain more time for themselves and their own emotional and physical needs.

Session 9: Planning for Maintenance and Generalization

Many dementias, such as Alzheimer's disease, involve progressive deterioration. Depression is often a recurrent condition. It is, therefore, likely that additional problems will emerge once treatment is completed. Consequently, before the end of treatment, plans are developed for continuing pleasant events and implementing problem-solving strategies that have been learned. Generalization of the caregiver's behavioral skills to new or different problem behaviors in the future is also encouraged. The final session serves as a summary session to review treatment and as a planning session to develop strategies for ongoing care.

PROGRAM EVALUATION

In several clinical settings, the behavioral strategies discussed here are being successfully implemented. As clinical experience with this approach grows, a necessary next step will be to standardize the treatment in such a way as to maximize what has been learned over time and yet maintain the individualized nature of the approach. To this end, a treatment manual has been developed to guide clinicians in using this approach. (A copy of this manual is available from the author.) Aspects of the program have been incorporated into other treatment packages and developed as the clinical need arose. For example, as already mentioned, a videotape training program on the ABCs has been developed and is currently available. An independent evaluation of this program revealed that these videos are being used by almost 300 Veterans Affairs Medical Centers, academic medical centers, hospitals, and other health care facilities. More than half of the videos currently in circulation are being used as part of an ongoing training program for family caregivers and caregivers in facilities. The overwhelming response to these videos has been favorable; requests for additional copies are received regularly.

Teri and Uomoto (1986, 1991) reported on four cases in which caregivers were taught behavioral skills similar to those just detailed. Caregivers were successful in increasing patients' involvement in pleasant activities, and a subsequent reduction in patients' depression was seen. In each case, the patient's mood was highly associated with both the duration and the frequency of pleasant activity. Over time, both activity and mood improved. Figure 6.2 illustrates the association between mood and activity, and the increase in both over the course of treatment.

Although this initial success is encouraging, it is necessary to continue to evaluate this protocol critically. As stated at the beginning of this chapter, clinical practice and clinical research interact and enrich each other. Consequently, in order to evaluate the effectiveness and efficacy of this approach, a controlled clinical trial was designed in which subjects were randomly assigned either to the Seattle protocol or to control conditions including a waiting list. *Patient measures* evaluated four primary

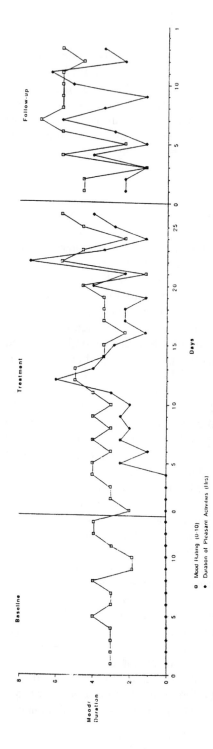

FIGURE 6.2 Case 3 data with mood ratings and duration of pleasant activities plotted across time using an AB/follow-up single-case design.

domains hypothesized to be important to the patient's status and associated with depression: (1) depression, (2) behavioral disturbance, (3) functional impairment, and (4) cognitive status. It was hypothesized that treatment would reduce depression and associated behavioral problems but would not significantly alter either cognitive or functional status, because those were hypothesized to be more closely related to the progression of disease than to depression. *Caregiver measures* included assessments of depression and burden. It was also hypothesized that the caregiver's depression and burden would not be significantly affected by treatment, given that the treatment focused on the patient's problems. All measures were completed pretreatment, posttreatment, and at 6 and 12 months after termination of treatment.

Table 6.4 summarizes the demographic characteristics of the subjects enrolled in this trial. As can be seen, in accordance with the intent of the intervention, all patients had mild to moderate levels of cognitive impairment (as evidenced by the Mini-Mental State Exam; Folstein, Folstein, & McHugh, 1975) and depression (as measured by the Hamilton Depression Rating Scale; Hamilton, 1967). Interestingly, patients had an average duration of 17 months of untreated depression. Some had been depressed as long as 3 years. Thus, depression in these patients can be a chronic condition, if left untreated.

Caregivers in this study were predominantly spouses. Most of the caregivers were female; this is consistent with the literature on caregiving. Unexpectedly, most of the caregivers in this study were significantly depressed. Seventy-four percent met Research Diagnostic Criteria (Spitzer, Endicott, & Robins, 1978) for major or minor depression. This high percentage of clinically depressed caregivers is a matter of concern for several reasons. First, it indicates a high degree of distress in these families. Caregivers and patients must cope not only with their own emotional distress but also with each other's. Second, recall that this intervention was designed for patients. These caregivers were, then, seeking help for the patient, not for themselves, despite their own high level of depression. Last but not least, this additional depression on the part of the caregiver may well have an impact on the care and quality of life of both patient and caregiver.

The caregivers' own moods may also bias their assessment of the patients' moods. This would have direct implications for any treatment program, whether for research or clinical practice. Because of the cognitive problems associated with dementia, patients may be unable or unwilling to provide the information necessary to assess depression accurately. For this reason, caregivers are often relied on to provide such information, even if the information is modified by a clinical evaluation by a trained

TABLE 6.4   Demographic Characteristics

Patient	
Age (x ± SD)	75 ± 7.2
Education (x ± SD)	13 ± 3
Gender, N (%)	
Female	38 (53%)
Male	34 (47%)
Dementia duration (months)	33.3 ± 23.0
Depression duration (months)	17.5 ± 16.0
Mini-Mental State Exam (x ± SD)	16.3 ± 7.3
Hamilton Depression Rating Scale (x ± SD)	16.5 ± 5.0
Caregiver	
Age (x ± SD)	66.15 ± 12.5
Education (x ± SD)	14 ± 3
Gender, N (%)	
Female	45 (63%)
Male	27 (37%)
Relationship, N (%)	
Spouse	56 (78%)
Adult child	12 (17%)
Other	4 (5%)
Depression diagnosis	
Major or minor	53 (74%)
Not depressed	19 (25%)

diagnostician. Clinicians are often dependent on the caregiver to provide information that they themselves cannot observe and that the patient may not reliably provide, such as sleeping and eating patterns. Thus, the ability of the caregiver to provide accurate information and the relationship between caregivers' depression and patients' depression become critical to accurate assessment.

Two studies were conducted to determine whether caregivers could accurately assess depression in their patients and whether there was a relationship between caregivers' depression and their reports of patients' depression. (These studies were conducted with subjects not enrolled in the intervention trial.) For the first study, trained clinicians rated 75 patients with Alzheimer's disease on the Hamilton Depression Rating Scale (HDRS, Hamilton, 1967; a commonly employed assessment of depression in older adults) in three ways: one based solely on the patient's report; a second based on the caregiver's report; and the third based on their own clinical judgment, using both reports and direct clinical observation (Teri & Wagner, 1991). Patients rated themselves as less depressed than did caregivers or clinicians, and caregivers rated patients as less depressed than did clinicians. Clinicians' ratings were strongly associated with caregivers' assessment of patients' depression, and this relationship was maintained on those items found most predictive of clinical diagnosis. The level of patients' dementia did not affect the different ratings. Caregivers, therefore, did not overrate depression in patients relative to clinical judgment and in fact were influential in the decisions made by clinicians.

For the second study, caregivers of patients with Alzheimer's disease were randomly assigned to observe one of two video vignettes and make ratings of depression based on the Hamilton Depression Rating Scale (Truax & Teri, 1990). One video depicted a depressed patient and the other a nondepressed patient. Depressed and nondepressed caregivers were included, and their mood was assessed with the HDRS. Findings indicated that caregivers were able to differentiate depressed from nondepressed patients on video. Further, caregivers' ratings were unaffected by their own mood, or the mood of the patient for whom they provided care. Thus, caregivers seemed accurate in assessing patients' depression, and this assessment seemed unrelated to their own mood.

These findings have important implications for the Seattle protocol, and for other treatment approaches with dementia patients and their caregivers. Caregivers play an important and integral role in treatment. They are responsible for providing the information necessary to facilitate diagnosis and the consistency necessary to carry out treatment. Patients without involved caregivers suffer an added disability.

CONCLUSION

Years of clinical and empirical study in dementia and depression have led to several important findings with direct implications for the accurate assessment and treatment of depression in patients with dementia. This chapter has provided a brief overview of the development of the field and provided one example of how a single intervention strategy was developed and is being evaluated.

The Seattle protocol is a coordinated treatment program aimed at reducing depression through a systematic behavioral approach to identifying and modifying problems. It provides patients and caregivers with information and education about depression and dementia, a rationale for behavioral intervention, systematic strategies for behavioral change, methods for identifying and increasing pleasant events, methods for maximizing current cognitive and functional abilities, effective problem-solving techniques, assistance with caregiving responsibilities, and plans for maintaining and generalizing treatment gains. Patients have benefited from this program. They have shown evidence of significant improvements in mood and behavior. Caregivers have been shown to be accurate reporters of patients' depression, and to be able to implement this program without difficulty. The clinical formulation of this approach and its empirical evaluation, however, are still very much in their infancy. More clinical application and research are needed.

It is hoped that this presentation of one treatment approach to depression in dementia patients—how it evolved from preexisting clinical and research knowledge, how it is used in clinical settings, and how it is being subjected to controlled empirical study—has helped illustrate the importance of applied clinical research and the excitement surrounding it. We can only hope that clinicians and researchers continue to collaborate and to stimulate each other. There is unlikely to be a "quick fix" to the problems of our older adults living with dementia, either as patients or as caregivers. Effective strategies are desperately needed for the seemingly endless array of problems and difficulties they encounter. What strategies work? For whom? Under what conditions? What is the role of pharmacological or nonpharmacological treatments? How do they compare? How can they augment each other? What is the impact of these treatments on patients, caregivers, and the larger health care community? Do caregivers and patients who receive help early experience less difficulty later? Is the progression of disease the great equalizer? What affects the outcome of treatment? How can we help patients without involved caregivers? The questions are endless. The need for answers is urgent.

REFERENCES

American Psychiatric Association. (1994). *Diagnostic and statistical manual of mental disorders* (4th ed.). Washington, DC: American Psychiatric Association.

Baltes, M. M., & Werner-Wahl, H. (1987). Dependence in aging. In L. L. Carstensen & B. A. Edelstein (Eds.), *Handbook of clinical gerontology* (pp. 204–221). New York: Pergamon.

Baltes, M. M., & Zerbe, M. B. (1976). Independence training in nursing home residents. *The Gerontologist, 16*, 419–432.

Barnes, R. F., Raskind, M., Scott, M., & Murphy, C. (1981). Problems of families caring for Alzheimer's patients: Use of a support group. *Journal of the American Geriatrics Society, 29*, 80–85.

Blackman, D. K., Howe, M., & Pinkston, E. M. (1976). Increasing participation in social interaction of the institutionalized elderly. *The Gerontologist, 16*, 69–76.

Burns, A., Jacoby, R., & Levy, R. (1990). Psychiatric phenomena in Alzheimer's disease: 3. Disorders of mood. *British Journal of Psychiatry, 157,* 81–86.

Drinka, J. K., Smith, J. C., & Drinka, P. J. (1987). Correlates of depression and burden for informal caregivers of patients in a geriatrics referral clinic. *Journal of the American Geriatrics Society, 35,* 522–525.

Folstein, M. F., Folstein, S. E., & McHugh, P. R. (1975). Mini-mental state: A practical method for grading the cognitive state of patients for the clinician. *Journal of Psychiatric Research, 12,* 189–198.

Gallagher, D., Rose, J., Lovett, S., & Silven, D. (1986, November). *Prevalence, correlates and treatment of clinical depression in family caregivers.* Paper presented at annual meeting of Gerontological Society of America.

Greene, J. G., Smith, R., Gardiner, M., & Timbury, G. C. (1982). Measuring behavioral disturbance of elderly demented patients in the community and its effects on relatives: A factor analysis study. *Age and Aging, 11,* 121–126.

Haley, W. E., Brown, S. L., & Levine, E. G. (1987). Family caregiver appraisals of patient behavioral disturbance in senile dementia. *Aging and Human Development, 25,* 25–33.

Haley, W. E., Levine, E. G., Brown, S. L., Berry, J. W., & Hughes, G. H. (1987). Psychological, social and health consequences of caring for a relative with senile dementia. *Journal of the American Geriatrics Society, 35,* 405–411.

Hamilton, M. (1967). Development of a rating scale for primary depressive illness. *British Journal of Social and Clinical Psychology, 6,* 278–296.

Hussian, R. A. (1983). A combination of operant and cognitive therapy with geriatric patients. *International Journal of Behavior Geriatrics, 1,* 57–61.

Hussian, R. A., & Brown, D. C. (1987). Use of two-dimensional grid patterns to limit hazardous ambulation in demented patients. *Journal of Gerontology, 42,* 558–560.

Hussian, R. A., & Lawrence, P. S. (1981). Social reinforcement of activity of problem-solving training in the treatment of depressed institutionalized elderly patients. *Cognitive Therapy and Research, 1,* 57–69.

Kahn, R. L. (1975). The mental health system and the aged. *The Gerontologist, 15,* 24–31.

Konarski, E. Q., Johnson, M. R., & Whitman, T. L. (1980). A systematic investigation of resident participation in a nursing home activities program. *Journal of Behavior Therapy and Experimental Psychiatry, 11,* 249–257.

Linsk, N. L., & Pinkston, E. M. (1984). Training gerontological practitioners in home-based family interventions. *Educational Gerontology, 10,* 289–305.

Logsdon, R., & Teri, L. (1988, November). *Neuropsychological and behavioral assessment in the identification and treatment of DAT.* Paper presented at the meeting of the Association for Advancement of Behavior Therapy, New York.

McDonald, M. (1978). Environmental programming for the socially isolated aging. *The Gerontologist, 18,* 350–354.

Niederehe, G., Furge, E., Woods, A.M., et al. (1983). *Caregiver stress in dementia: Clinical outcomes and family considerations.* Paper presented at the meeting of the Gerontological Society of America, San Francisco.

Pagel, M. D., Becker, J., & Coppel, D. B. (1985). Loss of control, self-blame and depression: An investigation of spouse-caregivers of Alzheimer's disease patients. *Journal of Abnormal Psychology, 94,* 169–182.

Panella, J. (1986). Toileting strategies in day care programs for dementia. *Clinical Gerontologist, 4*, 61–63.

Pearson, J., Teri, L., Reifler, B., & Raskind, M. (1989). Functional status and cognitive impairment in Alzheimer's disease patients with and without depression. *Journal of the American Geriatrics Society, 37*, 1117–1121.

Pinkston, E. M., & Linsk, N. (1984). Behavioral family intervention with the impaired elderly. *Gerontologist, 24*, 576–583.

Pinkston, E. M., Linsk, N., & Young, R. N. (1988). Home based behavioral family treatment of the impaired elderly. *Behavior Therapy, 19*, 331–344.

Raskin, A., & Rae, D. (1980). Distinguishing depressive pseudodementia from true dementia. *Psychopharmacology Bulletin, 16*, 23–25.

Raskind, M. A. (1989). Organic mental disorders. In E. Busse & D. Blazer (Eds.), *Geriatric Psychiatry* (pp. 313–368). Washington, DC: American Psychiatric Association.

Reifler, B. V., Larson, E., & Teri, L. (1987). An outpatient geriatric psychiatry assessment and treatment service. *Clinics in Geriatric Medicine, 3*, 203–209.

Reifler, B. V., Teri, L., Raskind, M., Veith, R., Barnes, R., White, E., & McLean, P. (1989). Double-blind trial of imipramine in Alzheimer's disease patients with and without depression. *American Journal of Psychiatry, 146*, 45–49.

Rosberger, Z., & McLean, J. (1983). Behavioral assessment and treatment of "organic" behaviors in an institutionalized geriatric patient. *International Journal of Behavioral Geriatrics, 1*, 33–46.

Rovner, B. W., Broadhead, J., Spencer, M., Carson, K., & Folstein, M. F. (1989). Depression and Alzheimer's disease. *American Journal of Psychiatry, 146*, 350–353.

Schnelle, J. F., Traugber, B., Morgan, D. B., Embry, J. E., Binion, A. F., & Coleman, A. (1983). Management of geriatric incontinence in nursing homes. *Journal of Applied Behavior Analysis, 16*, 235–241.

Small, G. W. (1988). Psychopharmacological treatment of elderly demented patients. *Journal of Clinical Psychiatry, 49*, 8–13.

Spitzer, R. L., Endicott, J., & Robins, E. (1978). Research diagnostic criteria. Rationale and reliability. *Archives of General Psychiatry, 35*, 773–782.

Teri, L. (1990). *Managing and understanding behavior problems in Alzheimer's disease and related disorders* [Training program with videotapes and written manual]. Seattle: University of Washington.

Teri, L. (1992). Non-pharmacological approaches to management of patient behavior: A focus on behavioral intervention for depression in dementia. In G. M. Gutman (Ed.), *Shelter and care of persons with dementia* (pp. 101–113). Vancouver, BC: Gerontology Research Centre, Simon Fraser University.

Teri, L. (1994). Behavioral treatment of depression in dementia patients. Behavioral symptoms in dementia: Theories and therapies. In *Alzheimer's disease and associated disorders* (Vol. 8, pp. 66–74). New York: Raven.

Teri, L., Baer, L., & Reifler, B. (1991). Depression in Alzheimer's patients: Investigation of symptom patterns and frequency. *Clinical Gerontologist, 11*, 47–57.

Teri, L., Larson, E., & Reifler, B. V. (1988). Behavioral disturbance in dementia of the Alzheimer's type. *Journal of the American Geriatrics Society, 36*, 1–6.

Teri, L., & Logsdon, R. (1991). Identifying pleasant activities for individuals with Alzheimer's disease: The pleasant events schedule-AD. *The Gerontologist, 31*, 124–127.

Teri, L., Logsdon, R., Wagner, A., & Uomoto, J. (1994). The caregiver role in behavioral treatment of depression in dementia patients. In E. Light, G. Niederehe, & B. Lebowitz (Eds.), *Stress effects on family caregivers of Alzheimer's patients* (pp. 185–204). New York: Springer.

Teri, L., Truax, P., Logsdon, R., Uomoto, J., Zarit, S., & Vitaliano, P. P. (1992). Assessment of behavioral problems in dementia: The Revised Memory and Behavior Problems Checklist. *Psychology and Aging, 7,* 622–631.

Teri, L. Truax, P., & Pearson, J. (1988, November). *Caregiver depression and burden: What are the correlates?* Paper presented at the Gerontological Society of America, San Francisco.

Teri, L., & Uomoto, J. (1986). *Treatment of depression in Alzheimer's disease: Helping caregivers to help themselves and their patients.* Paper presented at the annual meeting of the Gerontological Society of America.

Teri, L., & Uomoto, J. (1991). Reducing excess disability in dementia patients: Training caregivers to manage patients depression. *Clinical Gerontologist, 10,* 49–63.

Teri, L., & Wagner, A. (1991). Assessment of depression in patients with Alzheimer's Disease: Concordance between informants. *Psychology and Aging, 6,* 280–285.

Teri, L., & Wagner, A. (1992). Alzheimer's disease and depression. *Journal of Consulting and Clinical Psychology, 3,* 379–391.

Truax, P., & Teri, L. (1990, November). *Are caregiver depression ratings of demented patients biased by their own mood?* Paper presented at the annual meeting of the Gerontological Society of America, Boston.

Wragg, R. E., & Jeste, D. V. (1989). Overview of depression and psychosis in Alzheimer's disease. *American Journal of Psychiatry, 146,* 577–587.

Zarit, S. H., Orr, N. K., & Zarit, J. M. (1985). *The hidden victims of Alzheimer's disease: Families under stress.* New York: New York University Press.

CHAPTER 7

Effects of Cognitive Group Interventions on Depressed Frail Nursing Home Residents

IVO L. ABRAHAM
LISA L. ONEGA
SALLY J. REEL
AMY B. WOFFORD

BACKGROUND

Work by Thompson and Gallagher-Thompson (see Chapter 8 in this book) has established that individual psychotherapeutic interventions within the cognitive-behavioral framework are effective in alleviating depression and depressive symptomatology among community-dwelling older adults. The effects of cognitive interventions with depressed nursing home residents, many of whom might be physically frail and suffer from some degree of cognitive impairment, are less well established. Abraham, Neundorfer, and Currie (1992) noted that 24-week-long cognitive group interventions—such as cognitive-behavioral group therapy and "focused visual imagery" group therapy, administered by nurses to long-term care residents—did not produce significant changes in total scores on depression, hopelessness, and life dissatisfaction over four points in time (4 weeks before interventions, 8 and 20 weeks after treatment initiation, and 4

Note: Supported by grants from the National Institute for Nursing Research and the National Institute of Mental Health.

weeks after termination). These interventions produced significant and lasting improvements in overall cognitive status in nursing home residents with slight to moderate cognitive impairment, as compared with a control (attention) intervention involving educational discussion groups.

The results reported by Abraham et al. (1992), though, are to be interpreted with reservation because they constitute one of the first formal studies with frail depressed nursing home residents and concerned global outcomes of cognitive function and depressive symptomatology. Abraham and Reel (1992) have since reanalyzed the cognitive data, focusing on the 15 neurocognitive parameters tested by the Modified Mini-Mental State Examination (Abraham et al., 1993; Teng & Chui, 1987). Effects were noted on neurocognitive operations involving brain functions at higher cortical and subcortical-limbic levels, where lower and more basic cortical functions were not affected.

In this chapter, we use these initial analyses as the basis for further exploration of the effects of cognitive group interventions on depressed frail nursing home residents. First, we briefly review cognitive-behavioral and focused visual imagery therapies for depressed older adults and the extent to which prior research offers insight and direction regarding the use of these interventions with depressed nursing home residents. Next we report on research that evaluates the effects of these treatments for depressed nursing home residents. Specifically, using the factor structure of the Geriatric Depression Scale (GDS; Abraham, Wofford, Lichtenberg, & Holroyd, 1994), we reanalyzed our data to examine whether the original findings on the outcome of depression (Abraham et al., 1992) manifest themselves across the six dimensions of the GDS, or whether differentiated effects on selective dimensions of depression in late life can be identified. Similarly, using the factor structure of the Modified Mini-Mental State Examination (Abraham et al., 1993), we reanalyzed the data to look at differential effects across major dimensions of neurocognitive function in order to better understand the results presented by Abraham et al. (1992) and Abraham and Reel (1992). We undertook this reanalysis to further examine the absence of treatment effects on depressed mood and to elucidate the nature of the cognitive effects.

This dual focus on depression and cognition is not only predicated on our previous findings but also supported by epidemiological evidence on nursing home populations. For instance, Parmelee, Katz, and Lawton (1989) have shown that 26.5% of nursing home residents suffer from symptoms classifiable as major or minor depression according to *DSM-III-R*. Blazer (1989) reported that most depressed older adults have depressive symptoms associated with physical illness and adjustment to life stresses. Therefore, the prevalence of depressive symptomatology among elderly persons in nursing homes, with their multiple chronic illnesses and functional impairments, might well increase the 26.5% of depressive disorder identified by Parmelee et al. (1989; see Chapter 1, by Katz & Parmelee). Cognitive impairment, mostly due to irreversible forms of dementia, affects more than 60% of nursing home residents, and 15% of them present with both cognitive impairment and diagnostically classifiable depression (Parmelee et al., 1989; see also Chapter 6, by Teri). Because it is associated with apathy, decreased attention span, and diminished concentration, depression may further add to cognitive dysfunction ("pseudodementia"), even in elderly people without dementias (Blazer, 1989). Among depressed, physically ill, and functionally impaired institutionalized elderly people, cognitive status may be further compromised because of the lack of cognitive stimulation in the constrained physical and social environment of a nursing home.

Detailed reviews of studies on the efficacy of cognitive-behavioral interventions with community-dwelling depressed older adults provide a better argument in favor of this type of intervention than can be presented in this chapter (see Chapter 8 in this book; also Thompson, Davies, Gallagher, & Krantz, 1986). One additional study (DeBerry, Davis, & Reinhard, 1989), published soon after completion of our protocols, should be noted. Thirty-two subjects between ages 65 and 75 with complaints of anxiety and depression, but without major affective disorders or major medical illnesses, and not on psychotropic medication, received either relaxation-meditation imagery, cognitive-behavioral therapy, or a pseudo-treatment. All groups met for 45-minute sessions twice a week for 12 weeks, for a total of 24 sessions. The only statistically significant reduction from pretreatment to posttreatment was in state anxiety among subjects practicing meditation-relaxation imagery. There were no significant effects on depression. The investigators speculate that the study period of 12 weeks was too short a time to attempt modification of thoughts and behaviors, and suggest that if the groups had lasted another 12 weeks, the positive clinical trends noted might have resulted in significant reductions in anxiety and depression. Their recommendation for a 24-week protocol, although it was made after completion of our study, provides post hoc support for our longer treatment periods.

The clinical relevance of focused visual imagery group therapy may, however, need some further specification (see below for definition and description). There is ample clinical and anecdotal evidence, as well as some empirical evidence, that focused visual imagery is an effective clinical intervention for depression in younger adults. Hart and Means (1985) induced a dysphoric mood in subjects through hypnosis. Subsequently, these subjects were randomly assigned to the four cells of a factorial experiment that crossed mode of treatment (imagery versus cognitive). Cognitive treatment was found to reduce cognitively induced dysphoria; imagery was effective for both imaginally and cognitively induced dysphoria. Schultz (1978) compared four imagery strategies in a study with 60 depressed veterans: aggressive imagery, socially gratifying imagery, positive imagery, and free or unfocused imagery (where subjects had free choice of the content of imagery). Subjects in the three "focused imagery" groups had significantly lower levels of depression than those in the "unfocused imagery" condition. Gold, Jarvinen, and Teague (1982) studied the effects of no imagery and positive, neutral, and self-generated imagery on depression in depressed female students. All three types of imagery were found to be effective in alleviating depressive symptomatology in these subjects, as compared with the control group. It was also noted that the more vivid the imagery, the higher its therapeutic effect (Gold et al., 1982). The clinical efficacy of focused imagery in adults has also been documented in several other studies (Lipsky, Kassinove, & Miller, 1980; Propost, 1980; Reardon & Tossi, 1977), yet there is some evidence to the contrary as well (Smith, 1982). No studies were found that investigated the effects of focused visual imagery on cognitive functioning. Most likely this is due to the fact that studies have involved cognitively intact subjects. It may also reflect the belief that imagery can be practiced only by people with full cognitive capacity and, conversely, the belief that people suffering from cognitive impairment are poor candidates for imagery.

The effects of focused imagery on depression in older adults are less clear. Leja (1989) assigned 10 depressed postsurgical patients to either a visual imagery group or a control group. Depression scores among experimental subjects decreased significantly after the intervention, but this effect did not persist after discharge from the hospital. In a study on imagery as a pain control technique for use with geriatric patients, Hamm and King (1984) found a decrease in perceived pain. Further evidence for older adults' ability to practice imagery is the finding that people between ages 60 and 94 show a significantly higher frequency of eidetic imagery than younger adults, and, in fact, have the same capability as children age 5 to 7 (Giray, Roodin, Altkin, Flagg, & Yoon, 1985). Riccio, Nelson, and Bush (1990), studying a sample of 27 elderly women residing in supportive-care environments, found that imagery training significantly increased the amount and duration of repetitive, simple physical exercises practiced by subjects. Finally, the sensitivity of older adults to positive suggestion was demonstrated by Casler (1985). He gave nursing home residents positive suggestions about health and longevity and compared these subjects' survival with that of matched control subjects. Experimental subjects outlived controls by a factor of 4.25. The median number of days without hospitalization was 1,424 for experimental subjects and 365 for controls. These findings should be interpreted with caution, however: they may imply more causality than is warranted. At best, Casler (1985) reported a striking association between positive suggestion and very general measures of morbidity and mortality. This caution must be coupled with another caution that applies to the limited body of imagery research in general. The studies reviewed here varied greatly as to type of imagery (anywhere on the continua from passive to active, unstructured and unguided to structured and guided, content-unfocused to content-focused), the length and intensity of the intervention, and the outcome measures used. It is safe to say that empirical support for the effects of visual imagery is tentative, certainly in the elderly. The support for imagery may be found more often in belief in the intervention than in availability of data.

While admittedly the original intent was to have an impact on depression and its psychoemotional correlates, the effects on cognitive functioning have proved to be intriguing but perhaps understandable. Cognitive-behavioral and focused visual imagery therapy might, indeed, have a positive effect on cognition, not only because they reduce depression (and thus clear up associated pseudodementia) but also because of their different methods of stimulating cognitive activity. Cognitive-behavioral therapy engages people in rigorous examination of their thinking and behavior and encourages them to change faulty ways of thinking about themselves and their interactions with their social and physical environment. Imagery therapy is an intensely cognitive effort requiring unique cognitive skills involving imagination, memory storage, and retrieval in both verbal and visual codes (Hill, Evankovich, Sheikh, & Yesavage, 1987; Stern & Stern, 1989), recognition and recall, and naming to achieve the goal of ''thinking in pictures.'' At the clinical level, cognitive-behavioral therapy aims at influencing people's cognitive abilities and processes, whereas in imagery therapy these abilities and processes are the actual means to achieve therapeutic goals. And although in cognitive-behavioral therapy some of the cognitive processes are changed as a means of effecting therapeutic change, in imagery therapy different cognitive processes are used to achieve cognitively induced states of awareness.

The effects of cognitive-behavioral therapy and focused visual imagery therapy on frail depressed nursing home residents have not been studied. Prior research, including studies involving older adults, have suggested the relative efficacy of these cognitive interventions, yet these assumptions remain in need of empirical support. The intention of the study (for which new analyses are reported here) was to investigate the effects of these interventions in a population with a high prevalence of mood disturbance as well as cognitive impairment.

METHODS

Detailed descriptions of sample, design, dependent measures, procedures, and clinical protocols can be found elsewhere (Abraham et al., 1992; Abraham, Niles, Thiel, Siarkowski, & Cowling, 1991; Abraham & Reel, 1992; Neese & Abraham, 1992). We summarize the essentials here.

SAMPLE

The sample consisted of 76 older adults residing in seven nursing homes, who met the following sampling criteria: sufficient hearing and vision to participate in group activities and perform functions associated with the interventions (no near or complete loss of hearing or vision); sufficient verbal and comprehension skills to participate in group activities and perform functions associated with the interventions; and absence of major cognitive impairment. Because of the mix of physical and mental disability in residents of nursing homes, it was necessary to recruit subjects from seven different facilities (894 beds in total) in order to put together three cognitive-behavioral groups, three visual imagery groups, and two education-discussion groups. Only one nursing home yielded enough subjects for two groups; all the other facilities accommodated one group. Treatment conditions were randomly assigned to nursing homes. Of the 76 subjects admitted to the study, 30 participated in cognitive-behavioral groups, 29 in focused visual imagery groups, and 17 in education-discussion groups. There was some attrition among the subjects because of death and illness. Of the 76 subjects who began the clinical protocols, 42 (55.3%) completed the interventions and the follow-up data collection. Subjects ranged in age from 71 to 97 years ($M = 84.38$; $SD = 6.13$). The mean score on the Geriatric Depression Scale (Yesavage et al., 1983) at screening was 17.93 ($SD = 4.16$; range = 10–28). Length of stay ranged from 1 to 192 months ($M = 40.30$; $SD = 43.94$). In general, the subjects constituted a group of frail elderly of advanced age, with multiple impairments, who had been institutionalized for some time, who were physically quite ill, and who suffered from mild to severe depression. Subjects in the three conditions did not differ significantly on any of the demographic variables or in level of depression at screening.

DEPENDENT MEASURES AND FACTOR STRUCTURES

Geriatric Depression Scale (GDS)

This scale was developed specifically for measuring depression in elderly people for whom traditional depression scales may not be appropriate (Yesavage et al., 1983). Its 30 "yes-no" items yield scores between 0 and 30, on the basis of which patients are classified as severely depressed (21–30), depressed (11–20), or not depressed (0–10). Abraham et al. (1994) identified a six-factor solution consisting of the following factors: (1) life dissatisfaction, (2) dysphoria, (3) hopelessness and decreased self-attitude, (4) rumination and anxiety, (5) social withdrawal and decreased motivation, and (6) decreased cognition.

Modified Mini-Mental State Exam (3MS)

This instrument, developed to screen cognitive status and dementia (Teng & Chui, 1987), is an extension of the Mini-Mental State Examination (MMS; Folstein, Folstein, & McHugh, 1975), a widely used screening test for dementia. Scores may range from 0 to 100, with 80 or less indicating dementia. Abraham et al. (1993) proposed a five-factor structure involving the following dimensions: (1) memory and recall; (2) identification and association; (3) orientation; (4) concentration and calculation; and (5) psychomotor skills.

PROCEDURES

Three clinical nurse specialists with credentials and experience in the respective treatment modalities conducted the 24-week interventions. Four trained and blinded interviewers collected data 4 weeks before the interventions (t_1), 8 weeks (t_2) and 20 weeks (t_3) after treatment initiation, and 4 weeks after treatment termination (t_4).

CLINICAL PROTOCOLS

Detailed descriptions and discussions of the interventions with the cognitive-behavioral, focused visual imagery, and educational-discussion groups have been presented elsewhere (Abraham et al., 1991; Neese & Abraham, 1992). To summarize: *Cognitive-behavioral therapy* is focused on correcting the depressed patient's negative thoughts and attitudes and maladaptive ways of processing information (Kovacs, 1980). The rationale is that depression will be alleviated when the patient learns to identify and logically challenge irrational cognitions and replace them with rational, constructive cognitions. Cognitive-behavioral therapy begins by identifying the dysfunctional cognition underlying the depression. The clinician seeks to expose and test the patient's erroneous beliefs and ineffective methods of processing information. The patient is then engaged in examination and adaptive alteration of the problematic cognition (Beck, 1967).

Visual imagery, on the other hand, is "thinking in pictures." It assumes that people have control over their thoughts and mental processes and that this control can be exerted with little effort and without physical skill. The basic theoretical foundation for practicing imagery is that it provides distraction from a particular mood (e.g., depression) and assists in expressing and discharging suppressed affect. In turn, this leads to reduction in conflict and a corresponding decrease in level of depression. Focused visual imagery involves a progressive relaxation technique that facilitates a calm emotional state and attention to the imagery directives administered by the clinician. The clinician verbally leads the group through a sequence of directives aimed at achieving an imagery experience that is mostly visual but potentially could be experienced in other sensory modes. The client is awake and alert at all times. At the conclusion of the focused imagery experience, the client group and the clinician discuss features of the experience and the clients' impressions of the experienced imagery.

Participants in the *educational-discussion* groups selected topics to discuss, including favorite poetry, current events, health and illness topics, aging, and so forth. These groups, common in long-term care settings, did not conduct formal group therapy but instead emphasized learning and discussion focused on the here and now. The educational discussion groups, in a sense, served as a control for the more formal treatment groups. They equalized the amount of attention given to subjects that did not invoke specialized expertise for its delivery.

RESULTS

Depression

Abraham et al. (1992) did not report on any main or interaction effects on the total GDS score. Reanalysis of the data on depression did not reveal any main effects for either intervention or time on any of the six dimensions of the GDS. Only one interaction effect for intervention and time was observed, specifically for the dimension of *decreased cognition* ($F(6,105) = 2.56$; $p < .03$). Examination of the mean values revealed that the change observed here could be attributed to the improvements in cognition reported elsewhere (Abraham et al., 1992; Abraham & Reel, 1992).

COGNITION

Abraham et al. (1992) reported a main effect for type of intervention on the total 3MS score ($F(2,36) = 3.91$; $p < .03$). Reanalysis of the data revealed main effects for type of intervention on the dimensions of *identification and association* ($F(2,35) = 3.61$; $p < .04$) and *concentration and calculation* ($F(2,36) = 3.59$; $p < .04$). At the level of individual parameters, main effects for type of intervention were noted on *similarities* ($F(2,36) = 3.32$; $p < .05$), *mental reversal* ($F(2,36) = 3.59$; $p < .04$), and *writing* ($F(2,36) = 3.58$; $p <. 04$). Abraham et al. (1992) also reported a positive main effect for time on the total 3MS score ($F(3,108) = 89.42$; $p < .0005$), indicating improvement of cognitive function over time. The present reanalysis of cognition data revealed main positive effects for time on the dimensions of *memory and recall* ($F(3,105) = 7.80$; $p < .0001$), *identification and association* ($F(3,105) = 6.92$; $p < .0001$), and *concentration and calculation* ($F(3,108) = 2.93$; $p < .04$). Significant main effects for time were also noted on the parameters of *first recall* ($F(3,108 = 8.51$; $p < .0001$), *second recall* ($F(3,108) = 5.24$; $p < .002$), *four-legged animals* ($F(3,108 = 3.32$; $p < .03$), *naming* ($F(3,108) = 3.42$; $p < .03$), *similarities* ($F(6,108) = 3.13$; $p < .05$), and *copying pentagons* ($F(6,105) = 3.72$; $p <. 05$). These positive main effects for time indicate improvement over time on the dimensions and parameters cited here. All this is in contrast to the absence of interaction effects on total cognition scores (Abraham et al., 1992) and on any of the five major cognitive dimensions.

DISCUSSION

This reanalysis of depression and cognition scores along their major dimensions (GDS and 3MS) and their individual (ratio-level) items (3MS) provides further insights in the effects, and relative lack thereof, of cognitive group interventions administered to frail, depressed nursing home residents with slight to moderate degrees of cognitive impairment. Importantly, even differentiated analyses of the data on depression failed to confirm that either cognitive-behavioral or focused visual imagery group therapy, conducted over a 24-week period, reduces depressive symptomatology in this population. This is in contrast to studies on younger adults and community-dwelling elderly people.

Several possible reasons for this result should be considered. One reason could be the subjects' physical and mental frailty. Subjects were very old, and most of them were wheelchair-dependent, had impaired vision or hearing, suffered progressively worsening health, and had cognitive problems. Possibly, depressive symptomatology could have been reduced if the interventions had lasted longer than 24 weeks (which was already twice the length of most intervention studies). There is, however, no clinical support for longer treatment protocols based on previous studies with younger adults or community-dwelling elderly people. Furthermore, longer protocols would also have required more subjects as a buffer against the likely higher attrition rates. Suggesting extending the intervention, as others have done when they did not obtain significant findings using shorter protocols (e.g., DeBerry et al., 1989), may reflect belief in the intervention rather than trust in the data.

Another possible reason why depressive symptomatology was not reduced in our sample was suggested by Gatz and Hurwicz (1990). They found that older persons (age 70–98) had the highest depression scores of all age groups on the Center for Epidemiological Studies—Depression (CES-D) scale (Radloff, 1977), but almost exclusively because of elevated scores on the subscale ''lack of well-being.'' The investigators speculate that in old age, people's expressions of lack of well-being may represent not depression but rather a realistic coming to terms with some of the constraints on their lives. It may be for our sample, as well, that what we were measuring as various dimensions of depression was actually realistic acceptance of limitations in subjects' current lives that the interventions could not change.

As to cognition, we hypothesized that cognitive effects would occur primarily as a result of reducing depression and thus affecting the pseudodementia that often accompanies depression in the elderly. Yet, because the interventions did not influence depression, it is inferred that the improved cognitive performance of subjects in these two conditions may have been due to the activation of cognitive resources through cognitive-behavioral and focused visual imagery activities and exercises.

Why this is so is not well understood and should be further investigated. But it may be related to the amount, type, and intensity of cognitive resources that are activated in the course of the three group interventions tested in this study. Education-discussion groups rely on basic and primary cognitive skills used routinely by elderly people to communicate and converse. Cognitive-behavioral group therapy requires some of these same skills, but at a more intensive level. In addition, this mode of therapy requires the special cognitive skills of reflecting on one's own and others' cognitive errors, verbalizing these reflections and one's reactions to them, and learning less depressogenic modes of thinking and behaving. Visual imagery requires still different cognitive skills—namely, imagination, construction of mental images, storage into and retrieval from short- and long-term memory in both verbal and visual codes, recognition and recall, naming and other linguistic skills, and reproduction. The finding that visual imagery subjects in the visual imagery group showed a slightly greater improvement in cognitive functioning than cognitive-behavioral subjects may be due to the fact that this intervention is more unusual as regards the type of cognitive activities involved. We must also acknowledge, however, that these subjects began the study with a slightly higher (though not statistically significant) level of cognitive functioning.

The reanalyzed data about dimensions and their respective parameters yield additional insights into the cognitive gains achieved by the subjects. The main effect of intervention on total cognition score was caused largely by the differential impact of the interventions on the neurocognitive dimensions associated with the ability to recognize and associate objects and the ability to concentrate and execute; and on the specific functions of abstraction and conceptual thinking (similarities), concentration and linguistic manipulation (mental reversal), and execution of auditorily presented language skills (writing). These main effects for type of intervention, though limited to 3 of the 15 parameters and 2 of the 5 dimensions tested by the 3MS, were noted on cognitive dimensions involving higher cortical functions. Time was found to have a significant impact on the following cognitive operations: short- and medium-term recall (first recall, second recall); fluency of category retrieval (four-legged animals); abstraction and conceptual thinking (similarities); concentration and linguistic manipulation (mental reversal); and execution of visually presented commands (read and obey). It also significantly affected the overall dimensions of memory and recall as well as identification and association. Note that the absence of intervention by time interaction effects precludes firm inferences about the differential efficacy of the treatment. The significant main effects for time show that subjects, undifferentiated by the type of intervention received, improved over time; the overall effects were found almost exclusively among subjects in the two experimental conditions. The various main effects for intervention show the potential effects of the interventions. However, further research is needed to examine the true efficacy of the treatment as regards neurocognitive functions.

Time significantly improved subjects' ability to perform several cognitive operations, irrespective of the treatment condition to which subjects were assigned. May this have been caused by testing, and might it thus constitute a significant threat to the internal validity of the intervention? Both testing and maturation effects are unlikely. The choice of words used in recall tasks was altered from one administration to the next, and the only consistent feature was that they pertained to something to wear, a color, and a good personal quality—all of which are procedures embedded in the 3MS by Teng and Chui (1987). The fact that the subjects were consistently unable to generate 10 four-legged animals, as the test asks them to do, reflects the degree of difficulty subjects had with "fluency of category retrieval." The transposition of consonants in the word *world* makes it unlikely that reversed spelling of this word is influenced significantly by repeated administrations. The abstraction embedded in the "similarities" task, coupled with the fact that subjects are never given feedback about the accuracy of their performance on any of the 3MS items, also reduces the likelihood of a testing effect. The "read and obey" task is probably the only one where a testing effect may have occurred.

As to maturation caused by extraneous sources, such an effect is highly unlikely, as no other opportunities for learning or training were offered in the nursing homes during the implementation of our protocols. However, intentional maturation did occur experimentally in response to group participation. The main effect for time suggests that, above and beyond whatever effects specific group interventions might produce, longitudinal participation in meaningful group activity requiring cognitive efforts of some kind may lead to improvement in selective dimensions of cognitive functioning. Last, the interaction effects noted for "naming and copying pentagons" suggests that memory retrieval and linguistic identification, as well as the praxis of graphical transposition and reproduction, are significantly enhanced through differential group participation over time.

In terms of brain functioning, the main and interaction effects noted were all on cognitive dimensions and parameters that involve functions at higher cortical and subcortical-limbic levels. In contrast, cognitive tasks involving lower and more basic cortical functions were not affected. For instance, "registration" and "repetition," both of which involve the immediate reproduction of auditory information, concern only basic cortical operations, with, at most, "repetition" being somewhat more demanding as regards motoric speech. Similarly, the "three-stage command" elicits a sequence of praxic motor responses to a sequence of verbal (and auditorily processed) commands. The fact that orientation to time, place, and self were not affected by intervention or time lends further support to the assertion that the nursing interventions tested in this present study had an impact primarily on higher neurocognitive functions. It must also be recognized that detailed orientation to time and place is less pertinent to old and frail nursing home residents than to younger, community-dwelling elderly people.

CONCLUSION

It would be premature to conclude on the basis of this one study that cognitive interventions of the kind tested in this study are ineffective in alleviating depressive symptomatology in frail depressed nursing home residents, but that they may instead lead to improvements in cognitive performance. Yet the data from this one study have been analyzed and reanalyzed from sufficient angles to permit, at least, a new hypothesis: that for depressed nursing home residents (versus community-dwelling elderly people) with multiple impairments (versus relatively functional people) participating in group (versus individual) cognitive interventions may *help them think better* but may perhaps *not help them feel better*. Thus, these interventions may not have the same effect on depressive symptomatology that they have been argued and shown to have on younger adults or community-dwelling elderly people. More encouragingly, however, evidence is now emerging that cognition is sensitive to clinical manipulation, even in a clinically difficult population of frail, depressed nursing home residents with some degree of cognitive impairment.

It may very well be that the interventions studied alleviate depressive symptomatology only in certain subgroups of nursing home residents. If so, this would call for further differentiation in what is often seen as a homogeneous segment of the elderly population. Future research is also needed to clarify factors that possibly influence whether group interventions alleviate depressive symptomatology in nursing home residents, if this is indeed possible. A review of psychotherapy for the treatment of depression in general found no evidence for the relative superiority of any one approach (Robinson, Berman, & Neimeyer, 1990). As the authors of that review concluded, the focus of future research should be less on differentiating among psychotherapies for depression than on identifying the factors responsible for improvement.

These findings about the neurocognitive effects of the interventions, as administered by clinical nurse specialists, have significant implications for the growing involvement of psychogeriatric nursing in the clinical care of the people who are cognitively impaired. The findings attest to the fact that cognitive nursing interventions administered in a group format may lead to marked improvements in cognitive functions involving higher cortical and subcortical-limbic functions. The findings also underscore the fact that these interventions should not be limited to cognitively intact people, as prior studies have done, but can be used as effective therapeutic agents to achieve improvements in cognitive status. Given the relationships between cognitive status, functional ability to perform activities of daily living (ADL), and self-care, cognitive nursing interventions may have a potential to affect function and self-care indirectly through maintenance or improvement of cognitive function.

REFERENCES

Abraham, I. L., Manning, C. A., Boyd, M., Neese, J. B., Newman, M., Plowfield, L., & Reel, S. (1993). Cognitive screening of nursing home residents: Factor structure of the Modified Mini-Mental State (3MS) Examination. *International Journal of Geriatric Psychiatry, 8,* 133–138.

Abraham, I. L., Neundorfer, M. M., & Currie, L. J. (1992). Effects of group interventions on cognition and depression in nursing home residents. *Nursing Research, 41,* 196–202.

Abraham, I. L., Niles, S. A., Thiel, B. P., Siarkowski, K. I., & Cowling, W. R. (1991). Therapeutic group work with depressed elderly. *Nursing Clinics of North America, 26,* 635–650.

Abraham, I. L., & Reel, S. J. (1992). Cognitive nursing interventions with long-term care residents: Effects on neurocognitive dimensions. *Archives of Psychiatric Nursing, 6,* 356–365.

Abraham, I. L., Wofford, A. B., Lichtenberg, P. A., & Holroyd, S. (1994). Factor structure of the Geriatric Depression Scale in a cohort of depressed nursing home residents. *International Journal of Geriatric Psychiatry, 9,* 611–617.

Beck, A. T. (1967). *Depression: Clinical, experimental, and theoretical aspects.* New York: Harper & Row.

Blazer, D. G. (1989). Depression in the elderly. *New England Journal of Medicine, 320,* 164–166.

Casler, L. (1985). A simple verbal procedure for reducing the rates of psychosomatic enfeeblement and death in an aged population. *Death Studies, 9,* 295–307.

DeBerry, S., Davis, S., & Reinhard, K. E. (1989). A comparison of meditation-relaxation and cognitive-behavioral techniques for reducing anxiety and depression in a geriatric population. *Journal of Geriatric Psychiatry, 22,* 231–247.

Folstein, M. F., Folstein, S. E., & McHugh, P. R. (1975). "Mini-Mental State": A practical method for grading the cognitive state of patients for the clinician. *Journal of Psychiatric Research, 12,* 189–198.

Gatz, M., & Hurwicz, M. (1990). Are old people more depressed? Cross-sectional data on Center for Epidemiological Studies Depression Scale factors. *Psychology and Aging, 5,* 284–290.

Giray, E. F., Roodin, P., Altkin, W., Flagg, P., & Yoon, G. (1985). A life span approach to the study of eidetic imagery. *Journal of Mental Imagery, 9,* 21–32.

Gold, S. R., Jarvinen, P. J., & Teague, R. G. (1982). Imagery elaboration and clarity in modifying college students' depression. *Journal of Clinical Psychology, 38,* 312–314.

Hamm, B. H., & King, V. (1984). A holistic approach to pain control with geriatric clients. *Journal of Holistic Nursing, 2,* 32–36.

Hart, D. E., & Means, J. R. (1985). Cognitive versus imaginal treatments for cognitively-versus imaginally-induced dysphoria. *Journal of Mental Imagery, 9,* 33–52.

Hill, R. D., Evankovich, K. D., Sheikh, J. I., & Yesavage, J. A. (1987). Imagery mnemonic training in a patient with primary degenerative dementia. *Psychology and Aging, 2,* 204–205.

Kovacs, M. (1980). The efficacy of cognitive and behavior therapies for depression. *American Journal of Psychiatry, 137,* 1495–1501.

Leja, A. M. (1989). Using guided imagery to combat postsurgical depression. *Journal of Gerontological Nursing, 15,* 6–11.

Lisky, J. M., Kassinove, H., & Miller, N. J. (1980). Effects of rational-emotive therapy, rational role reversal, and rational-emotive imagery on the emotional adjustment of community mental health center patients. *Journal of Consulting and Clinical Psychology, 48,* 366–374.

Neese, J. B., & Abraham, I. L. (1992). Group interventions with the elderly. In K. C. Buckwalter (Ed.), *Geriatric mental health nursing: Current and future challenges* (pp. 75–83). Thorofare, NJ: Slack.

Parmelee, P. A., Katz, I. R., & Lawton, M. P. (1989). Depression among institutionalized aged: Assessment and prevalence estimation. *Journal of Gerontology: Medical Sciences, 44,* M22–M29.

Propost, L. R. (1980). A comparison of the cognitive restructuring psychotherapy paradigm and several spiritual approaches to mental health. *Journal of Psychology and Theology, 8,* 107–114.

Radloff, L. S. (1977). A self-report depression scale for research in the general population. *Applied Psychological Measurement, 1,* 385–401.

Reardon, J. P., & Tossi, D. J. (1977). The effects of rational stage directed imagery on self-concept and reduction of psychological stress in adolescent delinquent females. *Journal of Clinical Psychology, 33,* 1084–1092.

Riccio, C. M., Nelson, D. L., & Bush, M. A. (1990). Adding purpose to the repetitive exercise of elderly women through imagery. *American Journal of Occupational Therapy, 44,* 714–719.

Robinson, L. S., Berman, J. S., & Neimeyer, R. A. (1990). Psychotherapy for the treatment of depression: A comprehensive review of controlled outcome research. *Psychological Bulletin, 108,* 30–49.

Schultz, K. D. (1978). Imagery and control of depression. In J. L. Singer & K. S. Pope (Eds.), *The power of human imagination: New methods in psychotherapy* (pp. 281–307). New York: Plenum.

Smith, D. M. (1982). Guided imagination as an intervention in hopelessness. *Journal of Psychiatric Nursing and Mental Health Services, 20,* 29–32.

Stern, J. M., & Stern, B. (1989). Visual imagery as a cognitive means of compensation for brain injury. *Brain Injury, 3,* 413–419.

Teng, E. L., & Chui, H. C. (1987). The Modified Mini-Mental State (3MS) Examination. *Journal of Clinical Psychiatry, 48,* 314–317.

Thompson, L. W., Davies, R., Gallagher, D., & Krantz, S. (1986). Cognitive therapy with older adults. In T. Brink (Ed.), *Clinical gerontology* (pp. 245–279). New York: Haworth.

Yesavage, J. A., Brink, T. L., Rose, T. L., Lum, O., Huang, V., Adey, M. B., & Leirer, V. O. (1983). Development and validation of a geriatric depression screening scale: A preliminary report. *Journal of Psychiatric Research, 17,* 37–49.

CHAPTER 8

Psychotherapeutic Interventions with Older Adults in Outpatient and Extended Care Settings

LARRY W. THOMPSON
DOLORES GALLAGHER-THOMPSON

The focus of this chapter is a brief description of several predominant psychotherapeutic techniques that have been modified for use with elderly depressed patients living in the community, along with a few lesser known but promising approaches for working with depressed elders in extended-care settings. A thorough and scholarly review of literature on the efficacy and outcomes of these various approaches (which is beyond the scope of this chapter) can be found in Gallagher-Thompson and Thompson (1995).

PSYCHODYNAMIC PERSPECTIVES

Although Freud maintained that psychodynamic therapy was not appropriate for elderly people (because it was too late for them to work through issues and make changes), psychodynamically oriented clinicians were among the first to modify and apply therapeutic principles to elders both in the community and in extended-care settings. There are at least three different perspectives within the psychodynamic tradition: (1) Some thera-

Note: This research was supported in part by grant MHR01-37196 to L.W. Thompson, principal investigator.

pists focus on developmentally oriented issues in late life; (2) others focus on changes in the self due to negative life events; and (3) still others emphasize the interplay of intrapsychic processes (Newton, Bauer, Gutmann, & Grunes, 1986). In general, these theoretical and clinical positions share some similarities. All, however, emphasize the importance of internal psychological processes in coping with late-life problems, believing that the outcome of late-life challenges depends on how early developmental issues were resolved. They also have in common a belief that negative life events foster the reemergence of unresolved conflicts which were handled by reasonably intact defenses during early adulthood.

Both the content and the process of psychodynamic treatments are often different for older patients and younger, middle-aged patients (Silberschatz & Curtis, 1991). Themes of grief and fear of death and sickness occur much more often, as do guilt and despair over past failures. Supportive therapy may also be incorporated into the dynamic therapy in order to help shore up previous defenses and improve self-esteem. The focus of therapy is typically on the relationship between therapist and patient, and how that is a microcosm for other current (and past) relationships; it is believed that understanding and working through key interpersonal conflicts will reduce symptoms and improve quality of life. Psychodynamic therapists generally take a more active stance with an older adult than they do with a younger patient, they pay more attention to age-related problems and they are less formal; all this often strengthens the relationship between patient and therapist. There is greater flexibility in the duration and frequency of sessions. Increased contact with the patient's family and other professionals involved with the patient occurs much more often than it does in working with young adults. Also, crises frequently occur, which require changes in strategy to support and assist patients in coping, before other, more typical aims of therapy can be addressed.

Use of the "life review" is one variant of psychodynamic therapy that has received considerable attention in recent years. It is consistent with Erikson's theoretical work (1982) describing a specific developmental task of later life, normally to resolve the conflict between ego integrity and despair. This unique conflict of later life requires that elders find meaning in their life even when the situations and relationships that once gave it meaning are no longer available. One's perception of being generative during the late-adult years facilitates this ability to find meaning and greatly enhances self-worth. Butler (1963) first described the life review as an intervention strategy. He viewed life review as "a naturally occurring universal mental process characterized by the progressive return to consciousness of past experiences, and particularly the resurgence of unresolved conflicts'' (p. 66). Older people typically ask existential questions such as "Who am I?" and "How did I live my life?" If the answers to these questions are generally positive, a sense of ego integrity (rather than despair) will result. Life review techniques include imagery, guided recollection, and written or spoken autobiographical exercises; these can be used in both group and individual settings. Life review programs are popular with well elders but also can be very effective when used with institutionalized elderly people, particularly in a group format. When there is little else that is positive in one's life, reflection on past good deeds, and public recognition, and the like can often be extremely helpful in bolstering one's feelings of self-worth.

COGNITIVE-BEHAVIORAL PERSPECTIVES

In most cognitive and behavioral approaches, there is little emphasis on exploring intrapsychic processes; however, there is a great deal of emphasis on forming a strong collaborative working relationship between the therapist and the patient, which is pivotal to the development of new skills for coping with life stresses. Most cognitive-behavioral (CB) approaches were developed from conceptual models that emphasize the interrelationship of physical, cognitive, behavioral, and affective processes in reacting to and coping with environmental events. For example, a negative event might occur that affects one's thoughts, which in turn affect one's mood, which in turn might affect one's behavior. Frequently, this can become a circular process in which any one of the components might have a negative or positive impact on any other. Thus, the more negatively one thinks, the more negatively one feels and the less likely one is to engage in pleasant activities; this makes one's mood even more negative, and that again decreases activity, etc. The therapist using cognitive or behavioral models (or both) then targets thoughts and behaviors as points of entry in this circular process, in order to treat affective disorders—most notably depression and anxiety disorders, for which these models were specifically developed.

Figure 8.1 shows four components that are critical to therapy in CB approaches. First, patients must learn to *monitor* carefully what they are doing and what is happening around them in real-world situations. They must learn to pay attention to their mood, their thoughts, and their behaviors, so that they can appreciate the interconnection among these and other real-world events.

Second, therapist and patient must work collaboratively to *set goals*, both short-term and long-term, that they hope to achieve during the course

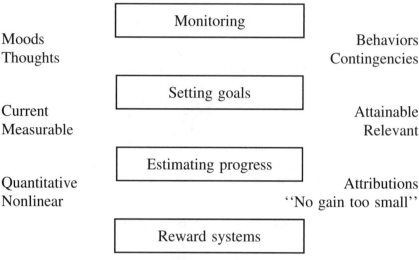

	Monitoring	
Moods		Behaviors
Thoughts		Contingencies
	Setting goals	
Current		Attainable
Measurable		Relevant
	Estimating progress	
Quantitative		Attributions
Nonlinear		"No gain too small"
	Reward systems	

FIGURE 8.1 Cognitive-behavioral perspectives.

of therapy. Such goals should be measurable, so that progress in therapy can be assessed. They also ought to be attainable, so that patients can have some assurance of success as a result of their efforts. To increase the likelihood of some resolution to the patients' problems, the goals should be current and relevant to the primary complaints.

Third, the therapy must include strategies for *estimating progress*. It is most helpful if these strategies can be quantitative. This enables patients to detect even small gains and provides a basis for the therapist and patient to make attributions about the patient's improved efficacy.

Fourth, the use of *rewards* for making changes increases the probability that any improvements will persist and encourages patients to continue trying to reach their goals.

A number of therapeutic techniques fall within the CB framework. In our work with elderly depressed patients, we have focused on cognitive therapy as described by Beck and his associates (Beck, Rush, Shaw, & Emery, 1979), and behavioral therapy as developed by Lewinsohn and his colleagues (Lewinsohn, Biglan, & Zeiss, 1976). We use either approach or both approaches with an individual patient, depending upon the patient's characteristic pattern of coping with stress, the general nature of the patient's problems, and the goals formulated collaboratively by patient and therapist at the outset of treatment. A fuller description of our approach with depressed elders can be found in Thompson et al. (1991) and Gallagher-Thompson and Thompson (1992).

COGNITIVE THERAPY

The cognitive approach emphasizes that depression is likely to occur when individuals develop a negative view of the self, the future, and the current situation. Typically these negative perceptions occur as a result of characteristic distortions of incoming information or unhelpful patterns of thinking. For example, the glass is never half-full but always half-empty. We refer to these as dirty tricks that we play on ourselves. Burns (1989) has described at least 10 of these, which he refers to as "unhelpful thinking patterns." Two examples of such patterns that occur regularly in elders are "all-or-nothing" thinking and jumping to conclusions:

- *All-or-nothing thinking.* In this kind of distortion, people classify features of their environment into two distinct categories—either good or bad. Whatever a situation might be, it is typically conceptualized by the patient as being either all-black or all-white, with no shades of gray. A common example of this in an elderly person would be: "The only way I can be happy is to have everything as it used to be—my job back, my children at home, etc. Without all this, nothing else can be meaningful." Another example involves declining performance: "I can't do things as well as I used to. Therefore I'm really of no use to anyone." This is a variation of another theme: "Unless I do something perfectly, I'm a failure."
- *Jumping to conclusions.* In this pattern, people are likely to put a negative construction on a series of events, even if there is no real evidence to support that construction, and then proceed to plan future actions on the basis of this premise. "Mind reading" is one variation of this pattern: People assume that someone else won't like them or won't like what they have to offer; consequently, they won't make an effort to state their position or even, at times, to make contact with others. A common variant of this pattern implicates ageism: "They think I'm too old to fit in at their get-together." "My son wouldn't accept my idea because he thinks I'm out of it." In another variant, patients view a possible negative outcome as an already established fact. Here again, ageism often plays a role: "If I go down there to find out about my license, I'll just get a runaround. When you get old, they just don't try to help you."

Cognitive therapy targets these unhelpful thinking patterns as factors in the development of mood disorders, and therefore a substantial component of therapy is focused on modifying such patterns. A first step is to have patients learn to monitor their thoughts in situations where their mood has changed for some reason. A helpful tool in this process is the "daily thought record" (DTR). Table 8.1 shows a completed 5-column DTR. The number of columns can vary, depending on the sophistication of the patient and on what the therapist is trying to accomplish at a given stage of therapy. Using only a 3-column DTR may be a good way to introduce the technique of monitoring thoughts. A DTR helps patients begin to focus on the thoughts that occur when they are feeling down, see the connection between these thoughts and their emotions, and identify unhelpful thinking patterns. It also sensitizes them to the idea of quantifying their thoughts and feelings—an important first step in learning how to modify both.

Once patients learn to monitor their negative thoughts and identify their unhelpful thinking patterns, the next step is to help them develop ways to challenge their negative thinking. There are many different strategies one might use, which are described in detail by others (Beck et al., 1979; Burns, 1989). Two that we have found particularly helpful with many older patients are "examining the evidence" and "experimenting":

• *Examining the evidence.* Rather than assume that a negative construction is true, the patient asks specific questions to challenge that construction and also lists specific evidence that disproves it. For example, when elderly people make an error on a task, they may conclude that they are no longer capable of doing anything right. This, obviously, would be a very depressing thought. When that thought occurs, then, a person might ask, "Is this really true all the time? Are there times or situations when I do things well?" If the person can momentarily assume an objective attitude and address the question by listing things he or she has done successfully, that will help counteract the negative construction.
• *Experimenting.* In this technique, patients are asked to do an experiment to test the validity of their negative thoughts. They are encouraged to assume a scientific attitude, momentarily, and to try to be objective in collecting data relevant to their negative assumptions. For example, if they think that they will not fit in at a social gathering, because of their age or their lack of social skills, they are encouraged to attend anyway, and to attempt to interact with other guests for the sake of collecting information about what happens. In this way, they may obtain data to refute their negative assumption. If the negative assumption is upheld, they will probably get data that can help them plan constructive behavioral changes for future social situations.

Once again, a DTR can be a useful tool for illustrating the effectiveness of learning to counteract negative thoughts that occur in emotionally

TABLE 8.1 Daily Thought Record: Jane Doe, Widow, Age 60, in Poor Health

(1)	(2)	(3)	(4)	(5)
Describe the situation or event that led to your negative feelings.	What are your unhelpful thoughts? What does this situation mean to you? How strongly do you believe in these thoughts (from 0 to 100%)?	What are you feeling (sadness, anger, anxiety, etc.)? How strong are these emotions (from 0 to 100%)?	Please challenge your negative thoughts and replace them with more helpful and adaptive thoughts.	Now, how strongly do you believe in your original negative beliefs from (0 to 100%)?
Date 6/15 Alone in my home after returning from dinner with Steve; reflecting a lot on the past.	If I need someone, Steve is the only one who will help me. I'm not sure how I really feel about him, though. Since my husband's death, I don't know if it's possible for me to have another close relationship with anyone. (90% belief)	Lonely: 80% Anxious: 70% Sad: 70% Trapped: 55%	Steve *isn't* the only one: I have my daughter in New York. (That's far away, but we talk a lot on the phone and I know she'd come out on short notice if I really needed her.) I also have Jewell and Elsie right here. There are others that I just don't know well enough yet. I don't have to be feeling so alone or so trapped.	Lonely: 40% Anxious: 30% Sad: 25% Trapped: 10%

Note. Ratings for intensity: 0% = not at all; 100% = completely

(0 to 100%)?Trapped: 10%charged situations. Note that in column 4 of Table 8.1, the patient challenges the negative thoughts listed in column 2 with more rational reconstructions. Then, in column 5, the patient reassesses the intensity of her feelings. In this particular example, the strength of the negative feelings decreased substantially when the patient challenged her original thoughts. Experiencing this type of success can be very encouraging to patients, in that it provides them with several tools to use to reduce the intensity of their negative affect. The example also shows the value of learning to think of feelings in quantitative terms, rather than simply as being present or absent (in an "all or none" sense).

BEHAVIOR THERAPY

Other methods that we use frequently stem from Lewinsohn's model, which holds that depression occurs when individuals have much too little pleasure in their lives or far too much unpleasantness (or both). Thus, increasing the amount of pleasure in a person's life can reduce depression. This approach is usually very appropriate for elders who are severely depressed. It is also easily modified for patients with some cognitive impairment.

Essentially, patients must first learn to monitor their moods and begin to note life events, situations, and activities that might be affecting their moods from day to day. The next step is to identify activities that are feasible on a regular basis and that might give the patient some pleasure or satisfaction. A vacation trip to France might lift a patient's spirits but may not be practical, whereas for a patient who is socially isolated, beginning to meet regularly with a former friend for coffee or a snack might indeed be practical and might be done often enough to affect the patient's mood. We have found that the Older Persons' Pleasant Events Scale (OPPES; Gallagher & Thompson, 1981) can be a helpful tool for highlighting appropriate categories of pleasant activities from which specific events can be identified in collaboration with the patient. This scale contains 66 activities that are frequently rated as pleasant by elderly community residents and are also usually easy to do. Examples are: "Looking at clouds." "Seeing beautiful scenery." "Reading a good book." "Having people show an interest in what I say." "Listening to music." The scale requires people to indicate how frequently they do each of the activities listed, and how pleasurable each might be (whether or not they have actually done it in the past month).

Once an appropriate list of activities—known as pleasant events, or PEs—is agreed upon (usually about 6 to 10 can be listed), patients are encouraged to do several of these daily, or as often as possible. They also continue to monitor their mood, so that a graph can be constructed showing coincident changes in PEs and mood. Such graphs are typically very compelling: Patients can understand and accept the relationship between PEs and mood. This "Aha!" effect usually heightens patients' motivation for finding ways to increase the frequency of pleasurable events or decrease unpleasant events in the future. Much of the remainder of therapy focuses on teaching the patient techniques for doing this, or developing ways of coping with stresses that might be preventing pleasurable activities.

In general, the cognitive and behavioral perspectives both emphasize the acquisition of new skills for dealing with stressful life situations. As in any other type of learning situation, the development of new techniques for minimizing psychological distress can be enhanced by following certain systematic principles. In Table 8.2 we give several concrete suggestions for increasing the likelihood that older adults will learn the skills being presented in therapy. These suggestions are particularly relevant for older persons who are frail or who are experiencing some cognitive impairment.

TREATMENT OF DEPRESSION IN LONG-TERM CARE PATIENTS

Application of cognitive and behavioral principles can also be very effective in treating depression (and related negative affects such as anxiety and frustration) in long-term care patients. Typically, such treatment strategies rely heavily on personnel within the long-term care setting as therapeutic agents in the treatment process.

TABLE 8.2   Maximizing Learning Opportunities

---

1. Present material in several modes—say it, write it, demonstrate it.
2. Have the client repeat it in his or her own words, to clarify misconceptions and improve mutual understanding.
3. Have the client keep a record of what takes place in therapy:
    Tape sessions.
    Write down homework assignments.
    Give client a folder, to keep papers organized.
    Encourage the client to keep a "therapy log."
4. Repeat as often as necessary. (Avoid labeling the client as "resistant" if he or she forgets.)
5. Help the client plan environmental memory "prompts":
    Use the folder—always keep it in the same place.
    Link assignments to events that occur on a regular basis.
    Have the client prepare signs and post them in obvious places.

A Pleasant Events Schedule

For example, Teri and colleagues have developed an outpatient program in which family caregivers are trained to identify and implement a very specific behavioral approach for reducing depression in patients with Alzheimer's disease. This approach is very appropriate for use with other demented patients as well, both in their homes and in institutional settings (Teri, Logsdon, Wagner, & Uomoto, 1994).

Typically, this approach helps both the demented patient and his or her primary family caregiver. It grew out of Lewinsohn's "pleasant events" model, but it has an added feature: Patient and caregiver are encouraged to do *shared* pleasant activities which can enhance their relationship and lessen the caregiver's sense of being burdened and helpless. As in the "basic model," moods and frequency and enjoyability of activities are tracked, in order to increase the frail elder's rate of engagement in pleasant activities.

The cornerstone of the approach is use of a Pleasant Events Schedule (PES) specifically designed for patients with Alzheimer's disease (Teri & Logsdon, 1991). This 53-item questionnaire is completed primarily by the caregiver, but whenever possible with the patient's input—particularly on the "enjoyability" ratings. Many caregivers report that just filling out the PES often gives them ideas for activities they had forgotten about, or did not realize the patient would still find pleasurable, such as reviewing old photo albums or going for a brisk walk. Repeated use of this questionnaire as the patient changes over time can help the caregiver keep discovering appropriate activities even when the patient's impairment worsens. This helps keep both in better spirits. Besides using this with patients and families, we have trained the staff in the nursing home of our medical center to administer this measure to residents, and to complete it themselves on the basis of observation and questioning. We have found it an easy, practical way to identify enjoyable activities, reducing depressive symptoms in the residents.

A Multifaceted Approach

A second approach to treating depression in long-term care settings was developed and evaluated by a clinical research group at Vanderbilt University (Ray, Meador, Taylor, Gallagher-Thompson, & Thompson, in press). This is a multifaceted approach involving nursing home residents, their families, and the staff of the facility, who work to reduce depression in frail elders with physical or cognitive impairments. Their therapy expands Lewinsohn's basic model to the nursing home setting, and there is a detailed manual describing the intervention process (which is available from the authors on request). Their strategy significantly involves the staff and emphasizes ways to improve communication and interaction between staff and residents.

Table 8.3 shows the steps involved in this type of treatment program. Initially, a therapist works collaboratively with the depressed patient and appropriate staff members, orienting them to the treatment model and identifying recurring activities and events that are pleasant and unpleasant for a particular patient. Pleasant and unpleasant events are then monitored to obtain baseline frequencies and to determine the antecedents and consequences of targeted events. Consultation with staff and patient is held to identify significant problem areas amenable to change. Feasible plans for change are initiated with the staff's assistance. Finally, evaluations are completed to determine whether the plan should be modified.

Table 8.4 shows baseline data on depression and key somatic morbidity for two of the depressed nursing home residents for whom data were collected in the Vanderbilt research program. Table 8.5 lists the actual interventions used with each of these residents, and Table 8.6 reports changes in depressive symptoms and overall functioning for the same two patients over a 3-month treatment period.

Overall, these data indicate that there was a 45% decrease in depression scores from baseline to conclusion of treatment. Also, by the end of the active phase of therapy neither of these two cases (nor other patients enrolled in the treatment program) met the formal diagnostic criteria for major depression. Cooperation by the staff was very high: It is noteworthy that 94% of the planned interventions for patients in this study were implemented. From this, the Vanderbilt team concluded that systematic application of this enhanced behavioral therapy is effective and clearly has a place in the long-term care setting.

Simulated Presence Therapy

Two other approaches are less widely used but seem to be promising methods for managing depression in extended care settings: Simulated

TABLE 8.3   Steps in Behavioral Therapy in a Nursing Home

1. *Preparation* of staff for the behavior therapy process
2. *Measurement* of baseline frequency of pleasant and unpleasant events and behavior problems
3. *Identification* of primary problems amenable to change
4. *Institution* of feasible plan for change
5. *Evaluation* of the effect of the plan

TABLE 8.4   Example of Staff-Assisted Behavioral Therapy in a Nursing Home: Baseline Diagnostic Evaluation

Age/sex	Mini-Mental Status	Geriatric Depression Scale	Hamilton Rating Scale for Depression	Depression history	Medications	Key Somatic Comorbidity
Patient 1. 84/M	22	17	17	Nervous breakdown, 1960; many consults	Imipramine (300 mg); lorazepam (2 mg); temazepam (15 mg)	S/P TURP, Foley catheter
Patient 2. 91/F	15	21	13	Denied	Isosorbide dinitrate, carbidopa, levadopa	Urinary and bowel incontinence, bedridden, Parkinson's disease

Presence Therapy and music therapy (discussed below). Simulated Presence Therapy was originally designed by a relative of a patient with dementia to reduce the patient's agitation and other disruptive behaviors in the home. It is a novel combination of cognitive and behavioral features that is well described by Woods and Ashley (1995). Essentially, this technique uses selected memories to calm patients, help engage them in mentally stimulating activity, and provide some pleasure in their lives. Favorite past memories of people and events are determined through consultation with family members. These are then recorded on audiotape by a close family member whose voice is quite familiar. The tape might start by saying, "Hi, George. This is William, your older brother. Boy, we had some good times together! Remember the time when we went to Uncle Clyde's and he let you drive the tractor? You were so proud sitting at that steering wheel, and I . . . " This one-sided but personalized "conversation" is played for the patient, who uses an auto-reverse player with a headset. It has been described as at least temporarily effective in improving mood, particularly with more demented patients (Camber et al., 1996).

Individualized Music Therapy

Finally, individualized music therapy is an effective approach that has not been studied a great deal, but that some research (at least) has found

TABLE 8.5   Example of Staff-Assisted Behavioral Therapy in a Nursing Home: Interventions

	Event	Planned intervention	Result/frequency
Patient 1	Loss of privacy from catheter (*u*)	1. Obtain portable leg bag	Obtained
	Wearing own clothes (*p*)	2. Dress in clothes from home	2–3 days/week
	Looking at photos (*p*)	3. Ask family to bring photos	Done
	Talking about past (*p*)	4. Engage in reminiscence with staff	2–3 days/week
	Forgetting things (*u*)	5. Remind patient of what he can remember	3–5 days/week
	Seeing children (*p*)	6. Arrange visit with child	One visit
	Having visitors (*p*)	7. Arrange weekly visits	Done
Patient 2	Reading (*p*)	1. Ophthalmologic examination	Done
		2. Obtain new glasses	Done
		3. Construct bed shelf	Done
	Listening to music (*p*)	4. Obtain tape player	Done
		5. Arrange hearing evaluation	Not done
	Unpleasant interactions with staff (*u*)	6. Assign favorite nurse more	Done
	Not being changed as needed (*u*)	7. Reduce time for changes	Done
	Physical affection (*p*)	8. Increase affection	3–5 days/week
	Seeing children (*p*)	9. Arrange visits	Two visits

Note: *p* = pleasant; *u* = unpleasant

to be a viable form of treatment for depressed patients, and possibly also for patients with combined depression and dementia. One controlled study of the effects of music therapy on older adult outpatients who were diagnosed with a major or minor depressive disorder was recently completed by Hanser and Thompson (1994). In this study, a series of planned "active listening" sessions were developed for each patient after consultation concerning his or her specific preferences in music. In one treatment condition, the music therapist went to the patient's home to conduct the

TABLE 8.6   Example of Staff-Assisted Behavioral Therapy in a Nursing Home: Change in Symptoms and Severity Over Time

	Hamilton Rating Scale for Depression			Global Assessment Scale		
	Baseline	Week 8	Week 12	Baseline	Week 9	Week 12
Patient 1	17	5	0	45	75	80
Patient 2	13	8	8	45	55	60

sessions. In the second treatment condition, the music therapist visited the home on one occasion to familiarize the patient with the music materials and tape recorder, and then telephoned weekly to discuss the music sessions with the patient. Results from these two groups were compared with a delayed-treatment control group. Both treatment groups showed a substantial decline in depression when compared with the control group; there was no statistically significant difference between the treatment groups. These data suggest that music therapy might be a useful strategy for frail elders who are unable to come to a clinic for treatment. These results need replication in a nursing home setting, but (as noted above) they are clearly promising and suggest a cost-effective way to improve quality of life for many older adults. Although controlled studies with dementia patients are lacking, numerous vignettes in our setting (as well as other institutional settings) strongly suggest that music therapy can be effective in reducing depression in cognitively impaired patients in long-term care.

This brief, selective review should encourage the reader to utilize a variety of existing psychotherapeutic interventions with frail and cognitively impaired elderly people, according to the patient's needs and capabilities. At present, the most widely used methods derive from psychodynamic and cognitive-behavioral perspectives, but newer approaches are being developed and implemented as well. Future research in this very exciting and fast-growing field also needs to address issues of cultural diversity in long-term care settings. At present, so little research has been done on this topic that virtually no intervention studies have included culturally diverse patients and staffs. Yet the growing minority population in the United States, and the increasing longevity of elderly people in minority groups, makes this a topic deserving of future research attention (Yeo, 1990).

REFERENCES

Beck, A. T., Rush, J., Shaw, B., & Emery, G. (1979). *Cognitive therapy of depression.* New York: Guilford.

Burns, D. D. (1989). *The feeling good handbook: Using the new mood therapy in everyday life.* New York: Morrow.

Butler, R. N. (1963). The life review: An interpretation of reminiscence in the aged. *Psychiatry, 26,* 65–76.

Camber, L., Ooi, W., Hurley, A., Ashley, J., Woods, P., Volicer, L., & Odenheimer, G. (1996). Methods to evaluate on audiotape intervention for Alzheimer's patients. *Gerontologist, 36,* 7–8.

Erikson, E. H. (1982). *The life cycle completed.* New York: Norton.

Gallagher, D., & Thompson, L. W. (1981). *Depression in the elderly: A behavioral treatment manual.* Los Angeles: University of Southern California Press.

Gallagher-Thompson, D., & Thompson, L. W. (1992). The older adult. In A. Freeman & F. Dattilio (Eds.), *Comprehensive casebook of cognitive therapy* (pp. 193–200). New York: Plenum.

Gallagher-Thompson, D., & Thompson, L. W. (1995). Psychotherapy with older adults in theory and practice. In B. Bongar & L. E. Beutler (Eds.), *Comprehensive textbook of psychotherapy* (pp. 359–379). New York: Oxford University Press.

Hanser, S. B., & Thompson, L. W. (1994). Effects of a music therapy strategy on depressed older adults. *Journal of Gerontology, 49,* P265–P269.

Lewinsohn, P. M., Biglan, T., & Zeiss, A. (1976). Behavioral treatment of depression. In P. Davidson (Ed.), *Behavioral management of anxiety, depression, and pain* (pp. 91–146). New York: Brunner/Mazel.

Newton, N. A., Brauer, D., Gutmann, D. L., & Grunes, J. (1986). Psychodynamic therapy with the aged: A review. *Clinical Gerontologist, 5,* 205–229.

Ray, W., Meader, K. G., Taylor, J. A., Gallagher-Thompson, D., & Thompson, L. W. (in press). Behavior therapy for major depression in nursing home residents: Model description and feasibility study.

Silberschatz, G., & Curtis, J. T. (1991). Time-limited psychodynamic therapy with older adults. In W. Myers (Ed.), *New techniques in the psychotherapy of older patients* (pp. 95–108). Washington, DC: American Psychiatric Press.

Teri, L., & Logsdon, R. (1991). Identifying pleasant activities for individuals with Alzheimer's disease: The Pleasant Events Schedule–AD. *Gerontologist, 31,* 124–127.

Teri, L., Logsdon, R., Wagner, A., & Uomoto, J. (1994). The caregiver role in behavioral treatment of depression in dementia patients. In E. Light, G. Niederehe, & B. D. Lebowitz (Eds.), *Stress effects on family caregivers of Alzheimer's patients* (pp. 185–204). New York: Springer.

Thompson, L. W., Gantz, F., Florsheim, M., Delmaestro, S., Rodman, J., Gallagher-Thompson, D., & Bryan, H. (1991). Cognitive-behavioral therapy for affective disorder in the elderly. In W. Myers (Ed.), *New techniques in the psychotherapy of older patients* (pp. 1–20). Washington, DC: American Psychiatric Press.

Woods, P., & Ashley, J. (1995). Stimulated presence therapy: Using selected memories to manage problem behaviors in Alzheimer's disease patients. *Geriatric Nursing*, *16*(1), 9–14.

Yeo, G. (1990). *Ethnicity and nursing homes: Review and suggested components for culturally sensitive care*. Working Paper Series No. 9. Stanford, CA: Stanford Geriatric Education Center.

CHAPTER 9

Psychotherapy in Residential Settings: Preliminary Investigations and Directions for Research

DEBORAH W. FRAZER

Few studies have been conducted on psychotherapy with the elderly. Indeed, many of the randomized, controlled studies of psychotherapy specifically exclude elderly subjects. Weissman and Myers (1979) noted that all 17 therapy outcome studies that they reviewed excluded elderly subjects. A decade later, a landmark study by the National Institute of Mental Health (NIMH) on the effectiveness of therapy in the treatment of depression (Elkins, Shea, Watkins, & Imber, 1989) excluded subjects over age 60.

It is known that the prevalence (Parmelee, Katz, & Lawton, 1989) and incidence (Parmelee, Katz, & Lawton, 1992a) of psychiatric disorders in long-term care facilities is exceedingly high. Yet until 1990, when changes were made in Medicare reimbursement for mental health services and in nursing home regulations regarding mental health care (OBRA, 1987; 1989; 1990), psychotherapy was rarely available to residents of long-term-care facilities. Now that reimbursement is available, practitioners are rapidly expanding their services into long-term care facilities. It is critical that this burgeoning practice be informed by clinical research.

A handful of investigators have systematically explored outcomes of therapy with the elderly over the last decade. Teri, Curtis, Gallagher-Thompson, and Thompson (1994) summarized the empirical findings on the use of cognitive-behavior therapy with depressed older adults. Niederehe (1994) reviewed the quantitative research on psychodynamic (including interpersonal therapy), psychoeducational, and reminiscence–

life review therapy with older adults. These authors conclude that there is evidence that cognitive-behavioral and psychodynamic therapies are both effective and equivalent modalities, and that therapeutic gains are sustained at follow-up. However, the studies reviewed generally had to do with elderly people who lived in the community, were cognitively intact, and were physically healthy. To date, there have been no randomized, controlled therapy outcome studies on elderly people who are depressed, physically or mentally frail, and living in residential facilities.

In contrast to therapy outcome studies, several investigations have been made of the therapy process. These studies have focused largely on the low rates of use of services by older consumers (Knight, 1985–1986; Lasoski & Thelen, 1987; Lundervold, Lewin, & Bourland, 1990). Others have looked at dropout rates (Mosher-Ashley, 1994; Pruchno, Boswell, Wolff, & Faletti, 1983; Trepka, 1986). Although a few of these studies have included frail elders living in residential facilities among their subjects, none has specifically focused on this population and its unique concerns.

THREE STUDIES OF PSYCHOTHERAPY IN RESIDENTIAL CARE

This chapter presents three preliminary investigations of the process and outcome of psychotherapy, conducted at the Philadelphia Geriatric Center with residents of nursing homes and senior apartments. This work, in combination with work done on psychotherapy with older adults living in the community, helps us conceptualize the therapeutic process with elderly people in residential facilities. These concepts, in turn, will, it is hoped, provide the basis for further clinical research with this population.

STUDY 1: SOCIAL SKILLS TRAINING

Bellack and his associates have developed an efficacious treatment modality targeting the poor social skills of schizophrenics (Bellack & Hersen, 1978). Known as *social skills training*, this modality has also proved effective with a variety of other disorders and populations (Bellack, Hersen, & Himmelhoch, 1983; Donahoe & Driesenga, 1988). Social skills training is a focused behavioral training strategy designed to teach specific skills needed to deal with problematic social situations. In accordance with principles of modeling and rehearsal, each skill is broken down into specific steps, and group members observe and participate in role playing incorporating each step. A social skills training session consists of: establishment of the rationale for learning the skill; presentation of the steps in a skill; role playing by two group leaders to model the skill; role playing with each group member; and feedback from the group after each episode of role playing.

Social skills training seems to be a promising approach for geriatric residents of nursing homes. A nursing home is an intensely interpersonal environment, with residents sharing intimate spaces, such as bedrooms and bathrooms, that were once private. In addition, residents are faced with many unfamiliar staff members who provide care and control the details of their lives. Newly admitted residents are particularly vulnerable to anxiety and depression associated with navigating in a new and complex interpersonal world. Interpersonal conflict is frequently reported among staff and residents; and among residents—especially roommates.

Social skills training has the potential to ease interpersonal tensions among residents, and between residents and staff; it may also promote a sense of personal efficacy and psychosocial well-being. Previous research using social skills training with nursing home residents (Fernandes-Ballesteros, Isai, Diaz, Gonzalez, & Sonto, 1988; Praderas & MacDonald, 1986) targeted the same skills used in work with other populations and may, therefore, have been limited by their failure to tailor the content and structure of the intervention to this particular population.

In the first of the three preliminary investigations presented in this chapter, Frazer, Winter, and Bellack (1993) developed a three-stage social skills program whose purpose was to determine the feasibility of using this well-established therapeutic technology with nursing home residents. The first stage was designed to determine empirically the major social requirements and difficulties of nursing home residents. The second stage involved testing an assessment battery. The third stage was a small pilot intervention study.

In the first stage of the study, semistructured interviews with 45 residents and 36 staff members elicited 63 unduplicated specific examples of interpersonal problems encountered in the nursing home. These problems were then sorted into categories by staff psychologists, who determined which social-skill deficiency contributed to the problem and what steps would lead to mastering that skill. This process identified three broad domains (each with several subdomains) of social skills that are most relevant in the nursing home environment. Table 9.1 summarizes the identified domains. Asterisks indicate which subdomains occurred most often.

The investigators used the most frequently cited subdomains of social skills to form a treatment module consisting of: a definition of the skill

TABLE 9.1   Social Skills in the Nursing Home

I.	Making friendships; conversational skills
a.	Initiating conversations
b.	Joining/maintaining conversations
c.	Ending conversations
*d.	Interacting with people with handicaps
e.	Selecting a potential friend
II.	Positive assertion
*a.	Requesting information or help
*b.	Expressing affection and positive feelings
c.	Following up on requests
d.	Giving and receiving compliments
III.	Negative assertion
*a.	Compromising and negotiating
b.	Refusing unreasonable requests
c.	Responding to negative comments
d.	Requesting new behavior from others
*e.	Expressing negative emotions

*Items marked with an asterisk occurred most frequently.

and an explanation of why it is useful; examples of problem situations where the skill is lacking; and the steps involved in mastering the skill.

In the second stage, the investigators tested Bellack's Social Problem Solving Assessment Battery (Bellack, Morrison, Mueser, Wade, & Sayers, 1990) for use with this population. On initial review of that set of four instruments (Self Evaluation Task, Response Evaluation Task, Role Play Task, and Response Generation Task) only two (Role Play Task and Response Generation Task) seemed relevant and feasible for this population. After pilot testing, the Role Play Task was also discarded, as the nursing home residents had unexpected and considerable difficulty with role playing.

In the third stage, 20 residents participated in a pilot social skills training intervention. Subjects were residents who had been admitted to the nursing home within the previous 6 months and who displayed either of two qualifying conditions: (1) they suffered from at least mild depression, determined by a Geriatric Depression Scale (GDS) score greater than 10 (Yesavage et al., 1983); or (2) they displayed adjustment difficulties as reported by nursing staff, with cognitive status either intact or borderline, demonstrated by a score of 10 or less on the Modified Blessed Dementia

Rating Scale (Blessed, Tomlinson, & Roth, 1968; Fuld, 1978). Mean age was 85 years.

Social skills training was conducted with small groups of experimental subjects twice a week for 5 weeks. Each session lasted 1 hour and focused on one social skill, with each skill receiving attention for two sessions. The original study design called for training in two groups, with one group serving as a waiting-list control. However, because of high attrition due to illness and death, the crossover design was modified. Twelve residents who completed training and participated in both a pretest and a posttest were considered the experimental group; the eight who completed two assessments but did not receive the training were defined as a comparison group. Because this was a pilot study, statistical analysis was not considered appropriate; however, comparison of group means yielded mildly encouraging results. Specifically, the experimental group demonstrated somewhat improved scores on three of the four domains of the Response Generation Task and even stronger improvement on the fourth domain ("Fit"). The comparison group, in contrast, showed small declines on the first three domains and a sharper drop on the fourth. These trends were all in the expected direction. No group differences were evident on the measures of general adaptation; this suggests either that training effects were not generalizing, or that the measures were not sensitive enough to pick up effects.

The experience with this pilot study suggests that interpersonal problems and problems with social skills are salient in nursing home life, that the Response Generation Task is the most useful assessment tool from the Social Problem Solving Assessment Battery, and that measures of general adaptation to the nursing home may be too broad to indicate effects of interventions. The investigators noted that social skills training is heavily dependent on role playing, a task which seemed particularly difficult for this population and whose utility is therefore limited. In a follow-up study, Winter (1993) suggested that the source of difficulty with hypothetical situations, such as role playing, may lie in deficits in the capacity for abstraction. This approach is also severely limited by the availability of participants because of the criteria for inclusion in the study. In the rather large nursing home ($N = 550$) used in this study, an initial pool of 111 potential subjects finally yielded only 12 persons who were appropriate in terms of the cognitive, medical, and sensory status; who were depressed; and who were willing to participate in 10 group sessions. The requirements of this approach may be far too rigorous to be useful in a more typical, smaller nursing home. On a more positive note, those who participated thoroughly enjoyed the sessions; the group was still continuing 1 year after the study in a less structured format.

STUDY 2: THE EXPERIENCE OF PSYCHOTHERAPY FOR THE OLD-OLD

Controlled prospective psychotherapy studies in a nursing home population such as study 1 above are few; but to this author's knowledge, there
has been only *one* study using a qualitative methodology to explore
residential clients' perceptions of their experience of psychotherapy. In the
second preliminary investigation presented here—study 2—Ruckdeschel
(1994) reported on a retrospective analysis of the reported experience of
psychotherapy for 10 elderly residents of a nursing home and senior
apartment complex. Such a study suffers from a lack of randomization,
a lack of control over variables, and a lack of standardized measures.
However, as an intermediate step between clinical anecdote and controlled
study, it serves to raise important questions and generate hypotheses to
be tested in future studies.

The average age of the clients in this study was 87.2. Three resided
in the nursing home and seven in the senior apartments. All had participated
in at least five sessions of therapy and had completed therapy within the
last 12 months. All had a diagnosis of major or minor depression; all had
cognitive status in the intact or borderline range (Blessed Test < 10).
The method of investigation consisted of chart reviews, interviews with
residents, and interviews with the therapist.

Through the interviews, Ruckdeschel attempted to address the following
questions: (1) How was the experience of being in treatment perceived
by the residents? (2) To what extent did they understand the purpose of
the psychotherapy they received, and the reason they were designated as
in need of such services? (3) Was the psychotherapy perceived by client
and therapist as effective in treating the depression?

The following are examples of the interview questions, which were
presented in a semistructured format: Why was (the therapist) coming to
see you? How was the therapy helpful? (Or: Why was it not helpful?)
Did (the therapist) help you solve problems? What kind of problems?
What were the solutions? Did you feel that (the therapist) understood you?

Among other findings, Ruckdeschel reported that four residents thought
the therapy was clearly helpful; three gave conflicting or ambiguous
answers regarding its helpfulness; and three stated clearly it was not
helpful. All three of those who felt that it was not helpful had a secondary
diagnosis of personality disorder. Two thirds of the "ambiguous" subjects
had borderline cognitive impairment and may have had trouble recalling
the experience with clarity.

Residents described the depressing impact of physical illness, pain,
sensory deficits, and loneliness; and the limitations of psychotherapy in
"helping" with those very real issues.

Generally, the residents perceived the therapist not as a teacher, guide, or expert but as an advocate and supporter. Therapy was seen as an opportunity to ventilate fears, disappointments, concerns, and joys. Therapy was perceived as helping people come to accept and cope with the negative aspects of their lives. The therapists were perceived, for the most part, as warm and caring persons who had a genuine interest in and respect for the clients. These clients felt that they had been treated like whole persons with a lifetime of experiences—something that they may not feel often enough in an institutional or medical setting.

Of all the beneficial factors, the one cited most frequently and most strongly was the relationship with the therapist. The specific content of the therapy, the techniques used, the skills learned—all were either not remembered or not seen as important. This finding is consistent with therapy outcome studies with younger adults showing equivalent efficacy across modalities, perhaps because of "nonspecific" or "common" factors. Prominent among these factors is the therapist-patient relationship (Lambert & Bergin, 1994).

This study was limited by its retrospective nature, its reliance on recall in a cognitively questionable population, the small size of its sample, and the fact that to some extent the clients' current depression could have influenced their recall of therapy interactions. However, even with these limitations, the study points up at least three important issues: the perceived value of therapy, even when the client is cognitively compromised; the perceived importance of the relationship rather than the specific modality or techniques; and the clients' report that although therapy did not necessarily "cure" their depression, it helped them learn to cope with and adapt to their losses.

STUDY 3: PSYCHOTHERAPY PERSISTENCE IN RESIDENTIAL SETTINGS

In a recent report, Mosher-Ashley (1994) analyzed therapy dropout rates and associated factors among 180 clients, some living in the community and some in nursing homes; they were aged 60–98 and were receiving therapy from a community mental health center. Mosher-Ashley found greater perseverance in therapy among the nursing home clients: 69.8% attended 20 or more sessions. Among clients living in the community, only 35.7% attended 20 or more sessions. Similarly, only 16.2% of the clients in long-term care terminated therapy after 4 or fewer sessions, whereas 35.7% of community clients terminated it after 4 or fewer sessions. The general adult population has been reported to have a dropout rate of 50% to 60% by the fourth session (Kelner, 1982).

Mosher-Ashley found that dropout patterns were unrelated to source of referral, diagnosis, education, age, or gender. Reimbursement was similar for all subjects, with third-party payments eliminating all or most direct fees from the clients. Receiving therapy at home, stated religious beliefs, and residence in a nursing home were associated with persistence in therapy.

A retrospective review, such as Mosher-Ashley's, is fraught with methodological problems. However, such naturalistic studies on the prevalence and distribution of disorders and the use of therapy can serve as a starting point for controlled, randomized studies on the process and outcome of therapy with frail elders residing in long-term care facilities.

In that context, Frazer and Parmelee (1994) reported the third preliminary investigation presented here, study 3: a retrospective analysis of ongoing individual psychotherapy services provided over a 2-year period to people who lived in nursing homes and senior apartments. These researchers looked at the distribution of psychiatric disorders, changes in diagnosis over the course of therapy, and natural patterns of perseverance, termination, and use through the following questions:

1. Of all those residential clients who received psychotherapy services in 1992 to 1993, what was the distribution of diagnostic categories? How is this distribution similar or different for nursing home residents versus apartment residents? How is this distribution similar to or different from that previously reported for these populations?

2. As these clients continue in therapy, do the therapists change their diagnoses? How? Is the pattern the same for nursing home versus apartment residents?

3. What is the natural pattern of use of therapy, persistence, and termination for all clients? Does this pattern differ between nursing home clients and apartment clients? Is it similar to or different from that reported by Mosher-Ashley?

4. Are we able to predict diagnostic changes from initial cognitive or functional status? Is age, gender, or diagnosis associated with persistence and termination?

Subjects

In the first set of analyses (questions 1 and 3), data were available on a total of 329 persons, of whom 208 resided in a nursing home and 121 in senior apartments. These represented men and women over age 65, who had been referred for mental health services, evaluated by both a psychologist and a psychiatrist, and recommended for individual therapy (with or without psychotropic medication), and who had participated in at least one therapy session during 1992–1993. The total number of sessions provided for all subjects over a 2-year period was 3,529. The second set of analyses (question 2) used a subset of therapy participants from 1992 alone. The third set of analyses (question 4) used a subset of participants who had also agreed to be subjects in a study by the National Institute of Mental Health Clinical Research Centers (NIMH-CRC). Thus for these subjects the researchers had available a battery of assessments of psychological function.

Intervention

Individual therapy was provided by the Clinical Psychology Department staff, consisting of six doctoral-level and three master's-level psychologists, and three postdoctoral fellows. Therapists were trained in cognitive-behavioral, psychodynamic, and behavior therapy. They used the approach or approaches that seemed to best fit each client and each referral problem. Trainees received individual weekly supervision; all licensed staff participated in weekly peer supervision.

Results

As can be seen in Table 9.2, diagnostic distribution at the beginning of the therapeutic intervention was weighted toward minor depression. This category, representing 42.9% of all clients, includes the *DSM-III-R* (Amer-

TABLE 9.2   Diagnostic Distribution of Clients ($N = 329$)

	Location					
	Nursing home		Apartments		Total	
Diagnosis	N	(%)	N	(%)	N	(%)
Minor depression	83	(39.9)	58	(47.9)	141	(42.9)
Major depression	38	(18.3)	24	(19.8)	62	(18.8)
Dementia with depression	34	(16.4)	8	(6.6)	42	(12.8)
Dementia	17	(8.2)	12	(9.9)	29	(8.8)
Dementia with delirium	6	(2.9)	2	(1.6)	8	(2.4)
Anxiety	5	(2.4)	8	(6.6)	13	(4.0)
Conduct	10	(4.8)	3	(2.5)	12	(4.0)
Other	15	(7.2)	6	(5.0)	21	(6.4)
Total	208	(100)	121	(100)	329	(100)

TABLE 9.3   Diagnostic Reclassifications of Clients (*N* = 297)

| | Location | | | | | |
| | Nursing home | | Apartments | | Total | |
Diagnosis	*N*	(%)	*N*	(%)	*N*	(%)
Severer (minor to major depression)	8	(3.9)	2	(2.2)	10	(3.4)
More prolonged (adjustment disorder to dysthymia or prolonged depressive reaction)	21	(10.2)	6	(6.5)	27	(9.1)
More dementia (major or minor depression) to dementia with depression	11	(5.4)	3	(3.3)	14	(4.7)
Unchanged	165	(80.5)	81	(88.0)	246	(82.8)
Total	205	(100)	92	(100)	297	(100)

ican Psychiatric Association, 1987) diagnoses of adjustment disorder with depressed mood; adjustment disorder with depressed and anxious mood; dysthymia; and depression not otherwise specified. Of all clients seen, 18.8% were diagnosed with major depression; 12.8% with dementia with depression; 8.8% with dementia, uncomplicated; 2.4% with dementia with delusions; 4% with anxiety disorders (including adjustment disorder with anxious mood and generalized anxiety disorder); 4% with conduct disorders (adjustment disorders with disturbance of conduct and adjustment disorder with disturbance of emotions and conduct); and the remaining 6.4% with an assortment of other diagnoses, including atypical psychosis, residual schizophrenia, organic affective syndrome, organic personality syndrome, and organic delusional syndrome.

Diagnostic distribution in the nursing home was similar to the total, but the apartment clients had a higher proportion of minor depression (47.9%) than the nursing home (39.9%), and lower levels of dementia with depression (6.6% vs. 16.4%). Conduct disorders were slightly more prevalent in the nursing home (4.8% vs. 2.5%). Anxiety diagnoses were somewhat more prevalent in the apartments than in the nursing home (6.6% vs. 2.4%).

To show change in diagnosis over time, Table 9.3 indicates the diagnostic reclassifications made by therapists as the clients continued in therapy over 1 year's time. Although most diagnoses were unchanged, shifts did occur toward greater severity of depression and toward perception of the depression as associated with a dementia. In addition, changes in diagnoses reflected a longer duration of depression, as adjustment disorders (which are by definition limited to 6 months) were changed to dysthymia (which by definition must be present for a minimum of 2 years) or prolonged depressive reaction. These shifts were particularly noticeable in the nursing home setting.

To address use of therapy and persistence-termination, Table 9.4 shows the distribution of all clients over a 2-year period ($N = 329$) by length of therapy and diagnostic category. Most striking is the high percentage of terminations after one to two sessions (35.8%). Of most concern is that of all major depressives who begin therapy, fully 29% terminate after one to two sessions. Patterns were similar in the nursing home and apartments, but the termination rate for major depression was particularly high in the nursing home (37%). Some 17.9% of all clients persist in long-term therapy (more than 21 sessions): 18.8% in the nursing home and 16.5% in the apartments.

A subset of these clients, who had also participated in a NIMH-sponsored Clinical Research Center study, were further analyzed ($N = 241$) to examine factors associated with early termination (i.e., two sessions or fewer). Chi-square χ^2 analysis yielded no significant effect for diagnosis, $\chi^2 = 3.01$, not significant (NS); or gender, $\chi^2 (1) = 2.00$, NS. Analysis of variance showed that termination was not associated with age, activities

TABLE 9.4   Distribution of All Clients by Diagnosis and Length of Therapy ($N = 329$)

Diagnosis	Number of Sessions					
	1–2	3–10	11–20	21–30	31+	Total
Minor depression	50	42	19	7	23	141
Major depression	18	27	8	2	7	62
Dementia with depression	16	12	6	4	4	42
Dementia	14	12	2	0	1	28
Dementia with delusion	5	2	0	1	0	8
Anxiety disorders	2	7	1	2	1	13
Conduct disorders	8	3	0	1	1	13
Other	5	9	2	1	4	20
Total	118	114	38	18	41	329
	(35.8%)	(34.6%)	(11.6%)	(5.5%)	(12.5%)	(100%)

of daily living (ADL; Physical Self-Maintenance Scale, Lawton & Brody, 1969), length of stay, or mood (Geriatric Depression Scale, GDS; Yesavage et al., 1983) at the beginning of therapy. However, initial cognitive status, as evidenced by performance on Fuld's (1978) modification of Blessed, Tomlinson, and Roth's Information-Memory-Concentration test (Blessed test, 1968), was significantly associated with early termination, $f(1,128) = 4.60$, $p < .035$, with poorer cognitive performance associated with early termination.

Discussion

Regarding diagnostic distribution, initial diagnostic categories among clients were closer to a 2:1 ratio of minor depressives to major depressives than the 3:1 ratio reported for this institution's general nursing home population (Parmelee, Katz, & Lawton, 1989). This suggests that disproportion in identification, referral, or initiation of therapy is appropriately weighted toward severer pathology.

Regarding change in diagnoses during the course of therapy, the reclassifications reflected greater severity, duration, and association with cognitive decline. These shifts, particularly evident in the nursing home population, reflect the sober reality of therapists and clients confronting chronic deterioration of medical and cognitive conditions.

Regarding persistence-termination patterns, Frazer and Parmelee's findings were distinctly different from those of Mosher-Ashley, with only 18% of their clients continuing past 20 sessions (compared with Mosher-Ashley's 70%) and 36% of clients dropping out after two sessions (compared with Mosher-Ashley's 16% after four sessions). Reimbursement mechanisms were similar for the two groups and would not account for the differences. This may reflect a difference in populations or in referral patterns. Mosher-Ashley's pattern prompted her to express concern about the ethical issues of treating a "captive population." Frazer and Parmelee's pattern suggests a need to encourage more engagement in the therapeutic process.

Patterns of use of therapy revealed a small subset (9%) of clients receiving 38% of the sessions. When clients receiving 31 or more sessions ($N = 41$) are compared with clients receiving 3 to 10 sessions ($N = 114$), the long-term clients have a higher percentage of minor depression (56% vs. 37%), and lower percentages of major depression (17% vs. 24%) and dementia-related disorders (12% vs. 23%). The group of users of intensive therapy needs further analysis. Is there a secondary personality disorder? Does this group require a larger "dose" of therapy? Do these clients or their therapists have difficulty terminating? Finally, regarding prediction of early termination, poorer cognitive status was identified as an associated factor. What is still unknown is whether early termination is initiated by a therapist who has determined that potential benefit is limited or by a cognitively compromised client who is dissatisfied with the service.

RESEARCH AND PRACTICE PROCEDURES FOR RESIDENTIAL SETTINGS

ISSUES

Preliminary investigations of each of these three issues—social skills training, experience of therapy, and patterns of therapy—raise other important issues regarding the design of controlled, randomized studies in residential settings for the elderly.

In the general population, studies of therapy process and outcome have developed substantially over the last 15 years. Large-scale, multisite studies, such as the NIMH Treatment of Depression Collaborative Research Program (Elkin et al., 1989) have spurred the development of therapy manuals, use of standardized diagnoses and procedures, identification of appropriate outcome measures, and delineation of "specific" and "nonspecific" effects. Current trends in managed care have added an emphasis on measures of consumers' satisfaction and fast relief of symptoms.

Can we translate the methodology from these therapy studies to the nursing home environment? Our preliminary investigations suggest that modifications of criteria for inclusion and exclusion predictor variables, therapeutic procedures, and outcome variables are called for in this population.

Older adults in residential facilities differ in several key respects from the younger depressives in studies of treatment outcomes. First, these "residential elders" are likely to have comorbid physical disease—often, of one or more chronic, deteriorating conditions. These comorbid conditions have complex interactions with depression and its treatments (Robinson & Rabins, 1989). Second, residential elders often are suffering from comorbid cognitive impairment; these are also typically chronic and progressively deteriorating conditions. Modifying treatments and measuring outcomes are complicated by cognitive deterioration over the course of treatment. Third, elders in residential settings are often facing a host of "adjustment" issues—relocation; roommates; and loss of home, spouse, friends, independence, and function—and must face these losses simultaneously or in quick succession. These stressors, in turn, interact with physical and mental disease. Fourth, elders in residential settings are often receiving a complex web of care and medications from a variety of disciplines and family members. It becomes difficult to isolate positive or negative effects of any one therapeutic regimen on the comorbid conditions. Fifth, residential elders are rarely self-referred for treatment of depression. More typically, a nurse, physician, or family member identifies the depression and requests treatment for the elder. Self-report measures may not fully or accurately reflect either the manifestations of the depression or its resolution.

STEPS IN PLANNING PSYCHOTHERAPY

How, then, does one disentangle the web of symptomatology, etiology, treatment, and outcome of interrelated cognitive, affective, and physical disease processes, each of which may be chronic and progressively deteriorating? The following procedure, developed from experience with the preliminary research reported above, suggests guidelines for the delivery of mental health services as well as a starting point for clinical research on the efficacy of those services.

Evaluate Cognitive Status

Cognitive status has been shown to be associated with depression (Parmelee, Katz, & Lawton, 1992b; Teri & Reifler, 1987), and increased depression to be associated with cognitive impairment. Cognitive status has also been identified as a key component in therapy modality, with modifications of behavioral programs (Teri & Logsdon, 1991), grief work (Lichtenberg, 1994), and other therapies (Knight, 1986) described. Research is needed to explicate the relationship between cognition and therapy outcome. Preliminary research reported above showed a positive association between poor cognition and early termination. Is this the patient's decision, the therapist's decision, or a mutual decision? When, if ever, is someone "too demented" to show effects of individual "talking" psychotherapy? Can one develop a modular therapy protocol, with more cognitive supports added as the client becomes more impaired (e.g., use of a therapy "log"; more environmental cues; more concrete, direct language; integration of modalities, such as art, music, or movement, into the more traditional talking therapy)? What aspects of patient education should be in a therapy protocol for clients in the early stages of dementia?

Evaluate Physical Medical Status, Including Medications

Clearly, in good service delivery, all medical conditions and medications should be handled to optimize mental as well as physical functioning. As with clients in the early phase of dementi, depressed medically ill residents may need an educational component to their therapy, regarding their particular disease or diseases, treatments, and prognosis. At times, simply knowing that a particular disease is frequently accompanied by depression (e.g., Parkinson's disease) may help the patient, family, and staff cope with the issues. Close coordination with the primary care team is essential. Medically ill and dying patients are perhaps most susceptible to Frank's (1961) "demoralization" triad: hopelessness, powerlessness, and isolation. Visits from the family, the clergy, or volunteers may be sufficient support to allow some patients to cope with demoralization; but other patients may need psychotherapy to prevent their demoralization from developing into despair and clinical depression. Research is needed on how specific diseases or their stages are related to therapy outcome, and whether there is a cumulative effect on depression and its treatment from the number of diseases and the severity of their symptoms.

Evaluate Functional Status

Medical, functional, and affective status have been shown to be closely correlated in the frail elderly population, with functional status being a strong predictor of mortality and morbidity (Parmelee, Katz, & Lawton, 1992). As with medical status, research is needed on the relationship of functional abilities to therapy outcome and whether there is a cumulative effect of functional disability on depression and its treatment.

Evaluate for Personality Disorder

Costa and MacCrae (1986) have demonstrated the stability of personality into late adulthood. Others have suggested that poor personality functioning may accompany depressive affect and interfere with treatment outcome (Thompson, Gallagher, & Czirr, 1988). Alexopoulous and his colleagues (Abrams, Alexopoulos, & Young, 1987; Alexopoulos, Young, Meyers, & Abrams, 1988) have introduced a distinction between early- and late-onset depression, with early onset presumably more highly associated with personality features. As neither medication nor psychotherapy has been shown to alter character structure in older adults, personality features may be a constraint on the effectiveness of therapy. For example, intriguing new findings suggest that among demented residents, certain positive personality features as rated by relatives (extroversion and task-centered assertiveness) declined with increasing cognitive impairment, whereas hostility and neuroticism remained stable (Van Haitsma, Lawton, & Klapper, 1995). Extroversion was positively correlated with positive affect and participation in activities, whereas hostility was related to expression of anger. Further research is necessary to identify the contributing role of personality features to depressive symptomatology among both cognitively intact and demented individuals, and the degree to which personality may limit the efficacy of treatment. Clinically, an individual with a personality disorder may require further modification of a basic protocol, with more involvement of the care team and family.

Evaluate for Anxiety

Parmelee, Katz, and Lawton (1993) have noted the strong association of anxiety with depression in a geriatric residential population. Individuals whose depression has a strong component of anxiety may need a medication protocol that targets reduction of anxiety. Similarly, the psychotherapy protocol may need to include techniques for reducing anxiety, before therapy for depression can be used. Research may explicate the interaction of anxiety with depression in treatment outcome, with the possibility that higher anxiety may be associated with lower efficacy of treatment.

Evaluate for Behavioral Difficulties

In the highly controlled, highly public world of the nursing home, behavioral problems are often the first observed and most bothersome manifestation of depression. "Inappropriate" behaviors—sexual, aggressive, agitated, or "demanding"—are frequently cited as the reason for a mental health referral. Such behavioral difficulties may arise because of poor environmental contingencies or an individual's cognitive problems as well as depression (Lichtenberg, 1990). They may also become manifest when there is a poor fit between a person's motivational style and the environmental opportunities (O'Connor & Vallerand, 1994). Careful evaluation of the relative contributions of the person and the environment to the behavioral outcome should determine the target or targets of change. If the behavioral difficulties are thought to be primarily depression-related, research is needed to determine if the treatment of an underlying depression resolves the behavioral difficulties, or if additional, behaviorally focused treatment modules are necessary.

Evaluate for Interpersonal Difficulties

Interpersonal difficulties, defined in the broad terms of Klerman, Weissman, Rounsaville, and Chevron's Interpersonal Therapy (1984), include role disputes, role transitions, social isolation, and grieving. From the preliminary investigations reported above on social skills and the experience of therapy, all issues that were identified by residents, staff, and therapy clients can be subsumed under one of the four domains described by Klerman et al. It has been shown (Elkin et al., 1989) that the interpersonal therapy (IPT) framework provides an appropriate way to classify depressive symptomatology, assess its severity, and treat it psychotherapeutically. Clinical research is needed to test the IPT therapy protocol in a geriatric residential setting and to develop modifications, if necessary. Specifically, IPT for the frail elderly may need to be somewhat more concrete and directive, adapted for sensory impairment; and the examples in the therapy manual may need to be tailored for a residential rather than a community environment.

Outcome Measures

It may be that improving the symptoms of depression is not a realistic goal when the depression is in the context of chronic, progressive, debilitating conditions. For example, the more "biological" or "vegetative" signs of depression may be linked to the physical disease as well as to the depression itself. Although suicidal ideation or intent, or actual attempts at suicide, should be triggers for active treatment, "hopelessness" or "thoughts of death" may be appropriate responses, not pathological symptoms, when the patient is near the end of life. This is not to imply a stance of therapeutic nihilism, but to suggest that goals and, therefore, outcome measures must be tailored for this population. The preliminary investigations reported above on the experience of therapy suggest that traditional outcome measures, such as self-reports of depression and checklists of symptoms, may not capture the perceived and self-reported value of therapy. Measures that capture the strengths of coping with and adapting to realistically negative events may better reflect the goals of treatment. These would include measures of adaptation, coping, self-efficacy, self-esteem, perceived meaningfulness, anxiety, and loneliness. Of interest from the perspective of policy is whether these proximal, individual measures of outcome relate to more distal system variables, such as demand on nursing or medical staff, medications or hospitalizations required, or intensity or amount of interpersonal conflict.

Nonspecific Treatment Factors

Frank (1961, 1973, 1982) has identified four nonspecific factors observed in virtually all effective psychotherapies: (1) an emotionally charged, confiding therapeutic relationship; (2) a designated healing setting; (3) a rationale for the patient's symptoms and recommended treatment, and (4) a treatment procedure that is believed by both patient and therapist to be efficacious in restoring health. Frank and Frank (1991) suggest that these nonspecific factors combat patients' feelings of demoralization.

The preliminary investigations cited above highlight the unique role of nonspecific factors in therapy with frail elders. Clearly, the therapeutic relationship, the healing setting, and the rationale for depressive symptoms are possible in the nursing home setting. However, the fourth factor (mutual belief in an efficacious procedure to restore health) is much more problematic in a chronically ill or dying population. Can one remain hopeless about restoration of physical health and function, and yet be "remoralized"? Using Frank's triadic concept of demoralization, the therapeutic procedure can address feelings of powerlessness and isolation, but it usually cannot induce hope of extrication from physical or functional distress. Frank's concept of remoralization through belief in the restoration of health was based on a different model: acute illness. In the long-term-care population, illness is more typically experienced as one or more chronic conditions, followed by death. For these patients, remoralization may be achieved through belief in a positive quality of life despite illness, followed by an "appropriate death." Adaptation and coping become the therapeutic strategies of choice (Levy, 1990; Taylor & Aspinwall, 1990). Clinical research with this population must address a way to maximize the power of nonspecific factors and specifically address the procedure and efficacy of "remoralization" in a chronically ill or dying population.

CONCLUSION

This chapter has used knowledge gained from three preliminary investigations of therapy with residential elders to outline key issues in the development of clinical procedures and research with this population. The design of such research must be multifactorial, including cognitive, medical, functional, psychiatric (affective, personality, and anxiety), behavioral, and interpersonal factors. Specific attention must be given to broadening outcome measures to include measures of adaptation and coping as well as symptoms of depression; and to include variables having an impact on the system as well as variables affecting the subject.

Whereas interpersonal therapy (ITP) appears to be an appropriate protocol for this population, the development of specialized procedures or modules may be necessary for clients who are cognitively impaired, have personality disorders, or are behaviorally disruptive. Nonspecific treatment factors may be unique (or nearly unique) in this population; further exploration of the role of "remoralization" is warranted.

In conclusion, the preliminary investigations cited here have begun a process of exploration of the process and outcome of therapy with residential elders. The time has now arrived for randomized, controlled clinical research in this relatively new and exciting area.

REFERENCES

Abrams, R., Alexopoulos, J., & Young, R. (1987). Geriatric depression and the DSM-III-R personality disorder criteria. *Journal of the American Geriatrics Society, 35,* 383–386.

Alexopoulos, G. S., Young, R. C., Meyers, B. S., & Abrams, R. C. (1988). Late-onset depression. *Psychiatric Clinics of North America, 11,* 101–115.

American Psychiatric Association. (1987). *Diagnostic and statistical manual of mental disorders* (3rd ed., rev.). Washington, DC: Author.

Bellack, A. S., & Hersen, M. (1978). Chronic psychiatric patients: Social skills training. In M. Hersen & A. S. Bellack (Eds.), *Behavior therapy in the psychiatric setting* (pp. 169–195). Baltimore: Williams & Wilkins.

Bellack, A. S., Hersen, M. G., & Himmelhoch, J. M. (1983). A comparison of social skills training, pharmacotherapy and psychotherapy for depression. *Behavior Research and Therapy, 21,* 101–107.

Bellack, A. S., Turner, S. M., Hersen, M., & Luber, R. F. (1984). An examination of the efficacy of social skills training for chronic psychiatric patients. *Hospital and Community Psychiatry, 35,* 1023–1028.

Bellack, A. S., Morrison, R. L., Mueser, K. T., Wade, J. H., & Sayers, S. L. (1990). Role play for assessing the social competence of psychiatric patients. *Psychological Assessment: A Journal of Consulting and Clinical Psychology, 2,* 248–255.

Blessed, G., Tomlinson, B. E., & Roth, M. (1968). The association between quantitative measures of dementia and of senile change in the cerebral gray matter of elderly subjects. *British Journal of Psychiatry, 114,* 797–811.

Brody, E., Kleban, M., Lawton, M., & Silverman, A. (1971). Excess disabilities of mentally impaired aged: Impact of individualized treatment. *Gerontologist, 11,* 124–133.

Burns, B. J., & Taube, C. A. (1990). Mental health services in general medical care and in nursing homes. In B. S. Fogel, A. Furino, & G. T. Gottlieb (Eds.), *Mental health policy for older Americans: Protecting minds at risk* (pp. 63–83). Washington, DC: American Psychiatric Press.

Byrne, K. J. (1984, November). *Psychotherapy with cognitively impaired older patients.* Paper presented at the annual meeting of the Gerontological Society of America, San Antonio, TX.

Costa, P. T., & McCrae, R. R. (1985). Hypochondriasis, neuroticism, and aging. *American Psychologist, 40,* 19–28.

Costa, P. T., & McCrae, R. R. (1986). Personality stability and its implications for clinical psychology. *Clinical Psychology Review, 6,* 407–423.

Donahoe, C. P., & Driesenga, S. A. (1988). A review of social skills training with chronic mental patients. In M. Hersen, R. M. Eisler, & P. M. Miller (Eds.), *Progress in behavior modification* (pp. 131–164). Newbury Park, CA: Sage.

Elkin, I., Shea, M. T., Watkins, J. T., Imber, S. D., Sotsky, S. M., Collings, J. F., Glass, D. R., Pilkonis, P. A., Leber, W. R., Docherty, J. P., Fiester, S. J., & Parloff, M. B. (1989). NIMH treatment of depression collaborative research program: General effectiveness of treatments. *Archives of General Psychiatry, 46,* 971–982.

Fernandes-Ballestros, R., Izai, M., Diaz, P., Gonzalez, J. L., & Sonto, E. (1988). Training of conversational skills with institutionalized elderly: A preliminary study. *Perceptual and Motor Skills, 66,* 923–926.

Frank, J. D. (1961). *Persuasion and healing.* Baltimore, MD: Johns Hopkins University Press.

Frank, J. D. (1973). *Persuasion and healing: A comparative study of psychotherapy* (2nd ed.). Baltimore, MD: Johns Hopkins University Press.

Frank, J. D. (1982). Therapeutic components shared by all psychotherapies. In J. H. Harvey & M. M. Parks (Eds.), *Psychotherapy research and behavior change* (pp. 5–37). Washington, DC: American Psychological Association.

Frank, J. D., & Frank, J. B. (1991). *Persuasion and healing.* Baltimore, MD: Johns Hopkins University Press.

Frazer, D. W., & Parmelee, P. A. (1994, November). *Psychotherapy within residential settings.* Paper presented at the annual meeting of the Gerontological Society of America, Atlanta, GA.

Frazer, D. W., Winter, L., & Bellack, A. (1993, November). *The transferability of schizophrenia assessment/treatment to depressed institutionalized elderly.* Paper presented at the annual meeting of Gerontological Society of America, New Orleans, LA.

Fuld, P. A. (1978). Psychological testing in the differential diagnosis of the dementias. In R. Katzman, R. Terry, & K. L. Bick (Eds.), *Alzheimer's disease: Senile dementia and related disorders* (pp. 185–193). New York: Raven.

Gottlieb, G. L. (1994). Barriers to care for older adults with depression. In L. S. Schneider, C. F. Reynolds III, B. D. Leibowitz, & A. J. Friedhoff (Eds.), *Diagnosis and treatment of depression in late life: Results of the NIH Consensus Development Conference* (pp. 377–396). Washington, DC: American Psychiatric Press.

Hussian, R. A., & Davis, R. L. (1990). *Responsive care: Behavioral interventions with elderly persons.* Champaign, IL: Research Press.

Ilardi, S. S., & Craighead, W. E. (1994). The role of nonspecific factors in cognitive—behavior therapy for depression. *Clinical Psychology: Science and Practice, 1,* 138–156.

Kelner, F. A. (1982). An evaluation of Jochim's PT scale in the prediction of premature termination from out-patient psychotherapy. *Journal of Clinical Psychology, 38,* 106–109.

Klerman, G. L., Weissman, M. M., Rounsaville, B. J., & Chevron, E. S. (1984). *Interpersonal psychotherapy of depression.* New York: Basic.

Knight, B. (1985–1986). Therapists' attitudes as explanation of underservice of elderly in mental health: Testing an old hypothesis. *International Journal of Aging and Human Development, 22,* 261–269.

Knight, B. (1986). *Psychotherapy with older adults.* Newbury Park, CA: Sage.

Lambert, M. J., & Bergin, A. E. (1994). The effectiveness of psychotherapy. In A. E. Bergin & S. L. Garfield (Eds.), *Handbook of psychotherapy and behavior change* (4th ed., pp. 143–189). New York: Wiley.

Lasoski, M. C., & Thelen, M. H. (1987). Attitudes of older and middle-aged persons toward mental health intervention. *The Gerontologist, 27,* 288–292.

Lawton, M. (1972). Assessing the competence of older people. In D. Kent, R. Kastenbaum, & S. Sherwood (Eds.), *Research planning and action for the elderly.* New York: Behavioral Publications.

Lawton, P., & Brody, E. (1969). Assessment of older people: Self-maintaining and instrumental activities of daily living. *Gerontologist, 9,* 179–186.

Levy, S. M. (1990). Humanizing death: Psychotherapy with terminally ill patients. In G. M. Herek, S. M. Levy, S. R. Maddi, S. E. Taylor, & D. L. Wertlieb (Eds.), *Psychological aspects of serious illness: Chronic conditions, fatal diseases, and clinical care* (pp. 185–213). Washington, DC: American Psychological Association.

Levy, S. M., Derogatis, L. R., Gallagher, D., & Gatz, M. (1980). Intervention with older adults and the evaluation of outcome. In L. W. Poon (Ed.), *Aging in the 1980's* (pp. 41–61). Washington, DC: American Psychological Association.

Lichtenberg, P. A. (1990). Reducing excess disabilities in geropsychiatric inpatients: A focus on behavioral problems. Mental health in the nursing home [Special issue]. *Clinical Gerontologist, 9,* 65–76.

Lichtenberg, P. A. (1994). *Psychological practice in geriatric long-term care.* New York: Haworth.

Lundervold, D., Lewin, L. M., & Bourland, G. (1990). Older adults acceptability of treatments for behavioral problems. *Clinical Gerontologist, 10,* 17–28.

Mosher-Ashley, P. M. (1994). Therapy termination and persistence patterns of elderly clients in a community mental health center. *The Gerontologist, 34,* 180–189.

Niederehe, G. T. (1994). Psychosocial therapies with depressed older adults. In L. S. Schneider, C. F. Reynolds III, B. D. Lebowitz, & A. J. Friedhoff (Eds.), *Diagnosis and treatment of depression in late life: Results of the NIH consensus development conference* (pp. 293–316). Washington, DC: American Psychiatric Press.

O'Connor, B. P., & Vallerand, R. J. (1994). Motivation, self-determination, and person-environment fit as predictors of psychological adjustment among nursing home residents. *Psychology and Aging, 9,* 189–194.

Omnibus Budget Reconciliation Act, Public Law 100-203. (1987). Washington, DC: U.S. Government Printing Office.

Omnibus Budget Reconciliation Act, Public Law 101-239. (1989). Washington, DC: U.S. Government Printing Office.

Omnibus Budget Reconciliation Act, Public Law 101-508. (1990). Washington, DC: U.S. Government Printing Office.

Parmelee, P. A., Katz, I. R., & Lawton, M. P. (1989). Depression among institutionalized aged: Assessment and prevalence estimation. *Journal of Gerontology: Medical Sciences, 44,* M22–M29.

Parmelee, P. A., Katz, I. R., & Lawton, M. P. (1992a). Incidence of depression in long-term care settings. *Journal of Gerontology: Medical Sciences, 47,* M189–M196.

Parmelee, P. A., Katz, I. R., & Lawton, M. P. (1992b). Depression and mortality among institutionalized aged. *Journal of Gerontology: Psychological Sciences, 47,* 3–10.

Parmelee, P. A., Katz, I. R., & Lawton, M. P. (1993). Anxiety and its association with depression among institutionalized elderly. *American Journal of Geriatric Psychiatry, 1*(1), 46–58.

Praderas, K., & MacDonald, M. L. (1986). Telephone conversational skills training with socially isolated, impaired nursing home residents. *Journal of Allied Behavioral Analysis, 19,* 337–348.

Pruchno, R. A., Boswell, P. C., Wolff, D. S., & Faletti, M. V. (1983). A community mental health program: Evaluating outcomes. In M. A. Smyer & M. Gatz (Eds.), *Mental health and aging: Programs and evaluations* (pp. 41–62). Newbury Park, CA: Sage.

Robinson, R., & Rabins, P. (1989). *Aging and clinical practice: Depression and coexisting disease.* New York: Igaku-Shoin.

Rovner, B. W., German, P. S., Brant, L. J., Clark, R., Burton, L., & Folstein, M. F. (1991). Depression and mortality in nursing homes. *Journal of the American Medical Association, 265,* 993–996.

Ruckdeschel, H. (1994, November). *Psychotherapy with the old-old: Ten case studies.* Paper presented at the annual meeting of the Gerontological Society of America, Atlanta, GA.

Sadavoy, J. (1987). Character disorders in the elderly: An overview. In J. Sadavoy & M. Leszcz (Eds.), *Treating the elderly with psychotherapy: The scope for change in late life* (pp. 175–229). Madison, WI: International Universities Press.

Smith, M. C., & Kramer, N. (1992, November). *Psychotherapy with persons with dementia.* Paper presented at the annual meeting of the Gerontological Society of America, Washington, DC.

Taylor, S. E., & Aspinwall, L. G. (1990). Psychosocial aspects of chronic illness. In G. M. Herek, S. M. Levy, S. R. Maddi, S. E. Taylor, & D. L. Wertlieb (Eds.), *Psychological aspects of serious illness: Chronic conditions, fatal diseases, and clinical care* (pp. 3–60). Washington, DC: American Psychological Association.

Teri, L., Curtis, J., Gallagher-Thompson, D., & Thompson, L. W. (1994). Cognitive/behavior therapy with depressed older adults. In L. S. Schneider, C. F. Reynolds, B. Lebowitz, & A. Friedhoff (Eds.), *Diagnosis and treatment of depression in late life* (pp. 279–292). Washington, DC: American Psychiatric Association.

Teri, L., & Gallagher-Thompson, D. (1991). Cognitive-behavioral interventions for treatment of depression in Alzheimer's patients. *The Gerontologist, 31,* 413–416.

Teri, L., & Logsdon, R. (1991). Identifying pleasant activities for Alzheimer's disease patients: The Pleasant Events Schedule—AD. *The Gerontologist, 31,* 124–127.

Teri, L., & Reifler, B. V. (1987). Depression and dementia. In L. Carstensen & B. Edelstein (Eds.), *Handbook of clinical gerontology* (pp. 112–119). New York: Pergamon Press.

Thompson, L. W., Gallagher, D., & Czirr, R. (1988). Personality disorder and outcome in the treatment of late-life depression. *Journal of Geriatric Psychiatry, 21,* 133–146.

Thompson, L. W., Wagner, B., Zeiss, A., & Gallagher, D. (1989). Cognitive-behavioral therapy with elderly stage Alzheimer's patients: An exploratory view of the utility of this approach. In E. Light & B. Lebowitz (Eds.), *Alzheimer's disease treatment and family stress: Directions for research* (pp. 383–397). Washington, DC: Department of Health and Human Services.

Trepka, C. (1986). Attrition from an out-patient psychology clinic. *British Journal of Medical Psychology, 59,* 181–186.

Van Haitsma, K. S., Lawton, M. P., & Klapper, J. (1995). *Continuity and context: The role of personality features in dementia.* Manuscript under review.

Weissman, M., Klerman, G., & Budman, S. (1983). *A manual for interpersonal counseling for stress and distress.* Unpublished manuscript, Yale University School of Medicine, Department of Psychiatry, Depression Research Unit, New Haven, CT.

Weissman, M. M., & Myers, J. K. (1979). Depression in the elderly: Research directions in psychopathy, epidemiology, and treatment. *Journal of Geriatric Psychiatry, 12,* 187–201.

Winter, L. W. (1993, November). *Cognitive egocentrism, social judgment, and cognitive impairments in the elderly.* Paper presented at the annual meeting of the Gerontological Society of America, New Orleans, LA.

Yesavage, J. A., Brink, T. L., Rose, T. L., Lum, O., Huang, V., Adey, M., & Leirer, V. O. (1983). Development and validation of a geriatric depression scale: A preliminary report. *Journal of Psychiatric Research, 17,* 37–49.

Part III

Implications for Policy
and Future Researach

CHAPTER 10

Gaps and Failures in Attending to Mental Health and Aging in Long-Term Care

GENE D. COHEN

F ailure to attend adequately to issues of mental health and aging in long-term care settings continues to be a pervasive, major public health problem. On the one hand, gaps and failures are perpetuated by denial (if not ignorance) of the prevalence of mental health problems and the possibility of promoting mental health. On the other hand, therapeutic as well as preventive strategies are undermined by misdiagnosis, and by misinformation about potential treatments.

The public and policy makers continue to perceive the need for nursing home placement, in particular, as governed by the magnitude of physical frailty. But this perception fails to account for the fact that any community has so many people with comparable physical diseases and disabilities who do not require nursing home care. This apparent paradox can be largely explained by the role of mental health problems that combine and synergize, negatively, with physical health problems, to the point that patients can no longer adequately cope and be cared for at home; they and their caregivers are overwhelmed by these combined physical and mental problems. Even when patients' mental health problems, ranging from chronic depression to schizophrenia, are treated in the community, these problems may still persist to varying degrees—just as many people who are treated for diabetes, hypertension, pulmonary, liver, or renal disease continue to suffer from these illnesses. These are the individuals whose need for long-term care and nursing home care is high, especially in later life; and these are the individuals who need combined physical and mental health interventions in long-term care settings. But in the overall plan for long-term care, often the mental health component is too little or is not there at all. This chapter examines various aspects of that issue.

TODAY'S PUBLIC POLICY DEBATES ON AGING AND THE MYTH OF TITHONUS

Among the current concerns about practice, research, and policy with regard to aging and older adults is to what extent the pursuit of quality of life will keep pace with the quest for longevity. What many policy makers fail to recognize is that, on the whole, the field of aging has come to terms with the tension between these two domains, developing overall plans and approaches predominantly focused on enhancing quality of life and increasing the "health span." Tension between quantity and quality of life is not new; indeed, it was reflected in the ancient Greek myth of Tithonus more than 25 centuries ago and still informs discussions in this area. Tithonus is a mortal who falls in love with Eos, the goddess of dawn. Being immortal, Eos is distraught to think that she will eventually outlive her lover, so she goes to the almighty Zeus, king of the gods, and asks him to bestow immortality on Tithonus. Eos has approached Zeus with some hesitation and trepidation, not knowing what his response might be. To her astonishment, Zeus grants her wish. But, alas, as scores of years go by, Eos realizes that while Zeus has granted her wish, he has left out one essential factor. Though Zeus has bestowed immortality on Tithonus, he has failed to give him eternal youth. Hence, Tithonus, to this day, grows older and older and more and more frail. The myth of Tithonus has thus served as a reminder to those who conduct research on aging that quality of life must be ensured before one becomes obsessed with increasing longevity.

LESSONS FROM ANTHROPOLOGY

Gaps and failures in long-term care can be an outcome of value judgments or perspectives influenced by assorted misconceptions and misinformation. Consider the view, periodically expressed, that in developing social policies for the older members of society, perhaps we could learn from approaches taken by ancient cultures and other species—as if this will reveal some primordial truth or insight and thus provide a beacon showing us what path to follow. Often such a view is a preamble to advocating "benign neglect" of the elderly—a rationalization based on stereotyped notions about legendary, heroic early cultures and primitive species that either actively or passively abandoned their oldest members for the good of the rest.

But such stereotypes are often based on apocryphal or atypical examples. Consider the behavior of an earlier human species often regarded as brutish—the Neanderthals. Anthropologic and archaeologic studies have found skeletal fossils of a significant number of Neanderthal bones showing no fractures, despite advanced osteoarthritis (Diamond, 1989). In that advanced osteoarthritis is associated with advanced aging, for these bones to have been without fractures, and to have reached that stage of disease, means that the Neanderthals must have either passively or actively protected and taken care of their older members. In other words, this species had a culture that, despite the demands of a sparse and hostile environment, cared for its elders.

THE NURSING HOME PARADOX

Irony has never been in short supply. Consider, for example, much of the Omnibus Budget Reconciliation Act (OBRA) legislation focused on nursing homes since the late 1980s. Detailed stipulations were delineated as to what should or should not be done if a mental health problem is diagnosed in evaluating individuals for nursing home placement. It was as if nursing homes were being viewed as settings that were inappropriate for persons with mental illness—or that if one had a *DSM* diagnosis (a diagnosis in the *Diagnostic and Statistical Manual of the American Psychiatric Association*, American Psychiatric Association, 1994) and received proper treatment, a nursing home would not be needed. As suggested earlier, what such perspectives fail to consider or understand is that even if individuals with mental illness receive the best mental health interventions possible, some of them may still need to be in nursing homes.

Even more fundamental is the fact that studies have shown that in many nursing homes, more than 90% of the residents have *DSM* diagnoses, among which depression is significant (Rovner, Kafonek, Filipp, Lucas, & Folstein, 1986). That is, research shows that for a nursing home resident a mental health diagnosis (among other diagnoses) is the *rule* rather than the exception. Denial of this reality is still prevalent, however, and, as a consequence, there is insufficient recognition of mental health problems in nursing home settings, or of the associated responsibility to develop effective mental health interventions there. This is both a paradox and a tragic irony of so much of the regulatory history of nursing homes–however well-intentioned the regulations may be.

THE INTERFACE OF MENTAL AND PHYSICAL HEALTH IN LATER LIFE

The emotional toll of depression on older adults is often trivialized (with various rationalizations like, ''Wouldn't you be depressed if you were old and in a nursing home?''), and thus the responsibility for dealing with it is dismissed. Similarly, the adverse impact of depression on physical health in later life is largely overlooked—despite the extensive literature from both psychosocial and psychoimmunologic studies showing that the influence of mental health on overall health is strongest in later life. The relationship between the two in long-term care is highlighted in nursing home studies looking at the influence of depression on mortality. Such studies have found that over a 12-month period patients with depression have nearly a 60% increase in mortality (Rovner et al., 1991). Studies of prolonged stress in relation to depression in people (typically older adults) who are caregivers for victims of Alzheimer's disease also reveal a marked negative effect of mental health problems on the course of overall health. These caregivers showed immunological changes, increased prevalence of physical illness, increased frequency of primary-care medical visits, and greater use of medications in general (Haley, Levine, Brown, Berry, & Hughes, 1987; Kiecolt-Glaser & Glaser, 1989). Failure to treat depression not only prolongs psychological suffering; it compromises physical health and recovery from physical illness.

ADVERSE EFFECTS ON FUNCTIONING: DEPRESSION VERSUS GENERAL MEDICAL DISORDERS

Those who trivialize the impact of depression on functioning should look at what has been reported on depression in major medical journals. Research on medical outcomes has found that depression and depressive symptoms have a worse effect on ability to carry out tasks, and on days spent in bed, than the following eight major general medical problems: hypertension, diabetes, advanced coronary artery disease, angina, arthritis, back problems, lung problems, and gastrointestinal disorder (Wells et al., 1989). Not only is the magnitude of the adverse effect of depressive disorder on functioning noteworthy; another noteworthy point is that depressive symptoms alone (i.e., subsyndromal depression) have a similarly negative effect on overall functioning.

A FAMOUS CASE FROM LONDON, 1843

Misunderstanding, if not denial, of both the nature of depression and its treatment in later life has interfered with the development of more informed policy addressing mental health needs and gaps. It was not until the late 1980s that Medicare partially liberalized coverage for mental health interventions, including psychotherapy for depression—despite the fact that case reports of its efficacy have been published and noted by the public for over 150 years.

Consider a case reported in England in 1843 (Cohen, 1993). It had to do with an elderly Londoner who had apparently been misdiagnosed for decades. Up until his later years, he was viewed simply as a mean-spirited misanthrope. He made the lives of all around him miserable. Things kept getting worse, and everyone missed the correct diagnosis: a chronic depressive disorder that had become more symptomatic in later life, was increasingly manifested behaviorally, and was acted out more through negative interactions with others. Then, however, according to the account, this man—remarkably—received an enlightened home visit by a multidisciplinary team (even though this was more than a century before the community health movement, with its emphasis on outreach). The team's interventions included the use of dream work (more than 50 years before Freud's classic work on *The Interpretation of Dreams*).

What Dickens was really conveying when he presented the case of Ebenezer Scrooge in 1843, in *A Christmas Carol*, was a fourfold message: (1) that depression takes an atypical course with aging; (2) that even chronic disorders respond to treatment in later life; (3) that psychotherapy is of value for depression in the aged, including the use of dream work; (4) that when you help older adults, it need not be at the expense of other age groups—witness the positive impact on the man's community, especially the family of his employee Bob Cratchit.

MYTHS ABOUT THE COST OF HEALTH CARE

President Kennedy once said that the great enemy of truth is often not lies—deliberate, contrived, and dishonest—but myths: persistent, persuasive, and unrealistic. That is proving true among American journalists and various politicians who persist in telling the American public that among patients in their last year of life, it is the elderly who receive the lion's share of health care resources and that their care is frequently futile, heroic, high-tech treatment that is robbing youth of their birthright.

There is no denying that health costs for the elderly are high. It is another matter, though, to single out the elderly in their last year of life and to assert that these costs are in large part attributable to them, or that such costs are high because of overutilization of aggressively, too often futile, interventions. One needs to distinguish between ''end of life'' costs in general from such costs for the elderly, and between low-tech or no-tech basic humane care in the last year of life as opposed to a no-holds-barred application of costly, questionable medical procedures. In fact, the costs of hospitals and physicians (expenses that reflect aggressive or heroic high-tech interventions) in the last year of life for people over age 80 are significantly *less* than costs in the last year of life for people age 65–79 or for people under age 65 (Cohen, 1994b; Scitovsky, 1988; Temkin-Greener, Meiners, Petty, & Szydlowski, 1992). What the research shows is that *functional status* rather than age influences the aggressiveness and expense of clinical interventions, and that such costs are greater per capita in the younger groups.

The debate on long-term health care is distorted by blurring the distinction between costs of physicians and hospitalization and the costs of humanistic care that alleviates suffering and provides comfort for the patient. The need for long-term-care insurance has to do with humane care rather than crisis medicine. Moreover, many interventions in long-term care settings—interventions that can make a difference by alleviating symptoms and suffering, increasing coping, and enhancing quality of life—are low-tech or no-tech. Not to overlook the obvious, most mental health interventions are low-tech or no-tech.

THE "GERIATRIC LANDSCAPE"

The term *geriatric landscape* refers to the growing number of sites where older persons both reside and receive treatment (Cohen, 1994c). A generation ago it was common to think that residential options for older persons typically represented a choice only between home and nursing home. Today, the choices are considerably more varied and are increasing—representing a new phenomenon in need of more research, innovative approaches to on-site services, and better information for deliberations about policy. In addition to home and nursing home, the geriatric landscape includes settings like congregate housing, assisted-living facilities, life-care or continuing-care communities, senior hotels, foster care, group homes, day care, respite care, and others—not to mention the growing diversity of retirement homes and communities. Meanwhile, the market-place has discovered this new landscape and is adding its own stamp, with hotels like the Marriott and Hyatt corporations applying their skills to the senior residential environment.

To a large extent, these new options have been developed in response to historically perceived problems of nursing homes as the only major alternative to one's home where both home life and help, as necessary, are available. As the saying went, "Nursing homes had two major problems: they too often provided neither good nursing nor a good home." At one level, the evolving geriatric landscape represents a constellation of new approaches to dealing with issues of nursing (e.g., disease and disability) and home (e.g., psychosocial opportunities and growth) for older adults at a growing number of increasingly diverse sites. Nursing homes themselves have improved significantly as part of this evolution: progress in the *nursing* component is reflected in the development of "teaching nursing homes," and advances in the *home* component are reflected in the growing sophistication of social programs and community connections that many nursing homes have developed. Depending on the specific setting within the broader landscape of different sites, the balance of attention between intervention for illness and promotion of health will vary.

To address the nursing side is to draw on knowledge from the field of health care; to address the home side is to draw on knowledge from the humanities. Moreover, these two elements intersect—at times being additive in their effects, at other times being synergistic. In a related sense, the nursing or health care component can benefit from involvement of a medical center; the home or humanities component can benefit from involvement of a university outside the medical center. Together, the two components—nursing and home, health and humanities—represent a challenge and an opportunity for a medical center and university to collaborate in order to foster, through research, new approaches aimed at better synchrony, if not synergy of the linkages between these core elements.

In summary, the geriatric landscape is a construct within which to examine the depth and breadth of human experience in later life. A health and humanities focus offers a design for dealing with not just the problems but also the potentials that can occur in later life—a way of approaching limitations that accompany disability as well as opportunities for new creative expression with growing old. The geriatric landscape, with its health and humanities orientation, is a construct designed to promote new thinking in research, practice, and policy relevant to aging and generational interchange. It also represents a construct within which to examine issues of mental health and aging in setting-specific contexts, taking into consideration not just acute problems but also problems requiring long-term attention. However, there has been too little attention of this sort—indicating an increasingly apparent gap in current community-based planning efforts.

MENTAL HEALTH ISSUES—CREATIVITY AND AGING

In considering the home and humanities aspects of the geriatric landscape, another gap becomes apparent—inadequate attention to human potential, including creativity, with aging. Not to recognize the prevalence and potential for creativity in later life is to not be aware of important opportunities for promoting mental health—opportunities related to life satisfaction, quality of life, sense of control, and self-esteem.

Typically, examples of creativity in later life are trivialized or dismissed as special cases—the exception rather than the general rule. Consider the case of folk art in America. In 1980, the Corcoran Museum of Art in Washington, DC, exhibited works of black artists identified in a study of 50 years (1930–1980) of folk art in the United States. One thing the researchers found was that nearly half of the outstanding folk art in America during that period had been created by artists who were members of racial and ethnic minorities, especially African Americans. (The works of black artists, in fact, were among the best.) What had not been described about these artists, but became apparent to people attending the exhibit, was that of the 20 artists in the show, 16 (80%) were age 65 or older, and 30% were age 80 or older (Cohen, 1994a; Livingston & Beardsley, 1980). Moreover, most of these artists had begun their work or first reached their mature phase only after age 65. Bill Traylor, whose work was featured on the cover of the catalog for the Corcoran show, and who had been born a slave, created his first painting at age 85.

With regard to creativity in later life, one contribution to the psychoanalytic literature has pointed out:

> With increasing years artists say they are "more open" to the nuances of internal chaos and pure intuition, to "conceiving," and to the "unfolding of the self" than to reinforcing the ascendancy of the ego's executive functions over the entire psychic apparatus. It is as if ego is expected to give up control from the top down for the rewards of a more wholeness-fostering dialogue with creative unconscious processes. (Maduro, 1974, p. 308)

Upon further examination of folk art in America, it becomes apparent that, independently of racial or ethnic background, folk art is dominated by older artist (Hartigan, 1991). Grandma Moses, for example, was a folk artist who began painting at age 78. That an entire field of art should be *dominated* by older artists illustrates poignantly that these people cannot be stereotypically dismissed as outliers or cases for ''Ripley's Believe It or Not.'' Folk art, too, provides a way to appreciate that marked creative potential in later life is found not just in the Picassos but in ordinary people as well.

CREATIVITY IN CONJUNCTION WITH LOSS ASSOCIATED WITH AGING

Having a physical illness, or even a mental illness, does not mean that opportunities for mental *health* are precluded. Problems and potentials can coexist; areas of illness and health, and decline and growth, occur together in the same individual, regardless of age. Such co-occurrence becomes apparent when we examine creativity in conjunction with loss in later life.

In ancient Greek mythology, the Theban Tiresius (a mortal) has the misfortune of seeing the goddess Athena while she is undressing to bathe. In a burst of rage, Athena impulsively blinds Tiresius. But Zeus takes pity on him, and replaces this loss of physical vision with great insight and prophetic powers that grow over the years and facilitated a long life for the seer. It is Tiresius, in his later years, who predicts the fate of Oedipus. (It is worth noting that the play about Oedipus was written by Sophocles in his eighth decade.)

The myth of Tiresius is reflected in the life and work of the poet and physician William Carlos Williams. In his sixties, Williams suffered a stroke that ended his practice of medicine, followed by a severe depression that required lengthy hospitalization. But he emerged from these losses to write some of his best poetry, including work at age 79 that led to a Pulitzer Prize. In his later years, Williams wrote poignantly about ''an old age that adds as it takes away,'' illustrating the human capacity to mobilize creative responses to crises throughout the life cycle. This capacity to develop new strategies for coping in response to loss in later life has enormous relevance, both for maintaining independence and for achieving rehabilitation; it permits a synergistic linking of treatment of problems that compromise functioning with development of new skills that promote adaptation, and this includes people in need of long-term care.

Awareness of the potential for new creative orientations psychodynami-cally mobilized in response to disease or disability associated with aging identifies a new pathway toward maximizing overall functioning and mental health in later life. Tapping into this creativity offers important opportunities for innovative clinical practice, new directions in research, and creative social policies relevant to older adults and the family as a whole.

THE SOCIAL PORTFOLIO

What can individuals themselves do to prepare for their own later life with regard to mental health as well as creativity? Although people are advised to plan for economic security for their future—to develop a balanced financial portfolio—too little attention is paid to developing a balanced "social portfolio" based on sound activities and interpersonal relationships. The diagram of a social portfolio in Figure 10.1 reflects efforts to plan for the future, balancing *individual* with *group* activities, and balancing *active* endeavors (requiring significant effort) with *passive* endeavors (requiring little physical exertion). Hence, just as a balanced and comprehensive financial portfolio takes into consideration the possi-bility of disability (including attention to disability insurance), so too with the social portfolio: Activities that require low levels of physical effort can be drawn on should illness bring reduced physical capacity, and activities that one can do alone can be drawn on during a transition marked by the loss of a significant other.

The social portfolio is a way of helping people develop new strengths and satisfactions in later life—even in the face of loss and problems requiring long-term care. Keep in mind, too, that the educational level of older cohorts has changed fundamentally during the second half of the 20th century. In 1950, the median of schooling for persons age 65 and older in the United States was 8.3 years—significantly less than a high school education. By 1990, the median of schooling for the cohort age 65 and older was 12.1 years—more than a high school education. This change in level of education implies cohort changes not only in the types of activities that are interesting to today's older adults, but also in older people's curiosity and their capacity to explore new and creative domains. Individuals are encouraged to get together with family and friends to have a group of significant others who know them well to help them plan and fill out the four cells of their social portfolio.

	Group efforts	Individual efforts
Active **interests:** **High energy,** **high mobility**	*Group/active* Elderhostel Dance lessons Tennis Travel	*Individual/active* Gardening Cooking Nature walks Photography
Passive **interests:** **Low energy,** **low mobility**	*Group/passive* Volunteer visits Fine arts class Movie club Games club	*Individual/passive* Reading Writing Telephone work Internet travel

FIGURE 10.1   The social portfolio.

CONCLUSION

To paraphrase H. L. Mencken: "For every complicated problem, there's a simple solution—and that simple solution always fails." The good news is that many gaps and failures in attending to the promotion of mental health and to interventions for mental health in long-term care are readily identifiable; it is when problems are amorphous that solutions are so difficult to identify. The nature and adverse impact of mental disorders on overall functioning in later life is better recognized today than ever before. The recognition that mental health problems compromise physical health, and that mental health interventions speed recovery from physical illness in older adults, has improved our understanding of how to maximize overall health with aging. A more informed appreciation of how old age can add as it takes away defines new avenues for creative action in the face of disease and disability over time. The next steps for research, practice, and policy development to improve care and the quality of life for older persons and their families are ready to be taken. The gaps are not in identifying problems or formulating solutions, but rather in making decisions and taking action.

REFERENCES

American Psychiatric Association. (1994). *Diagnostic and statistical manual of mental disorders* (ed 4). Washington, DC: Author.

Cohen, G. D. (1993). A tale of two Decembers: The journal of December 1992 and the case of December 1843. *American Journal of Geriatric Psychiatry, 1,* 1–2.

Cohen, G. D. (1994a). Creativity and aging: Relevance to research, practice, and policy. *American Journal of Geriatric Psychiatry, 2,* 277–281.

Cohen, G. D. (1994b). Journalistic elder abuse: It's time to get rid of fictions, get down to facts. *The Gerontologist, 34,* 399–401.

Cohen, G. D. (1994c). The geriatric landscape—Toward a health and humanities research agenda in aging. *American Journal of Geriatric Psychiatry, 2,* 185–187.

Diamond, J. (1989). The great leap forward. *Discover, 10,* 50–60.

Haley, W. E., Levine, E. G., Brown, S. L., Berry, J. W., & Hughes, G. H. (1987). Psychological, social, and health consequences of caring for a relative with senile dementia. *Journal of the American Geriatrics Society, 35,* 405–411.

Hartigan, L. R. (1991). *Made with passion: The Hemphill folk art collection.* Washington, DC: Smithsonian Institution.

Kiecolt-Glaser, J. K., & Glaser, R. (1989) Caregiving, mental health, and immune function. In E. Light & B. D. Lebowitz (Eds.), *Alzheimer's disease treatment and family stress: Directions for research* (Publication No. [ADM]89-1569). Washington, DC: U.S. Department of Health and Human Services.

Livingston, J., & Beardsley, J. (1980). *Black folk art in America.* Jackson: University of Mississippi Press.

Rovner, B. W., Kafonek, S., Filipp, L., Lucas, M. J., & Folstein, M. F. (1986). Prevalence of mental illness in a community nursing home. *American Journal of Psychiatry, 143,* 1446–1449.

Rovner, B. W., German, P. S., Brant, L. J., Clark, R., Burton, L., & Folstein, M. F. (1991). Depression and mortality in nursing homes. *Journal of the American Medical Association, 265,* 993–996.

Scitovsky, A. A. (1988). Medical care in the last twelve months of life: The relation between age, functional status, and medical care expenditures. *Milbank Memorial Fund Quarterly/Health and Society, 66,* 640–660.

Temkin-Greener, H., Meiners, M. R., Petty, E. A., & Szydlowski, J. S. (1992). The use and cost of health services prior to death: A comparison of the Medicare-only and the Medicare-Medicaid elderly population. *Milbank Quarterly, 70,* 679–701.

Wells, K. B., Stewart, A., Hays, R. D., Burnnam, M. A., Rogers, W., Daniels, M., Berry, S., Greenfield, S., & Ware, J. (1989). The functioning and well-being of depressed patients. *Journal of the American Medical Association, 262,* 914–919.

CHAPTER 11

Depression in the Nursing Home: Developments and Prospects

BARRY D. LEBOWITZ

The chapters in this book represent a refreshing and much-needed antidote to much of the current discussion of long-term care. By putting illness and disability at the center of the discussion, through the focus on depression, the authors have reaffirmed the need to constantly remind all of us that our concern must be with the patients who are in need of care. The nursing home provides a setting for the care of the sickest and most disabled in our population. For us clinical investigators, that is a given. Nonetheless, this focus on illness is often lost in policy-level discussions of case-mix reimbursement, staffing levels, quality assurance, and chemical restraints.

This book returns us to first principles—namely, that the people in nursing homes are sick, and they have come to the nursing home (typically) because they have burned out the capacity of their families to care for them. For these individual patients, the nursing home needs to be seen as a critical and unique component of the continuum of care (Brody & Masciocci, 1980). There are no alternatives to nursing home care for those for whom such intensity of care is appropriate. Indeed, an argument can be made that various organizational types emerging as part of the long-term care service system have resulted in an intensification of the demand for nursing home care (Lebowitz & Niederehe, 1992). That is, the care provided by day care, "partial hospital," and a variety of supportive services results in substantial increases of life expectancy for disabled individuals who would not have lived as long in settings inappropriate to their needs (Gruenberg, 1977). In other words, "alternatives to institutionalization" (a concept that at one time had a great deal of political

223

and intellectual popularity) are not alternatives in the first place, and in the second place do not displace the need for institutional care.

The book also allows us to revisit the history of the neglect of the nursing home as a principal site for research on the mental disorders of late life (Harper & Lebowitz, 1986), and to recognize the pioneering efforts of the investigators of the Philadelphia Geriatric Center whose work has established the foundation for the entire field.

WHERE TO TREAT THE MENTALLY ILL FRAIL ELDER

STATE HOSPITAL TO NURSING HOME

It has been well established that the nursing home is a prime site for the care of patients with a complex mix of disabling conditions (Rovner & Katz, 1993). In particular, patients in the nursing home exhibit a heterogeneous mixture of symptoms of physical and mental illnesses. The extreme burden of mental-disorder morbidity in the nursing home has been known for a long time (Group for the Advancement of Psychiatry, 1965; Kramer, Taube, & Starr, 1968). Action based on this knowledge has been sporadic, however, and we have needed to rediscover this phenomenon many times over the past three decades.

Why is that so? Part of the reason is money: Who pays for the care of these patients? Until the implementation of Medicare and, particularly, Medicaid, public-sector care of the mentally ill was the responsibility of state governments. This care, located for the most part in large state mental hospitals, consumed almost the entire state mental health budget, which was based on revenue generated through state taxes.

The Medicaid program created a federal responsibility for a large part of the care of the so-called medically indigent. The federal proportion of the Medicaid program varied by state but was designed to cover at least half the cost of care to as much as 80% or more (Goldman & Frank, 1990). This objective remains in force today, though the costs of the state portion of Medicaid have been identified as a major source of problems, and of concern, in state budgets.

State hospital care of the mentally ill was still to remain totally a state responsibility, though convalescent care and nursing home care would be eligible for coverage through the Medicaid program. The designers of the program were concerned that states would take advantage of this distinction and simply redesignate their state mental hospitals as nursing care facilities, thereby being able to shift the financial responsibility from total reliance on the state budget to major reliance on the federal portion of

Medicaid. *Institutions for Mental Disease* (IMDs) was the term designated to differentiate mental hospitals from other institutions, and a 50% rule was arbitrarily established as the defining characteristic. That is, any long-term-care institution in which more than half of the residents, or patients, had been diagnosed with a primary mental disorder would be considered a mental hospital—not a nursing home—for purposes of applying Medicaid policies.

The result of this policy was the creation of a significant barrier to the recognition and treatment of mental illness in the nursing home. As long as those seeking admission to nursing homes had multiple coexisting illnesses and disabling conditions, it was easy to overlook one class of illness or to regard that class as incidental or secondary to the primary disabling condition. Thus, many studies based on patients' records and clinical charts, as opposed to direct assessment, concluded that there was little mental illness in the nursing home (Kramer, Taube, & Starr, 1968).

This state of affairs—that is, official nonrecognition of mental illness in the nursing home—had a significant impact on both care of patients and development of policy. Any attempt to mandate targeted mental health care, or even consultation, was countered by the "facts" of low prevalence.

At the same time, legislation and litigation were restricting standards for admission to mental hospitals and were defining standards of treatment for those admitted (such as the right to treatment and to refuse treatment, and the requirement that treatment be provided in the least restrictive environment). The result of all this change was that in the absence of "dangerousness to self or others," patients could not be admitted to mental hospitals. As a result, many older persons were transferred from hospitals to nursing homes or were diverted from the hospital and admitted to nursing homes directly. Even in these situations, in which a patient with a mental disorder was institutionalized in a nursing home, the right to treatment that would have attended a hospital admission did not transfer to the nursing home setting, and many patients were unable to receive proper care.

All the barriers to the recognition of mental disorder notwithstanding, the growth in the population of nursing home patients with Alzheimer's disease and other dementias was pushing nursing homes closer to the 50% criterion for designation as an IMD. Even the charmingly archaic terminology of the nursing home surveys ("organic brain syndrome with senile brain disease" or "mental disorders without senility") could not dampen this documentable increase in prevalence.

There was a problem—an increase in the number of patients with mental disorders in nursing homes was creating a situation in which services could not be provided in the nursing home setting. There were at least three possible solutions: admission to nursing homes could be restricted; the definition of an IMD could be changed; the criteria for mental illness could be redefined. This last approach was taken as the solution, and under the threat of a pending lawsuit, the Medicaid rules were altered in the early 1980s to define Alzheimer's disease as the behavioral manifestation of an underlying neurological disorder (thereby excluding Alzheimer's disease as a diagnosis countable in the determination of IMD status).

This solution would lead to difficulties in the future regarding treatments that could be provided to these patients. One immediate problem was that admission to a state mental hospital was denied to patients with Alzheimer's disease who met the "dangerousness" criterion for hospital admission—on the grounds that they were not mentally ill and that, therefore, the state mental health authority was not responsible for their care. In addition, the administrative declaration that Alzheimer's disease was outside the scope of mental illness flew in the face of everything we know about the disease. Alzheimer's disease is a brain disease for which all manifestations are behavioral, cognitive, and emotional. Under that standard, the definition is entirely consistent with the definitions of schizophrenia, major depression, and other mental disorders. Moreover, the care of patients with Alzheimer's disease, and the assistance provided to their families, was, and largely remains, the responsibility of mental health professionals.

Thus, a solution that was administratively clever, and was widely regarded as appropriate, planted the seed for what would later become a major territorial battle in academic health care over responsibility for care of patients with Alzheimer's disease.

OBRA 87 AND AFTER

By the mid-1980s, the situation for nursing home patients with a mental illness was reaching crisis proportions. Despite the body of data from many studies, advocates had been unsuccessful in creating legislative or regulatory requirements for adequate assessment and treatment, for training of staff, or for monitoring and assurance of quality.

The provisions for nursing home reform in the 1987 Omnibus Budget Reconciliation Act (OBRA 87) recognized that failure and proposed, through "preadmission screening and annual resident review" (PA-SARR), to restrict access to nursing home care for those patients with mental disorders. The message was clear. Given that advocates had been unsuccessful in translating research into public policy, they should stop trying. The best way to get care for these patients was to keep them out of the nursing home in the first place. Other sectors of the mental health and long-term care systems were seen as more appropriate for the needs of these patients, though it was evident to many observers that such patients could not be integrated easily into those programs.

Though direct in theory, in practice PASARR has done little to divert the admission of patients to nursing homes. This could have been predicted because of a fundamental flaw in the thinking behind this provision. That flaw was a failure to recognize the clinical characteristics and complex comorbidities of disabled patients seeking admission to nursing homes. These patients were in need of such a broad range of care that only the nursing home was able to provide it. Community or residential care for the mentally ill was not prepared to meet the physical needs of these patients, and community care for the elderly was not prepared to meet their mental health needs.

The experience with PASARR and related aspects of nursing home reform succeeded in teaching us once again that it is much easier to plan a health care system of boxes and arrows than it is to develop a plan of care for a single patient.

A second aspect of this legislation has been problematic as well: the introduction of the concept of *chemical restraint*. This unfortunate term took nearly a full page to define in the Federal Register (Federal Register, February 5, 1992) and created a circumstance in which the only ''good'' psychotropic drug in the nursing home was the one that was never used. The term also called into question much of the art of pharmacological treatment that involves the use of drugs for purposes other than those for which the drugs were approved. This practice, called off-label use, is common in pharmacological treatment. Examples of off-label use are anticonvulsants for mania, antidepressants for pain, and antipsychotics for behavioral symptoms of Alzheimer's disease.

There is much that is wrong with the use of drugs in nursing homes, and cases of possibly inappropriate underuse (Heston et al., 1992) are at least as demonstrable as cases of possibly inappropriate overuse (Beardsley et al., 1989; Beers et al., 1988). It should be no surprise that the need in the field is for more research in general, and more clinical treatment trials in particular, instead of attempts to control clinical care through bureaucratic pronouncements.

The proper note on this issue was struck in a position statement, ''Psychotherapeutic Medications in the Nursing Home,'' issued by the American Association for Geriatric Psychiatry and committees of the American Geriatrics Society and the American Psychiatric Association (1992). This statement makes clear that the central concern should be for the patient and that a full range of treatments should be made available to the patient by the treating clinician. Though this is hardly revolutionary, and seems to be common sense, it once again reaffirms a concept underlying many of the chapters in this book: that in debates about the appropriateness of care, the needs of the patients must be primary.

THE NIH CONSENSUS DEVELOPMENT CONFERENCE ON THE DIAGNOSIS AND TREATMENT OF DEPRESSION IN LATE LIFE

While all these changes in nursing home policy were developing, there was considerable activity concerning the whole question of depression in general and depression in late life in particular. The National Institutes of Health (NIH) Consensus Development Conference on the Diagnosis and Treatment of Depression in Late Life (NIH Consensus Development Panel, 1992) was a landmark event in the history of interest in geriatric psychopathology in the United States. The goal of the conference was to assess the scientific knowledge base on depression in late life and to develop a series of recommendations for practice and for research. Depression in the nursing home was a major focus of the conference. A Consensus Development Conference consumes about a 2-year process of planning and evaluation and is considered a major event in health research. Of the approximately 90 consensus conferences that had been held to that point in all areas of health, only four had focused on mental disorders. The approval of a request to hold a Consensus Development Conference indicates that a body of research is sufficiently well developed to support such a serious undertaking.

Such was the case in November 1991 with depression in late life. Twenty-four investigators presented overviews of different aspects of the field, their own work, and the work of others to a panel of scientists whose expertise was in areas outside the topic of the conference. This panel acted like a jury, in that it evaluated the evidence presented and issued a report.

The panel report addressed the following questions:

• How does depression in late life differ from depression earlier in life? What are the sources of heterogeneity within late-life depression?
• How prevalent is depression in elderly persons, and what are its risk factors?
• What constitutes safe and effective treatment for late-life depression? What are the indications and contraindications for specific treatments?

- What are the patterns of use of health services for late-life depression? What are the obstacles to the delivery of adequate treatment?
- What are the benefits of recognizing and adequately treating depression in late life? What are the consequences of unrecognized or inadequately treated depression in late life?
- What are the most promising questions for future research?

The points raised by the presenters at the conference made a strong case for the significance of depression in late life. The presentations had a number of themes in common, including acknowledgment of the nursing home as a significant setting for consideration of a broad array of issues related to depression in late life:

1. Depressive illness is widespread among the elderly. Of the 31 million Americans age 65 and over, nearly 5 million suffer from serious and persistent symptoms of depression, and 1 million suffer from major depression (as defined by *DSM-IV*). Prevalence is particularly high in nursing homes and other settings for long-term residential care.

2. Depressive illness in late life is a serious public health concern. Depression is a serious illness in its own right. It is not an outcome of natural processes of aging and should not be considered normal. Depression is associated with significant functional disability in older patients. If untreated, depression increases the risk of premature death. It represents the leading cause of death by suicide in the elderly.

3. Medical comorbidity with depressive illness is particularly problematic in the older patient. Depression influences physiological function and alters the pattern of psychosocial risk factors for disease. Consequently, depression represents a major factor contributing to additional morbidity and mortality. Depression coexisting with medical illness is a major source of excess disability in geriatric patients, and it significantly alters the course and outcome of treatment for medical illness.

4. Depression can be diagnosed in elderly patients and can be separated from normal aging. The diagnosis of depression is a clinical diagnosis according to *DSM-IV* criteria. Severity of symptoms may be assessed clinically and with use of standard clinicians' rating scales and instruments (e.g., Hamilton Depression Rating Scale). As in other adult depressions, no biological, electrophysiological, or radiological test shows sufficient specificity and sensitivity to be used for diagnostic purposes.

5. Acute treatment for depression has been shown to be safe and efficacious in elderly patients. The broad array of treatments for acute episodes of depression that has been shown to be efficacious in adult patients is appropriate for use with elderly patients. Considerable data

exist for psychopharmacological approaches and for electroconvulsive therapy, and suggestive data exist for psychotherapy and for selected psychosocial interventions.

6.   Depression is a recurrent illness, and close attention must be paid to continuation and maintenance treatment so as to prolong the period of remission and recovery. Recommendations on the advisability of long-term treatment are largely based on extrapolation from adult patients, however, and more specific guidelines await the completion of several important studies that are still ongoing. In the meantime, the Consensus Panel recommended that treatment be continued for at least 6 months beyond resolution of a first episode of depression in late life and that treatment be continued for at least 1 year for patients experiencing a recurrence of depression. In both situations, the recommendation is that the continuation treatment consist of the same treatment as that which was successful in the acute episode; there is no evidence to support the long-standing practice of reducing the dose after acute treatment.

One indicator of the significance of the conference was that the panel report was accepted for publication in the *Journal of the American Medical Association*. Publication in this journal, one of the most prestigious in the world, is not automatic for reports of Consensus Development Conferences—the subject matter must be seen as significant for public health and relevant to a broad range of providers, and not be restricted to a single specialty or subspecialty of practice.

EFFICACY OF TREATMENT AND
THE PROCESS OF HEALTH CARE REFORM

In mid-1992, the Committee on Appropriations of the United States Senate requested a report on the efficacy of treatment for severe mental illness as well as on the cost of providing coverage for severe mental illness commensurate with that provided for all other illnesses. A number of analyses, including one in geriatrics (Schneider, 1993), were commissioned to assist in the development of this report, and the report was presented to the Senate and published independently (National Advisory Mental Health Council, 1993). The full scope of treatment options were considered: pharmacological and other biological somatic treatments, psychotherapy and other psychosocial and environmental interventions, and combination approaches.

The results of this comprehensive review of treatment were eye-opening: the efficacy of treatment for mental illness is at least the equal of any other area of illness and in many instances exceeds the reported efficacy of well established treatments such as angioplasty, atherectomy (National Advisory Mental Health Council, 1993), and antihypertensive agents (Materson et al., 1993).

This solid foundation of data based on clinical trials was important in the early discussions of health care reform and in subsequent legislative proposals. These data have provided a scientific rationale for policy discussions of parity in coverage of mental and physical illnesses.

If this were all that was needed to change health care policy, then there would be no question about the prospect for positive change in the coverage of treatment for mental illness. Unfortunately, other factors, including the historical stigma of mental illness, continue to impede this much-needed change. Incremental improvements in the coverage of mental illness have been accomplished in the Medicare program and in some private insurance plans. The data on efficacy of treatment will continue to be developed, and we can expect that further changes in the system will take advantage of this important knowledge base.

EFFECTIVENESS OF TREATMENT AND DIRECTIONS FOR FUTURE RESEARCH

At the same time as the efficacy of treatment was being documented, investigators and policy makers alike became concerned about the fragility of this database. Most studies are based in academic health centers and apply restrictive criteria for the inclusion and exclusion of potential subjects. Clinicians have long noted that the results of these highly controlled clinical trials are not readily transferrable to more usual practice settings or to the patients typically seen in such settings. This concern, called *treatment effectiveness*, is emerging as an important perspective in clinical trials in mental disorders.

Unlike efficacy studies, which tend to examine treatments under highly controlled conditions with tightly selective patient samples, effectiveness studies examine treatment in a broad range of settings, such as primary care, community service agencies, and long-term-care facilities. Samples in effectiveness studies enroll a heterogeneous group of patients, including those with coexisting physical illness, substance abuse disorders, and other conditions that would exclude them from the usual clinical trial. Effectiveness studies also look beyond the reduction of symptoms as a measure of outcome and extend to consideration of function, disability, and quality of life.

The methodology for effectiveness studies is largely derived from geriatrics, where studies commonly include heterogeneous patient samples, many with complex comorbidities, and study sites are located in a variety of settings.

We can expect, therefore, that more investigators will take the opportunity to extend their work into the nursing home and will begin to take on the serious issues of morbidity and disability that afflict the residents of these facilities. In doing so, they will be taking advantage of the pioneering work of the investigators of the Philadelphia Geriatric Center, whose important research was summarized in this book.

REFERENCES

Beardsley, R. S., Larson, D. B., Burns, B. J., Thompson, J. W., et al. (1989). Prescribing of psychotropics in elderly nursing home patients. *Journal of the American Geriatrics Society, 37*, 327–330.

Beers, M., Avorn, J., Soumerai, S. B., & Everitt, D. E. (1988). Psychoactive medication use in intermediate-care facility residents. *Journal of the American Medical Association, 260*, 3016–3020.

Brody, S. J., & Masciocchi, C. M. (1980). Data for long term care planning by health systems agencies. *American Journal of Public Health, 70*, 1194–1198.

Federal Register. (1992, February 5). *57*, 4516–4531. Washington, DC: Government Printing Office.

Goldman, H. H., & Frank, R. G. (1990). Division of responsibility among payers. In B. S. Fogel, A. Furino, & G. L. Gottlieb (Eds.), *Mental health policy for older Americans* (pp. 85–95). Washington, DC: American Psychiatric Association.

Group for the Advancement of Psychiatry. (1965). *Psychiatry and the aged: An introductory approach.* New York: Author.

Gruenberg, E. M. (1977). The failure of success. *Milbank Memorial Fund Quarterly, 55*, 3–23.

Harper, M. S., & Lebowitz, B. D. (Eds.). (1986). *Mental illness in nursing homes.* Washington, DC: Government Printing Office.

Heston, L. L., Garrard, J., Makris, L., Kane, R. L., Cooper, S., Dunham, T., & Zelterman, D. (1992). Inadequate treatment of depressed nursing home elderly. *Journal of the American Geriatrics Society, 40*, 1117–1122.

Katz, I. R., & Parmelee, P. (1994). Depression in elderly patients in residential care settings. In L. S. Schneider, C. F. Reynolds, B. D. Lebowitz, & A. J. Friedhoff (Eds.), *Diagnosis and treatment of depression in late life* (pp. 437–462). Washington, DC: American Psychiatric Association.

Kramer, M., Taube, C., & Starr, S. (1968). Patterns of use of psychiatric facilities by the aged: Current status, trends, and implications. In A. Simon & L. J. Epstein (Eds.), *Aging in modern society* (pp. 89–150). Washington, DC: American Psychiatric Association.

Lebowitz, B. D., & Niederehe, G. (1992). Concepts and issues in mental health and aging. In J. E. Birren, R. B. Sloane, & G. D. Cohen (Eds.), *Handbook of mental health and aging* (2nd ed., pp. 3–26). San Diego: Academic.

Materson, B. J., Reda, D., Cushman, W. C., Massie, B. M., Freis, E. D., Kochar, M. S., Hamburger, R. J., Fye, C., Lakshman, R., Gottdiener, J., Ramirez, E. A., Henderson, W., & the Department of Veterans Affairs Cooperative Study Group on Antihypertensive Agents. (1993). Single-drug therapy for hypertension in men: A comparison of six antihypertensive agents with placebo. *New England Journal of Medicine, 328*, 914–921.

National Advisory Mental Health Council. (1993). Health care reform for Americans with severe mental illness: Report of the National Advisory Mental Health Council. *American Journal of Psychiatry, 150*, 1447–1465.

National Institutes of Health Consensus Development Panel on Depression in Late Life. (1992). Diagnosis and treatment of depression in late life. *Journal of the American Medical Association, 268*, 1018–1024.

P.L. 100-203. *The Omnibus Budget & Reconciliation Act of 1987 (OBRA '87), Subtitle C.* The Nursing Home Reform Act 42 U.S.C. 139i-(3(a)-(h) (Medicare); 1396r(a)-h(Medicaid)).

Position Statement. (1992). Psychotherapeutic medications in the nursing home. *Journal of the American Geriatrics Society, 40*, 946–949.

Rovner, B. W., & Katz, I. R. (1993). Psychiatric disorders in the nursing home: A selective review of studies related to clinical care. *International Journal of Geriatric Psychiatry, 8*, 75–87.

Schneider, L. S. (1993). Efficacy of treatment for geropsychiatric patients with severe mental illness. *Psychopharmacology Bulletin, 29*, 501–524.

Index

mood changes in, 136, 145, 146, 178
  questionnaire on, 136, 137–141, 178
mood changes in, 176–177, 178
  in dementia, 136, 145, 146, 178
  music therapy in, 180–182
  in nursing home, 176–177, 178
  simulated presence in, 179–180
Portfolio, social, 220, 221
Positive affect, 32–36.
  See also Affect
Positive suggestions, sensitivity of older
    adults to, 157–158
Preadmission screening, Omnibus Budget
    Reconciliation Act provisions on,
    2, 17, 213, 226–227
Prevalence of depression, 1, 3–7, 19, 55,
    229
  in aging, 119–124, 229
  and dementia, 4, 48, 131
  subdysthymic, 4, 5–6, 55, 60
Problem-solving techniques:
  in dementia and depression, 134, 142
  in social skills training, 188, 189
Psychodynamic psychotherapy, 169–171,
    185, 186
  life review in, 170–171
Psychological well–being, 31–32
Psychopharmacology. *See* Drug therapy
Psychosocial interventions in
    subdysthymic depression, 68, 70
Psychotherapy, 18, 69, 169–207
  client interviews on effectiveness of,
    190–191
  cognitive-behavioral approach in,
    171–182, 185, 186
  diagnostic distribution of clients in,
    193–194
    changes over time, 194–195
  dreams in, 215
  life review in, 170–171, 186
  nonspecific treatment factors in,
    201–202
  number of sessions in, 195, 196
  oldest residents in, 190–191
  outcome measures in, 201

persistence-termination patterns in,
    191–197
preliminary investigations in residential
    settings, 185–203
psychodynamic approach in, 169–171,
    185, 186
social skills training in, 186–189
Public policy issues on aging, 212

Quality of life issues, 212
  in cost of health care, 216

Rehearsal techniques in social skills
    training, 186–189
Relaxation techniques, 156
Remoralization concept, 202, 203
Responsibility for actions, in personal
    meaning of depression, 86, 87
Restraints, chemical, 227
Retirement behavior, 110–111
Reward systems in cognitive–behavioral
    therapy, 172
Risk factors for depression
  in aging, 120–121
  personal beliefs on, 90–93
Role playing in social skills training,
    186–189

Sadness:
  compared with personal meanings of
    depression, 89–90
  neurotic response to, 123
Screening:
  in admission to nursing home, 2, 17,
    213, 225, 226–227
    nonrecognition of mental illness in,
    225
    Omnibus Budget Reconciliation Act
    provisions on, 2, 17, 213,
    226–227
  for subdysthymic depression, 70
Seattle treatment protocol, 129, 134–150
  caregiver issues in, 132, 142–144,
    147–148, 149
  clinical program in, 134–145

evaluation of, 145–149
maintenance and generalization of
skills in, 144–145
pleasant events in, 134, 136, 137–141
problem-solving skills in, 134, 142
Self–care deficits:
albumin serum levels in, 17
resource utilization in, 10
Self-esteem and affect, 35
Self-management of depression, 93–94
Self-reports:
on affect, and lifetime personal
identity, 97–104
on depression, on admission to nursing
home, 9
on health status, and lifetime personal
identity, 97–104
in subdysthymic depression, 64–65,
67, 68
Separation, in personal meaning of
depression, 84
Simulated presence therapy, 179–180
Social interactions:
in balanced social portfolio, 220
in residential setting, skills training on,
186–189
self-management of, in treatment of
depression, 94
Social portfolio, 220, 221
Social skills training, 186–189
Sociocultural factors, in anthropological
approach to depression, 75–113
Socioeconomic status, and susceptibility
to depression, 120, 121
personal beliefs on, 93
Staff:
in multifaceted treatment approach,
178–179
rating of depression, sensitivity and
specificity of, 8
time spent in care of depressed
patients, 10
State mental hospitals, 224–226
Stereotypes, cultural, on old age,
120–121, 213

Stress and depression of caregivers in
dementia. *See* Dementia,
caregiver stress and depression in
Stroke, 11, 120
Subdysthymic depression, 55–71
affect variability in, 42–45
compared with low and high symptom
groups, 64–66
consequences of, 67–68
diagnostic criteria on, 59–60, 69
education programs on, 71
mortality rate in, 68
as normal reaction to hospitalization,
60–64, 70
prevalence and incidence of, 4, 5–6,
55, 60
prior history of depressive symptoms
in, 60–64, 70
recovery from illness in, 67
screening for, 70
self-rating of health status in, 64–65,
67, 68
treatment of, 68–69, 70
postdischarge, 70–71
Suggestions, positive, sensitivity of older
adults to, 157–158
Suicidal behavior, 7, 201, 229
Susceptibility to depression, 120, 121,
122–123
personal beliefs on, 91, 92–93
Symptoms of depression:
in dementia, 131–132
in group cognitive interventions,
162–163, 166

Temperament, 30–31
and affect, 34–35
and susceptibility to depression, 122
Themes, personal, 76, 78–79
in life stories, 104–111, 112
Thought patterns in cognitive therapy,
173–176
Tithonus, Greek myth of, 212
Traits:
compared with states, 31, 32

Springer Publishing Company

Mood and Cognitive Disorders
Facts and Research in Gerontology
Supplement 1995

Bruno J. Vellas, MD, PhD, **J.L. Albarede,** and
P.J. Garry, Editors

This authoritative research volume addresses an extensive range of mood and cognitive disorders in elderly populations. Major advances in the treatment of Alzheimer's and other mental disorders are discussed, along with aging-related depression, pain, and suicide. The volume is a valuable reference work for all health and mental health practitioners concerned with psychological disorders in the elderly. Published in cooperation with SERDI in France.

Partial Contents:

- Depression and Alzheimer's Disease: Separate Phenomena or Epi-Phenomena?, *D.G. Blazer*
- Specialist Memory Clinics: the Experience at the Hammersmith Hospital, *C.A. Kelly, et al*
- Beyond Verbal Memory — Enhancing Memory by Acting, *M. Knopf*
- Atrophy-Corrected Cerebral Blood Flow in Fronto-Temporal Dementia, *B. Miller, et al*
- Face Processing in Alzheimer's Disease. *R. Bruyer, M. Van Der Linden*
- Screening for Depression in Elderly Patients, *H.G. Koening, et al*
- Sleep After Hourly Forced Awakenings in Young and Older Adults, *A. Buguet, et al*

1995   208pp   0-8261-8176-7   hardcover

536 Broadway, New York, NY 10012-3955 • (212) 431-4370 • Fax (212) 941-7842

Springer Publishing Company

Life Beyond 85 Years
The Aura of Survivorship

Colleen L. Johnson, PhD
Barbara M. Barer, MSW

Those 85 years and older — the Oldest Old — are now the fastest growing group in the U.S. Using their original research, the authors examine how the oldest old adapt to daily challenges and what competencies are needed to survive and continue living in the community. The authors address the topics of health and physical status, family and social relationships, quality of life, as well as the implications that increases in life expectancy have for families and society. The book features illuminating vignettes that illustrate how the oldest old perceive and interpret their world, and thereby convey the aura of their survivorship.

Contents:
- Introduction
- Studying the Oldest Old: The Context of Survivorship
- Are Very Old People Different?
- Stability and Change in Physical Status: A Naturalistic Account
- Late Life Family Relationships
- Social Networks: A Continuum from Sociability to Isolation: The Processes of Adaptation
- Managing Daily Routines
- Discourses on Self and Time
- Sustaining Emotional Well-Being: The Content of Emotional Life
- Profiles in Survivorship
- Preparing for Death
- Summary and Conclusions
- Afterword by *Lillian Troll*

Springer Series on Life Styles & Issues in Aging
1996   280pp   0-8261-9540-7   *hardcover*

536 Broadway, New York, NY 10012-3955 • (212) 431-4370 • Fax (212) 941-7842

 *Springer Publishing Company*

Enhancing Autonomy in Long-Term Care

Lucia M. Gamroth, RN, PhD
Joyce Semradek, RN, MSN
Elizabeth Tornquist, MA, Editors

This volume assesses the importance of autonomy to quality of life in long-term care facilities. First addressing conceptual issues, the editors then pose such questions as: What is autonomy and what does it mean in the context of physically and/or cognitively impaired elders? What is the effect of nursing home financing and federal regulations? How does the traditional medical model, which casts residents as "patients," affect autonomy? How does the physical environment make a difference? The contributors describe six successful models of care that provide a more meaningful quality of life through promoting autonomy.

Partial Contents:

1994   264pp   0-8261-8680-7   hardcover

536 Broadway, New York, NY 10012-3955 • (212) 431-4370 • Fax (212) 941-7842

Managed Care & Quality Assurance: Integrating Acute & Chronic Care

Annual Review of
Gerontology & Geriatrics, Volume 16

Robert J. Newcomer, PhD
Anne M. Wilkinson, PhD, Editors

The contributors to this volume provide an overview of each component of the acute and long term care service continuum including managed health care, subacute care, nursing homes, community care case management, and private case management. This volume is one of the first efforts to place these varied approaches side by side highlighting the gaps and areas of duplication in the services delivery system.

In addition, chapters address the emerging practices in long term care financing and assisted living as well the conceptual issues that need to be resolved to achieve acute and chronic care integration. This volume is of primary importance to professionals involved in long term care including administration, community nursing, social work, case management, discharge planning, and policy.

Contents:

1996 252pp 0-8261-6498-6 hardcover

536 Broadway, New York, NY 10012-3955 • (212) 431-4370 • Fax (212) 941-7842